AF575412

THE FRIGHTFEST GUIDE TO GRINDHOUSE MOVIES

First published by FAB Press, August 2021

FAB Press Ltd.
2 Farleigh, Ramsden Road, Godalming
Surrey, GU7 1QE, England, U.K.

www.fabpress.com

Introductory essays and all film reviews copyright © 2021 Alan Jones
Foreword copyright © 2021 Jane Giles
Welcome to FrightFest copyright © 2021 Alan Jones
The moral rights of the authors have been asserted

Author's Dedication:
For the never-to-be-forgotten George A. Romero, it was a privilege to be your friend.

Picture research and layout by Kevin Coward
FrightFest Guide original book design, layout and pre-press origination by Harvey Fenton
Film cast and crew credits, additional research and index by Francis Brewster
Thanks also to Alan Jones and the FrightFest image archive

World Rights Reserved.
No part of this book may be reproduced or transmitted in any form or by any means, electronic or mechanical, including photocopying, recording, scanning, or by any information storage and retrieval system, including the internet, without the prior written permission of the Publisher.

Copyright of film stills and promotional artwork is the property of the production or distribution companies concerned.
These illustrations are reproduced here in the spirit of publicity, and whilst every effort has been made to trace the copyright owners, the editor and publishers apologise for any omissions and will undertake to make any appropriate changes in future editions of this book if necessary.
Acknowledgement for visual material is due to the following organisations and individuals:
Academy International, Admiral Pictures, Aetas Films, Aico Films, Allied Artists, Alpine Productions, American Films Ltd., American International Pictures, Anglo Amalgamated Film Distributors, Anglo-EMI, Apollon Films, Apple Films, Aquila Film, Arco Films, Arden Distribuzione, Argos Films Paris, Artists XVI, Arwin Productions, Associated British-Pathe, Atlas Films, Atlas International, Audubon Films, Avco Embassy, AVR, Barber Dann Films, Barrister Productions, BCD Entertainment, BCP Productions, Bema Films, BES, BFD, BIP, Blake Films, Blue Underground, Boulting Brothers, B.R.C. Produzione, Cambist Films, Caralan Productions, Carar Film, Caro Film, C.C.F.C., Charles Band Productions, Chevron Pictures, Churubusco Studios, Cinecom, Cinefilm S.A., Cinema Distributors of America, Cinema Entertainment Corporation, Cinema Overdrive, Cinema Shares, Cinemation Industries, Cinerama Releasing, Cineriz, Cinesco, Cinevid, C.I.P.I. Cinematografica, Cintel Productions, Cobra Films, Columbia Pictures, Commonwealth United, Compagna Cinematografica, Compton Films, Champion, Constantin Film, Cosmo Video, Cosmopolis Films, CRC, Crown International Pictures, CultVideo, DCA, D.E.A., Dear Film Distribuzione, Delta Films, Derann, Dimension Pictures, Distribuidora Negrete, Distribuzione Filmar, Duplivision, Dusashenka, Eagle Films, Ealing Studios, Julie Edwards, EMI, Euro-American Pictures, Europix Consolidated, Export Film Bischoff, Fair Film SpA, Famous Players Corporation, Filmadora Independiente, Filmica Vergara (Cinecomisiones S.A), Films Distributing Corporation, Filmways Pictures, Flamingo Productions, G and H Productions, Gala Releasing, General Film Corporation, GGP, Go Video, Golden Era Film Distributors, Goldstar Productions, Graffitti Productions, Grand National Film Distributors, G.R.P. Cinematografica, Hal Roach International, Hammer Film Productions, Hammer Seven Arts, Hemdale Film Distributors, Hemisphere Productions, Hickmar Productions, Hygienic Productions, Independent International Pictures, Infra-Associates, Interfilm, Intermedia Productions, International Amusement Corporation, International Gold Cinematografica, Intervision, Istituto Luce, Italian Film International, Italo American Films, Iver Film Services, Jack H. Harris Enterprises, Joanna Productions, Joseph Brenner Associates, K.E./Buccaneer Productions, Kenworth, Kino-Lorber, KKI Films, L'Atlantica Cinematografica, La Globe Films International, Landmark Films, Les Films Concordia, Les Productions Artistes Associes, Levine-Van Winkle Productions, Lippert Inc., Lira Films, London Screen Distribution, L.T. Films, Luxcine, Magna Pictures, John Maltby Collection (English Heritage), Mammoth Films, Manson Distributing Corporation, Mark L. Lester Pictures, Mariner Cinematografica, Mark Associates, Maron Films, Medallion Pictures, Medford Films, Media Cinema, Media Trend, Medusa Distribuzione, Mercurfin Italiana, Mercurio Films, Metromedia Producers Corporation, MGM, Michael Balcon Productions, Miracle Films, Monarch Films, Mundial Films, National General Pictures, Nazionalcine Distribuzione, New Line Cinema, New Realm Distributors, New World Pictures, P.A.C.-Caravel Productions, Pan American Pictures Corporation, Parade Releasing, Paramount Pictures, Paris Cannes Production, Pathe, Planet Film Distributors, Prodex Film, Producciones Sotomayor, Produzioni Europee Associate, Rank Film Distributors, Rapid Film, Raymond Stross Productions, Regal Films International, René Thevenet-Tanagra Productions, Republic Pictures, Rialto Film, Rizzoli Film, Romana Film, Roxy Film, Sage Productions, San Francisco Film, Scanbox Group Scandinavia, Schneider-Film, Seven Arts Productions, Seymour Borde and Associates, S.F. Film Distributors, Shaw Brothers, Shochiku, Societe Nouvelel de Cinematographie, Stellor-Mercury, Super Video, Superstar International, Sutton Pictures, Sword & Sorcery Productions, Tarquinia Internazionale Cinematografica, Tei International, TFC-2 Pacemaker Releasing, Tigon Pictures, Timely Motion Pictures, Times Films, T.I.T. Film Produktion, Toho, Tonylyn Productions, Tony Tenser Films, Trans American Films, Trans-International Films, Trans-Lux, TV 13 Filmproduktion, 20th Century-Fox, Ultra Film, UMC Pictures, Un-Ad, United Artists, United Feature Syndicate, United Producers Releasing Organization, Universal Films, Universal-International Esp., Victory Films, Video Rondo, VIP Distributors, Virginia Cinematografica, Viscount Associates, Walter Manley Enterprises, Warner Bros., Warner-Pathe, Weintraub-Heller Productions, Yongestreet Film Productions, Zenith International Pictures.

Front cover illustration:
Cover design by Harvey Fenton, based on original "Video Nasty" VHS artwork for Snuff (1976)
Frontispiece illustration:
Original promotional artwork for The Ultimate Warrior (1975)

Printed in the Czech Republic

A CIP catalogue record for this book is available from the British Library

hardcover: ISBN 978 1 913051 10 5
paperback: ISBN 978 1 913051 11 2

-THE DARK HEART OF CINEMA-

FRIGHTFEST® GUIDE

GRINDHOUSE MOVIES

Alan Jones

The famous steps at the entrance to Cineworld, Leicester Square, London, on the opening night of FrightFest, August 2019.

© Harvey Fenton, 2019

- THE DARK HEART OF CINEMA -

FRIGHTFEST®

Across more than 20 years of programming the cream of the horror, sci-fi, thriller and fantasy genres at its three hugely anticipated annual mega-events (as part of the Glasgow Film Festival in Scotland every Feb/March, in London over the August Bank Holiday, and its Halloween Shocktoberfest) and online too, FrightFest, the UK's most prestigious Party Central for fear fans has premiered thousands of movies.

But how many of those could be called Exploitation in the true blue Grindhouse tradition? Especially as the Red Light district fleapits, 42nd Streets and redneck Drive-In circuits have ceased to exist in our modern multi-platform era where everything is hyped up, nothing is co-featured and very little escapes into the suburbs unnoticed. Gone are the days of scouring the local listing guides and plotting routes from your house to the far-flung Odeons where the one film you've been longing to see has finally turned up on a Late Night double bill. Oh, you've missed that experience too!

A look at past FrightFest programmes throws up a few possible contenders though: **Cradle of Fear** (2001), **Bloody Mallory** (2002), **Bad Biology** (2008), **Vampire Girl vs. Frankenstein Girl** (2009), **Bring Me the Head of the Machine Gun Woman** (2012), **Zombeavers** (2014), **Lowlife** (2017), **Ghost Killers vs. Bloody Mary** (2018) and **Bullets of Justice** (2019). Will these titles be discussed in future volumes about the deliciously gonzo Grindhouse sensibility that captivated generations? Time will tell. But for right now you have this terrific follow up to 'The FrightFest Guide to Exploitation Movies' by one of the key authorities on the once much maligned, now lauded genre.

If you thought international film critic, broadcaster, author and FrightFest co-director Alan Jones's last delve into Grindhouse gratuitous gore, Go-Go girls and gob-smacking gruesomeness hit the shock spot, well, you ain't read nothing yet! Prepare yourself for the deviant delights of **The Bloody Brood** (1959), **The Christine Keeler Affair** (1963), **Kitten with a Whip** (1964), **Death Is Nimble, Death Is Quick** (1966), **LSD: Hell for a Few Dollars More** (1967), **Devil in the Brain** (1972), **The Violator** (1974), **Spermula** (1976) and **Amin: The Rise and Fall** (1981). You've been warned! Doubly so!

'The FrightFest Guide to Grindhouse Movies' is the fifth volume in a series intended to build the knowledge of the curious spectator and the cult connoisseur alike – the exact same maxim with which we meticulously produce our annual events that are globally famous and used by the international film industry as a litmus test for the future of the horror genre.

Enjoy this latest respected circling of the grimy rim of the rebellious, rancid and raucous with the same passionate enthusiasm that sets Frightfesters apart from the mundane fest rest. But FrightFest is not just a film festival or the friendliest community you could ever wish to join. It's an ever-increasing brand that includes FrightFest Presents, our multi-platform/VOD entertainment label that has released such diverse and popular titles as **Some Kind of Hate** (2015), **My Father Die** (2016), **Boar** (2017), **The Siren** (2019), **Videoman** (2018), **The Wind** (2018), **12 Hour Shift** (2020), the cultural phenomenon **The Love Witch** (2016) and the critically acclaimed **Relic** (2020).

~ Alan Jones, FrightFest co-director

Alan Jones

Alan Jones is an internationally renowned reporter on the Horror Fantasy genre in all media and extensively travels the world to cover the making of movies in production. The first movie he covered on location was the original **Star Wars** in 1977, the latest **Gunpowder Milkshake** and **Jetski**.

He was the London correspondent for the seminal 'CFQ' magazine between 1977-2002, reviewed almost every genre release for 'Starburst' between 1980-2008, was a featured film critic for 'Film Review' for two decades, contributed set-reports to 'Fangoria' for a decade and has remained a featured film critic in the 'Radio Times', the UK's biggest selling magazine, since 1995. He was editor of 'Shivers', 'Film Guide' and consultant editor of 'The Horror Collection' a New Line Cinema endorsed collectable figurine part work.

Other magazines and newspapers he has written for include 'Empire', 'Total Film', 'SFX, 'Wonderland', 'Heat', 'The Guardian', 'The Independent', 'GQ', 'Vogue', 'City Limits', 'FHM', 'Femme Fatales', 'The Dark Side', and 'Premiere'. His 'Total Film' feature The Splat Pack ensured that term entered film industry jargon.

He's an active member of the London Critic's Circle whose annual film awards gain worldwide recognition and has served on the critic's juries of every major global fantasy film festival including Sitges (Spain), Fantasporto (Portugal), Paris, Rome, Strasbourg, Neuchatel (Switzerland), Science+Fiction (Trieste, Italy), RazorReel (Bruges), Motel X (Lisbon, Portugal), Fantastic Fest (Austin, Texas) and Avoriaz (France).

After co-presenting the legendary Shock Around the Clock festival in London, and Fantasm at the National Film Theatre, he is now co-curator of FrightFest, the UK's biggest horror fantasy event that takes place every August Bank Holiday in central London. Two satellite FrightFest events also happen at Halloween, and within the Glasgow Film Festival every February. He oversees the artistic direction of the 'FrightFest Presents' multi-platform label in conjunction with the UK independent Signature Entertainment, the brand's biggest successes, **The Love Witch** and **Relic**.

An in-demand expert on Horror, Punk (he worked for designer Vivienne Westwood and was the Sex Pistols' DJ) and Disco, he has appeared on, researched and written numerous programmes for television including award-winning documentaries on the Italian horror directors Mario Bava and Dario Argento, and 'Eli Roth's History of Horror'. His Punk showcases include the BBC series 'Punk Britannia', SKY TV's 'Anarchy on Thames' and the feature documentary **Who Killed Nancy?** talking about his good friend Sid Vicious. His reminiscences about the Disco era have graced many BBC programmes and comprise the sleeve notes of the bestselling 25-plus CD collections 'Disco: Discharge' and 'Disco: Recharge'. He also wrote sleeve notes for the 'The Vault of Horror; The Italian Connection' vinyl albums of rare soundtracks.

His DVD commentaries continually receive acclaim including those for Alejandro Jodorowsky's **Santa Sangre**, Nicolas Winding Refn's **Valhalla Rising**, **Bronson** and **Fear X**, Tom Shankland's **WAZ**, Andrew Birkin's **The Cement Garden**, Tony Maylam's **The Burning** and Dario Argento's **The Bird with the Crystal Plumage**, **The Cat O'Nine Tails**, **The Card Player**, **The Stendhal Syndrome**, **Tenebrae** and **Suspiria**. Other *giallo* commentaries include **What Have You Done to Solange?**, **The Bloodstained Butterfly**, **Death Laid an Egg** and **The Red Queen Kills Seven Times**. His moderated commentary with Oscar-winning actress Helen Mirren for Tinto Brass's **Caligula** is considered a milestone in the form. He has also contributed to DVD extras for **Heavenly Creatures**, **Video Nasties: The Definitive Guide, Volumes 1** & **2** and the **A Nightmare on Elm Street** Blu-ray collection amongst many others.

His books include the critically acclaimed *Saturday Night Forever: The Story of Disco* (UK, US and Italian editions), the global bestseller *Tomb Raider: The Official Film Companion*, the SGM Award-winning and Rondo Award nominee *Dario Argento: The Man, the Myths & the Magic*, *The Rough Guide to Horror Movies* (British and French editions), *The FrightFest Guide to Exploitation Movies*, *The Act of Seeing* with Nicolas Winding Refn (British and French editions), and *Discomania!*

Alan Jones with horror icon **Dario Argento** during his Guest of Honour appearance at FrightFest, August 2019.

© Julie Edwards

INTRODUCTION BY JANE GILES

© Matt Hass

20:30 MONDAY 23 MARCH 2020

With clenched fists, Britain's Prime Minister broadcasts the news to the nation. Isolated cases earlier this year have officially escalated to the levels of a pandemic. The Chinese doctor who first blew the whistle soon died of his patients' virus, which then spread like wildfire from Wuhan around the world. It's the beginning of Britain's Lockdown. People must work from home. All non-essential shops, restaurants, bars, gymnasiums, playgrounds, places of education, entertainment and worship must close immediately. We must not leave our homes except for essential food and medication. We must wear surgical face masks and sanitise our hands. Police patrol the parks fining those who break the curfew or gather in groups. Anyone with symptoms must self-isolate.

Overnight, thriving urban streets turn into the silent, sullen, stultified suburbs we ran away from as adolescents, the places where everything shut early and there was fuck all to do. The events we booked tickets for and eagerly awaited were all cancelled, along with holidays and international travel. Stuck in our homes on our island we binge watch telly and the streamers until there's nothing left. Some desperate people even resort to jigsaws, both the mind-numbing puzzle kind or the power tool. There's no choice but to Do It Yourself. Others spend painful hours 'decluttering' precious VHS collections and overflowing bookshelves (then buy it all back again on eBay).

People start to go mad from depression, anxiety and loneliness. Fights break out between the masked and the unmasked. Young people sharing four to a flat are forced to sleep and work 24/7 in their bedrooms, like hostages or high security prisoners in cells. And there's never enough WiFi to go round for those endless video meetings. Bosses monitor their remote workers through Spycam. Irritable relationships turn septic. Abuse spirals. Our elders go senile. Friends and family get sick, fade away and die without saying goodbye. There are suicides. We turn into zombies.

It's Cronenbergian. Carpenterish. Ballardian. Chuck Palahniukianish. It's all the dystopian horror and sci-fi fiction we grew up loving. But this time it's real and we're the hapless actors in the longest, flattest, most boring genre movie ever. The lightboxes of shuttered cinemas spell out 'Lockdown Pt 3 – Worst. Trilogy. Ever'.

Days and weeks and months and years go by. Winter never ends. Summer is cancelled.

But look! Just when we thought we could stand no more a man appears on the horizon holding a battered book in his hand. It's Alan Jones, come to save us with his Grindhouse Diaries 1953-1987 (FAB Press)! The dusty, ancient tomes reveal a long-lost world when people read film reviews and looked up screening times in actual newspapers and magazines bought from newsagents, searching for the most lurid ads, stills and straplines to plan a trip to the cinema. It was a time when young minds and imaginations lit up like pinball machines at the sight of film posters and billboards promising thrills beyond our wildest dreams.

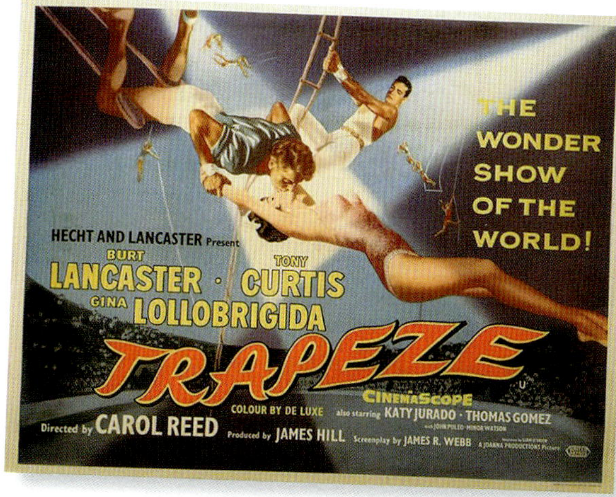

Jones' diary starts in his hometown of Portsmouth, 1956. We're teased with distant memories of Jones Snr taking his son to witness his first glimpses of a butch man in white vest and bulging tights (**Trapeze**, 1956) and half-naked slaves in chains (**The Ten Commandments**, 1956) before our hero breaks loose to brave the Gaumont Highland Road where he will embrace his destiny as a fright-obsessed lone viewer. Whether at the Saturday Kids' Matinees (Odeon Highland Road) or Sunday evenings with 007, swashbucklers and stop-motion SFX, these early childhood experiences shaped Jones' taste, like so many of his (okay, *our*) generation.

Jones' diaries lovingly detail his rise up the film classification ranks, from a U to the "must-see" A-certificated films. Adorably, our underage hero was forced to hang around outside cinemas trying to persuade single men to escort him into the auditorium. Thank goodness no harm became Alan in his desperate mission to watch the rubber-masked stars of **The List of Adrian Messenger** (1963).

As soon as Jones could pass for 16, he was in like Flynn to the forbidden fruit of X-certificated films, ripping off his school uniform to dress like a grown-up in an attempt to trick the hatchet-faced box office cashier and the terrifying ticket-tearing usher. It's a cinema's legal requirement to ensure that no one underage sees material deemed inappropriate for them by the standards of the BBFC. The management could lose its cinema license for breaching this regulation. But the less reputable the cinema, the more likely it was to turn a blind eye, a mixture of sympathy for an underage cinephiles' plight with the pitiful financial gain of a cheap ticket sale.

Cinemas attracted enthusiasts of all sorts, and Jones kindly introduces us to an assortment of Portsmouth's Dirty Old Men including the notorious 'Raspberry Ruffler' of the Essoldo Kings Road, the genital-flashing exhibitionist, and "the non-stop wanker" who prioritised Margaret Rutherford movies. Sadly I've never encountered such uninhibited characters, but over the years have come across plenty of eccentric cinema-going regulars, such as the Scala's Mrs Reeves and her adult son Melvin, Dr. Bonner (who proselytised about the benefits of drinking your own urine), and the NFT's 'Russian guy' who in later years had a permanent drip hanging from the end of his nose and would bark loudly with laughter in the most unlikely moments. Cinema managers always think these regulars come to them alone, and are horrified to discover that their punters promiscuously frequent other venues, travelling all over town to feed their insatiable habit.

Pre-digital, the 35mm film circuit was a place which began in the prestigious, expensive cinemas of London's West End where a film could run for as long as public demand held up, which could be weeks or months or even years. It was not unusual for audiences to go see the same film several times in a cinema. Jones describes his repeated viewings of **The Lords of Flatbush** (1974) in a way that's reminiscent of a fan's devotion to following a favourite band playing gigs around the country, and he's clear that the more effort made to see a film, the more it will impact. Having established demand, film prints were then sent around the country according to a rudimentary pecking order which prioritised the major chains leaving the single-screen owner operators, independents and rep houses until last. Programmes were packed with newsreels, adverts, trailers, and the supporting shorts which were the strange fruit of the Eady Levy (essentially a tax on American movies to subsidise the British film industry). Double-bills were not unusual and offered an affordable way to catch up on movies, although some couplings were bizarre beyond belief. Anyone up for **The Prime of Miss Jean Brodie** (1969) + Russ Meyer's **The Seven Minutes** (1971)? Both came from the same distributor, which was all that mattered to the blind booker at the Victoria Biograph, with its 100% male audience, leaky roof, and constant seat-banging traffic to and from the toilets.

Opulent 1,500 seat picture palace cinemas which had opened around the time of the First World War during the golden era of wildly popular silent film mostly survived the Blitz. But the coming of television and the family-owned motorcar in the 1950s presented the first major challenge to the existence of cinemas as audiences changed their recreational ways. Numerous 'electric theatres' were turned into live music venues, and later bingo halls or churches. Most cinemas which endured were multiplexed, their palatial auditoriums reduced to bland, odd-shaped shoeboxes. Once upon a time an entire audience would arrive at the cinema at the same time for the same film, creating a unified energy and purpose. Multiplexes diluted that experience.

But throughout the 1980s-90s British rep cinemas kept up the tradition of showing whatever the programmer wanted despite increasingly worn-out film prints in dilapidated venues which were nonetheless full of character, with their cracked marble floors, resident cats and unlikely murals. In these rep cinemas young female audiences felt at home to watch wild movies without being mistaken for prostitutes, firing the visual imaginations of a generation of creatives. Much of the inspiration for this post-punk cinema culture was imported directly from the Grindhouses of New York, Los Angeles and San Francisco, where sensationalist horror and sex movies were shown to audiences busy scoring drugs, fucking in the back row or yelling at the movie.

Alan Jones was at the centre of that scene, the man with his eyes fixed firmly on the screen, absorbing every detail to write up film reviews in his diary, and later for film magazines. This Volume ends in 1987, after the so-called 'Video Nasties' fiasco but before home video and digital technologies definitively transformed the film viewing landscape and before Jones embarked on his side line as the programmer of Britain's leading horror film festival. As we know, FrightFest was destined to leave the homely Prince Charles to move up in the cinema world. The festival's challenge was to retain its original spirit through a series of increasingly upmarket venues and that the fab four achieved this leaves me wondering what is the most important element to film exhibition. Is it the films, the venue or the people? Cinemas may be open or closed, the audiences packed together like sardines in a full-house or spread out so far you could drive a train between them, but at least now we have Alan Jones' picaresque diary to vividly evoke the memory of the Grindhouse while dissecting the value of the tat, titillation, trash, terror and treasure of the rarely-discussed Exploitation films they showed.

~ Jane Giles
Monday, 31 May 2021

Jane Giles is the author of ***Scala Cinema 1978-1993*** *(FAB Press), winner of the 2019 Kraszna-Krausz award for excellence in moving image book publishing. A feature-length documentary based on the Scala book is in production at the time of writing.*

FRIGHTFEST GUIDE

GRINDHOUSE MOVIES

INTRODUCTION

So, you've come back for more? More unwholesome shock, irresponsible sin, deplorable sensation and pious salvation – I knew you couldn't resist. And I know the feeling only too well. It's one that has remained with me ever since I could pretend I was just about old enough to see a forbidden X-certificate movie. Back when I was a teenager in the mid-1960s I didn't understand the term Exploitation because I had never heard the word used in relation to cinema. A movie was just a movie; a monster movie, a vampire movie, a sex movie, not under a derogatory umbrella category, so how could I recognize the idiom was vaguely snobby and insulting and that I was the quintessential prime target for the tag-line hustlers?! "A motion picture that peels off the dirty sweaters covering the raw emotions of youth!" (**The Bloody Brood**, 1959), "Photographed at the risk of the cameraman's lives!" (**Lash of the Penitentes**, 1936), "How would you solve the problem of not being able to fulfil your marital obligations?" (**Test Tube Babies**, 1948)... wow, count me in! During my deformative years I merely rushed ingenuously to see the latest Hammer horror, the new Amicus anthology, the hottest lurid science fiction, the racy 'adult issues' drama my family warned was 'too good' for me, the A.I.P. programmer and any Italian import that turned up magically at my local picturehouse.

For those readers new to such acquired tastelessness and who still haven't read my previous invaluable handbook to such habit-forming horrors – in the broadest sense – *The FrightFest Guide to Exploitation Movies*, let's quickly get you up to speed. Exploitation flicks earned their now fashionable soubriquet by taking advantage of taboo subject matter that major studios couldn't touch, even though they usually offered more in the way of enticing titles and explicit poster art than anything too hot to handle in terms of actual content. The Exploitation film business from the Dirty Thirties to the Swinging Sixties constituted a tangled web of Drive-In chancers and Grindhouse grifters working outside the film industry at large that mainly went ignored by all but a ready, willing and sensation seeking crowd who frequented their suburban fleapit or backwoods spit-and-sawdust venues hosting low-rent 'roadshow' sleaze like the legendary Kroger Babb's premarital sex shocker **Mom and Dad** (1945), complete with 'birth of a baby' footage and fake foyer doctors offering contraceptive advice.

Of course, peddling sin, scandal, sex and sordidness didn't begin with **Mom and Dad**. Prior to that male/female audience segregated crowd-pleaser, there was **Sex** (1920), **Trapped by the**

Mormons (1922), **Virtue's Revolt** (1924), **Party Girl** (1930), **Morals for Women** (1931), **Maniac** (1934), **Gambling with Souls** (1936) and all manner of dodgy carny-style entertainments. But the Babb blockbuster made so much money over so many years it couldn't help but prove alluring to other razor-blade smiling showbiz swindlers. And joining Babb in the con artist collective known as the Forty Thieves were the likes of Dwain Esper (**Marihuana**, 1936), Barry Mahon (**Cuban Rebel Girls**, 1959) and David F. Friedman (**Blood Feast**, 1963). Science fiction, nudist camps, softcore smut noirs and horror rapidly got thrown into the eclectic forbidden mix and soon such directors as Roger Corman would arrive on the scene to exploit the gap in the new burgeoning teenage market with his brand of assorted monsters on the loose, switchblade gang thrillers, and eventually Hells Angels westerns. The 1960s also opened up the field to such heavy-hitters as Russ Meyer, Herschell Gordon Lewis and Radley Metzger, to name the tip of the vice-berg.

But it was the rediscovery of the 1938 anti-dope chestnut **Reefer Madness** by the turned-on hippie generation who thought they had invented drug culture that really began putting the word Exploitation on the film buff discussion table. What was once a 'tell your children' moral tale was now a hilarious tawdry treasure trove of creaky camp, bad acting and misinformation that proved irresistible on the Midnight Movie and University Campus circuits. **Freaks** (1932), **Cocaine Fiends** (1935) and **Sex Madness** (1938) were also revived as such vintage edgy romps turned the spotlight on what similar contemporary delights were now available down the street at the local Grindhouse where a free-for-all attitude, crappy execution, seamy stories, trashy terror but high level entertainment value could all be counted on in crazy-for-kicks spades.

I mostly found out about such flicks in magazines like 'Continental Film Review'. But my genre bible was 'Castle of Frankenstein' magazine, well, when I could find copies in out-of-the-way dodgy newsagents, my local favourite being in New Road, Copnor, in my hometown of Portsmouth, Hampshire. I almost felt like that sleazy Miles Malleson customer character in **Peeping Tom** (1960) requesting to see some "views" when asking for the most recent copies of my favourite genre journal. 'Famous Monsters of Filmland'

being the derided poor substitute with its stupidly juvenile eyerolling puns ("You axed for it!") if 'Castle of Frankenstein' wasn't available. But looking back now in enlightened hindsight I can see clearly how I was very much indeed the Exploited, even though I didn't realise it at the time. All I knew was I loved the ritual of going out to see something forbidden, shocking and naughty. I adored being taken in by the impossible poster images and headline hype because I really never knew, maybe this time it would actually deliver. And I still do. That too often delusional anticipation has never left me.

My devotion to all things horror, sci-fi, fantasy and, okay, Exploitation related can be traced back to my very first solo outing to the cinema in Southsea, my seaside Portsmouth family enclave. While I can just about remember my father taking me to see the circus drama **Trapeze** (1956) and a rare family outing to Cecil B. DeMille's **The Ten Commandments** (1956), it wasn't until I braved the Gaumont, Highland Road, for the U-certificate **Abbott and Costello Meet the Mummy** (1955) and literally spent half the time cowering behind the seat during the Klaris the Mummy chases that I knew my life would never be the same again. From that moment on I became delicious-fright obsessed and read every horror paperback – the multi-volume 'Pan Book of Horror Stories' being a favourite – and true crime book I could lay my hands on. Still the scariest hardback I've ever read, and the one that kept me up at nights staring into the blackest shadows, is Charles Franklin's shockingly explicit and appalling 'The World's Worst Murderers' (Odhams, 1965), outlining in lipsmacking detail the notorious crimes of such psychopaths as Peter Kürten, Béla Kiss and Peter Manuel.

In common with many future movie buffs I also went through that rite of passage of attending Saturday Morning Pictures. I wonder how many other fledgling buffs caught the cinema bug solely because their mothers wanted them out of the house at the weekend? The ABC cinema circuit had a rival event, The ABC Minors, but the local Odeon in Highland Road, Southsea, was my nearest venue so the obvious choice come rain or shine. For sixpence (half a shilling, or 2½ pence in new money!) you lined up with the other raucous kids and got treated to a full morning programme permutation comprising of a Laurel and Hardy short, a Gene Autry mini Western or a Flash Gordon serial, and then either a naff Children's Film

Foundation release like **The Adventures of Hal 5** (1958) or **Soapbox Derby** (1958), or a been-around-the-block main feature like **The Day the Earth Stood Still** (1951), the one I remember making the most impression upon me.

It wasn't long before these anticipated outings transformed into proper regular cinema going (the whole point of them from a cinema business perspective), mainly on a Sunday evening because that's when the weekly programme changed, unless there was a holdover like the two I most vividly remember, **From Russia with Love** (1963) and **Casino Royale** (1967). Both James Bond movies, incredibly interesting that! Very quickly Hammer swashbucklers, historical adventures and fantasies, like **The Devil-Ship Pirates** (1964), **The Brigand of Kandahar** (1965) and **She** (1965), were being ticked off the looking-forward-to release calendar. And then there were, of course, the thrilling Ray Harryhausen flights of stop-motion imagination, and I know I'm not alone in recalling the timeless classic **Jason and the Argonauts** (1963) as another game-changer in crystallising my genre tastes for the rest of my life.

Then came the next rite of passage for every nascent young movie lover of the era; progressing up the certification ranks from the taken-for-granted U to the must-see A, because the latter meant you had to be over sixteen or accompanied by an adult. My parents weren't interested in helping advance my movie knowledge so I had to do what many will now see as totally unacceptable behaviour, but it was the norm for that time – hanging around outside the cinema and asking couples, but mainly single men, if they would pretend to know you and escort you into the auditorium. What were we thinking? But, of course, it was a vastly different and more innocent age. I can honestly say though that I was never put in any compromising position using this dubious begging method. I did it numerous times but the only memorable occasion was going to see **The List of Adrian Messenger** (1963), the mystery thriller with famous stars wearing rubber masks. Once in the Stalls I sat away from my 'guardian' until the manager, clearly seeing through the familiar ruse, insisted I go back and sit next to him for decorum's sake or else I would be shown the exit.

As soon as I could pass for sixteen, the age you had to be by rigid British law to see an X-certificate film, I did so. (Supplanting the loathed H certificate instigated in 1932, the far more enticing X was introduced by BBFC secretary Arthur Watkins on 1 January 1951). This was the last rite of passage for my Baby Boom generation; putting on grown-up clothes you thought made you look older (school uniform was out, the tie still in), pacing up and

down outside the cinema to summon enough courage to face the stern woman behind the glass ticket booth, the seemingly endless walk from the entrance through the foyer to said booth, sweating profusely as you asked for a ticket in the Stalls, your hand shaking as you handed over the cheapest admission fee (five shillings; 25p), relaxing slightly and breathing more steadily when the transaction was done, sweating again when giving the ticket to the grumpy-looking usher on the auditorium door to tear in half, floating on air, mission-accomplished thrilled as you took the nearest seat to get yourself out of sight as quickly as possible, and then being more scared of being found out than of anything shown on the screen! Always waiting for the manager's hand on your shoulder asking you to leave because you clearly were not supposed to be there and breaking the law. Or the hand on your knee from the Dirty Old Man who suddenly sat next to you despite the auditorium being practically empty. I learned to avoid 'The Raspberry Ruffler', named after the coconut sweets with which he tried to lure you into compliance, at the Essoldo Kings Road, once the usher got to know me well enough to warn me of his whereabouts. The other major pervert hazard was the exhibitionist who would flash his genitals when pushing past in the aisle. Then there was the non-stop wanker who only ever seemed to attend those Margaret Rutherford Miss Marple movies like **Murder She Said** (1961) and vibrate the whole row. Ah, yes, I remember it well.

Just as I remember the poster hoardings at the end of my home street in Southsea, because that ever-changing display of garish double-bill posters set the seal on my unknowing Exploitation choices for years. Every new pasting up would provide an awe-inspiring hard stare for ages that would keep me transfixed to the pavement on the way back from the

Southern Grammar School for Boys on Eastern Road. I didn't know his name at the time but Hammer/Amicus poster designer Tom Chantrell has a lot to answer for when it comes to defining my Exploitation temptations. From the Hammer double bill **The Kiss of the Vampire** (1963) and **Paranoiac** (1963) to **The Demon Doctor/The Awful Dr. Orlof** (1962) twinned with **Varan the Unbelievable** (1962), unbelievably fabulous artwork indeed! I can still picture myself standing in front of the shocking pink poster for **The Gargon Terror**, the British title for **Teenagers from Outer Space** (1959), because it featured a scary giant lobster-like monster menacing screaming crowds. Of course, when I finally saw it many years later, it turned out to be the more rock bottom interpretation – a very unscary shadow of a real lobster being waved in front of the camera with two people cowering. Exploited? Moi?

Years before I could actually see **Psycho** (1960) I could describe every detail on the iconic jagged logo poster to anyone who asked. More than you'd think actually, because my mother ran a summer guesthouse, and I'd bore anyone staying if they showed the slightest interest in films. One guest checked out as I kept giving him adverts for **Repulsion** (1965) I had cut out of the local newspaper because I wanted someone to urgently go and see it and tell me how scary it was. For some reason the double bill of **Frantic/Ascenseur pour l'échafaud** (1958) and **Confess, Dr. Corda/Gestehen Sie, Dr. Corda** (1958), with its purple/green day-glo images of a cowering heroine and a moody villain, really burnished itself on my memory, leaving an everlasting impression, and both movies delivered when I finally saw them, as you will read later on in this volume.

Another crystal clear recollection concerns the moment the poster for **The Day of the Triffids** (1963) double billed with **The Legion's Last Patrol** (1962) appeared at the end of my road. I thought the deadly giant space plant image, looking to all intents and purposes like a fiery artichoke with massive waving arms, was so stunning I crept out of bed at midnight and with a blunt pair of

scissors and tremendous difficulty cut the Triffid half of the poster off the billboard. Ironically, considering where my future writing career was mainly headed, I didn't want the Italian war movie part, whose theme tune by Angelo Francesco Lavagnino was riding high in the pop charts at the time.

Back at home I folded up the ragged torn poster, encrusted with multiple layers of previous attractions, and hid it under my bed. But a nosy neighbour had seen me in covert action and turned up at the front door to grass me out to my mother about my night mission the following day. I was firmly reprimanded and told to put it back. My questioning how I could do that exactly was ignored. So I was forced to leave my prize acquisition lying in front of the billboard I had hacked it from, whereupon it either got nabbed by someone else or was swept away by dustbin men. I was distraught for days afterwards. However, I learnt my lesson. The next time I stole a poster – **Corruption** (1968): "Is Not A Woman's Picture! Therefore: No Woman Will Be Admitted Alone To See This Super-Shock Film!!" – I made sure to cover my tracks, in this instance, the broken glass from the Odeon, Highland Road, display case. Yes, it was I, a juvenile delinquent, I finally confess! Just like Dr. Corda.

The first four X-certificate movies I saw when I was brave enough to endure the 'Long, Long Walk Through The Foyer To The Ticket Booth' were a Sunday evening retrospective screening of **Horrors of the Black Museum** (1959) double billed with its Anglo-Amalgamated stable mate **Circus of Horrors** (1960) at the Classic, Commercial Road, **Blood and Black Lace** (1964) at the Essoldo Kings Road and **Crypt of Horror** (1964) at the Essoldo Kingston Cross. The first three shockers ensured my absolute commitment to sleazy images, sordid stories, florid direction, fabulous photography, glorious soundtracks and nerve-jangling frights. **Circus of Horrors** had been an obsession ever since I saw the giant poster for it at Waterloo Station on my first ever trip to London.

The fourth made me realise, after popping my 'X Adults Only' cherry, that not all horror movies were good, despite even my desperate hopes. I can still bring to mind the depressing boredom I felt watching that dire blunting of Sheridan Le Fanu's classic novel 'Carmilla'.

That's the reason I began keeping a yearly diary on what movies I saw, where I saw them, on what date and my overall views and initial reactions. I kept this rigid protocol going for the next sixteen years, which is when I turned professional film critic and it became a time-consuming impracticality alongside being paid to write up the same titles. What you will read in the main body of this book are my embellished notes and thoughts, with spelling and fact-checked corrections based on those intricate, minutely hand-written diary entries. In one instance – and you'll have to guess which because I'm purposely not divulging it here – I used the completely unaltered review as I first wrote it in 1975 (a clue!)

So I can tell you with complete confidence that I saw **Night of the Big Heat** (1967) double billed with **The 10th Victim** (1965) on Monday 29 January 1968, at the Odeon, Highland Road, **Black Belly of the Tarantula** (1971) with **The Weekend Murders** (1970) on Monday 8 August 1972, at the New Victoria, London, **The Mutations** (1974)

with **Chosen Survivors** (1974) on Thursday 26 September 1974, at the Victoria Broadway, New York, and **The Crimes of the Black Cat** (1972) with **The Horrible Sexy Vampire** (1971) on Wednesday 19 May 1976, at the Hammersmith Broadway, London. And strangely enough I remember every detail about seeing those movies from that Grindhouse Golden Age more than I can recall what I saw at a multi-media preview screening last week.

Is it merely rose-tinted nostalgia or simply a yearning to recreate the key memories of the past that moulded my life and loves? Not at all! It's just that in those days of expectations fuelled by shameless PR and publicity in 'Photoplay' magazine (I had a monthly subscription), the 'ABC Film Review' (which I bought on occasion when a horror star featured on the cover) or the free pocket guides you picked up from the Odeon, 'Showguide' in Portsmouth or the 'West End Cinema Entertainment Guide' that later became 'Movie Goer' in London, anticipation was a crucial element; something that has never gone out of style.

Films of every type, from blockbuster to homegrown comedy, hung around for quite a while so they came with a certain sense of occupational charisma. Titles lingered longer because in London they opened as solo attractions first in the West End, then got a double bill release in North London, followed by South London usually a week later to save on 35mm print costs, and after a while they would appear on Late Night programmes at far-flung repertory cinemas you'd have to travel out to the London suburbs to catch. I always remember seeing **Myra Breckinridge** (1970) at the Rialto, Coventry Street, and

Beyond the Valley of the Dolls (1970) at the Carlton, Haymarket, and being furious I'd seen them separately and more ticket-expensively when they finally ended up together on a nationwide double bill. And despite popular accepted wisdom, not everything turned up at the wonderful Scala Cinema (known as the King's Cross Odeon in the 1960s and the King's Cross Cinema in the '70s)!

In the days before mobile phones, texting and instant communication, I often had standing movie dates with many casual film buff acquaintances. One of my favourite independent films of the era was **The Lords of Flatbush** (1974) and wherever that wonderful Fifties-set coming-of-ager showed – usually at the Paris Pullman in Drayton Gardens off the Finchley Road, or the Odeon, Croydon – I would religiously turn up, get in line – there was always a line – and meet my friends who had also scoured the listings magazines (like 'What's On in London' or my absolute favourite, 'Films Illustrated') for what would now be seen as a collective 'Singalong' experience. "Oh, what a Night for Love" indeed! Making that effort in the dim and distant days before easy access video, DVD or streaming meant the movies impacted more, they didn't just fly out of the mind the moment they finished unspooling, they had a real dominance and persuasive presence, a power differential that made them more a pillar of one's cultural consciousness. That's why they remain such a potent force in the early fanboy and fangirl's perceptions.

My formative years spent honing my naïve diary doodlings into something resembling a critical style would not have happened had I not been smack bang in the middle of what I called the Nine-Pointed Portsmouth Star. Some of those cinemas (now sadly mostly turned into supermarkets or Bingo halls) demanded either a brisk walk or a double bus journey, but not a week went by where you wouldn't find me frequenting the Essoldos – Kings Road and Kingston Cross – the Odeons – Highland Road, Cosham and North End (the nearest Roadshow venue) – the Gaumont London Road, the Classic and ABC on Commercial Road or the Palace on Guildhall Walk. Each picturehouse sparks off irreplaceable reminiscences that fuelled my desire to learn everything about what really seemed the poor relation to the already 'underground' cinema I adored. Uncongenial material that made a silk purse out of a sow's ear in my humble estimation, and while I still had no idea Exploitation movies weren't being taken seriously, all I knew was that I certainly did see their value, no matter how tattered and torn.

It was at the Odeon Highland Road that I saw the Jack the Ripper/Sherlock Holmes shocker **A Study in Terror** (1965) and for the life of me couldn't understand why people would take their seats halfway through the film and then watch the earlier bit they missed after the ice cream intermission. That really was the norm for the time. No wonder Alfred Hitchcock objected to that practice when he launched **Psycho** (1960) with that then controversial "The picture you must see from the beginning!" door policy. It was at the Essoldo Kingston Cross that I saw **The Horror of Party Beach** (1964) twinned with **The Curse of the Living Corpse** (1964), innocently wondering

how come Del Tenney had the time to direct both. Where the 1960s classic double bill of **Terror-Creatures from the Grave** (1965) and **Castle of the Living Dead** (1964), as shamelessly promoted in the short-lived but essential British horror magazine 'Supernatural' debuted. Plus where the controversial hag horror **Lady in a Cage** (1964) and the extraordinary double bill of the Japanese **Onibaba** (1964) and the snoozerama **Nudist Paradise** (1959) ended up because this Essoldo was the main cinema that showed GLC (Greater London Council) rated movies when refused a

certificate by the BBFC. Thank you Portsmouth City Council for just that one adopted policy alone – **Lady in a Cage** is seared on my memory for that prime copycat 'No Cert' reason. As is the delightful Danish sex comedy **Seventeen** (1965). And the Odeon Cosham is where **The Sorcerers** (1967) opened to cement my love of doomed director Michael Reeves.

The Palace was the infamous fleapit venue on the wrong side of town. Every city had one, usually by the main railway station. Being the nearest cinema to maritime Portsmouth's Dockyard, it was where the sailors on leave congregated, apparently to pick up prostitutes. Its Red Light reputation preceded it so much that even my docker father warned me about the place when I was desperate to go and see **Mondo Cane** (1962). However, I did steel myself for the 'Shock... Shock... Shock!!!' Hammer double bill of **The Evil of Frankenstein** (1964) and **Nightmare** (1964) because, for some reason I couldn't fathom, the programme didn't play at my nearest Essoldo. (I would learn about punishing distribution

patterns much later on in my career.) Needless to say I saw nothing untoward happening at all in the dark auditorium and the Palace soon became a regular haunt because all the interesting sounding and perversion-packed foreign sex movies ended up showing there.

It was also an object lesson in ignoring parental advice – Dire Warning equals Absolute Must-Have Exciting Experience. My mother never understood my horror mania. She told me time and again the only horror movie she ever saw was **Phantom of the Opera** (1943) and it scared her so much she never dabbled again. I told Dario Argento this story when he revealed it was his initiation movie too, only with far greater consequences obviously. Only once did my father react to my constant cinema going. After I saw Hammer's **The Witches** (1966), twinned with the crime mystery **Death Is a Woman** (1966), he asked what star Joan Fontaine looked like now because he'd been a big wartime fan. That was the sum total of my parents' shared interest but it suited me fine as I could indulge my passion without any unwanted attention or explanation.

It was at the Palace that I saw a film that would have an unusual and astonishing impact on my subsequent move to London. Michael Winner's **West 11** (1963) was a no-mark crime drama exploiting the contemporary hot topic of Notting Hill Gate slum landlords in the wake of the Profumo scandal. The amateur gangster character played by Alfred Lynch lived in a flat in Colville Terrace, off Powis Square (the famous location for Mick Jagger's house in **Performance**, 1970) and I ended up living at that exact West 11 address. I only realised this years later when I was watching the movie again on late night television and was astounded when Lynch was followed up the stairs by Winner's camera into the very same place I was at that time inhabiting. Now, I live around the corner from where **Horrors of the Black Museum** (1959) was filmed, so it seems that hard-won Exploitation atmosphere will continue to follow me forever. And I have never had any intention of complaining.

The London equivalent to the Palace was the now-demolished Biograph in Wilton Road, opposite Victoria mainline station. But while nothing really happened in the Palace as far as my innocent eyes saw, the seedy shenanigans at the Biograph were notoriously in your face. Managed by British heavyweight boxer Henry Cooper's identical twin brother George, the Biograph was a well-established gay haunt that kept attracting banner headlines – 'Close Down this Cinema of Vice' screamed the 'News of the World' one Sunday – due to the constant moving from seat to seat by the 100% male audience and frequent visits to the gent's toilet on the right hand side of the screen.

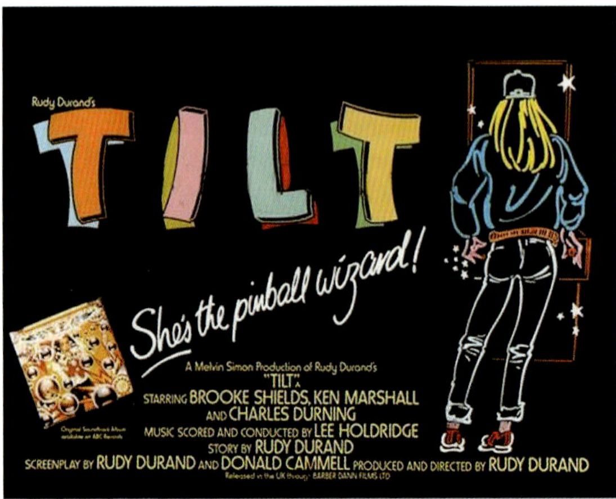

The trouble was the Biograph played some terrific double bills of little-seen cult items, from **Incense for the Damned** (1971) twinned with the Swedish erotic horror **Fear Has 1,000 Eyes** (1970) to 'Sunday Matinee Only' Roger Corman monster classics. I dared to enter the place a few times, the most memorable occasion being to catch a rare screening of **Four Flies on Grey Velvet** (1971). But the constant activity and seat-banging action was just too intrusive and being on guard for wandering hands all the time was exhausting. It always amused me that one of the final twin programmes before the place closed for good was **Tilt** (1979) and **Blow Out** (1981), not so much a double bill, I surmised, as instructions on the cruising protocol!

When I moved to London in 1969 to reinvent my teenage self into a Carnaby Street Dedicated Follower of Fashion, whole new cinemagoing avenues opened up and I lost no time exploring the delights of the glittering West End, even though the first horror movie I saw in the capital was **Eye of the Cat** (1969) at the Odeon Edgware Road. The ritzy Leicester Square venues mainly catered for the blockbuster crowd (the Leicester Square Theatre that became the Odeon West End even put on hour-long free lunchtime shows of trailers, a useful rest stop) and I soon gravitated more to my House of Schlock locations of choice – the Rialto in Coventry Street (where I saw **Doctor Death: Seeker of Souls**, 1973), the Odeon 2, Shepherds Bush (**Zoltan… Hound of Dracula**, 1977), the Classic, Praed Street (**Miss Leslie's Dolls**, 1973), The Broadway in Hammersmith (**The Bell of Hell**, 1973), The Metropole in Victoria (**The Fiend**, 1972), and between the latter and the Biograph, the New Victoria, which pretty much became my home from home because that's where every Hammer, Amicus and A.I.P. movie premiered.

Now a musical theatre venue, the cavernous New Victoria hosted **Countess Dracula**(1971)/**Hell's Belles** (1969), **Vampire Circus** (1972)/**Angels Who Burn Their Wings** (1970), **Dr. Phibes Rises Again** (1972)/**The Return of Count Yorga** (1971), **Bonnie's Kids** (1972)/**Scream… and Die!** (1973), **Blood Brides** (1970)/**The Creeping Flesh** (1973), **Blood and Lace** (1971)/**Psych-Out**

(1968), **Stanley** (1972)/**Blood Mania** (1970), **Something Creeping in the Dark** (1971)/**Night of the Damned** (1971)… far too many greats to list. Except to note that I saw practically every key *giallo* in this sorely missed rococo palace, something I only really appreciated in astonished hindsight. I also nearly caused the place to burn down. You could smoke in cinemas back then and when my movie-going companion at the time put his cigarette out, he didn't notice the girl sat in front of us had long hair and that strands were dangling in the ashtray fixed to the back of her seat. Before you could shout "Towering Inferno", I tried dousing the fire with my Kia-ora drink, which only made it far worse for some reason, causing a huge kerfuffle with the manager, ushers and ice-cream tray lady when the flaming haired punter ran down the aisle screaming… 'Wicked' indeed, just like the musical that is now entrenched in that remodelled Apollo theatre.

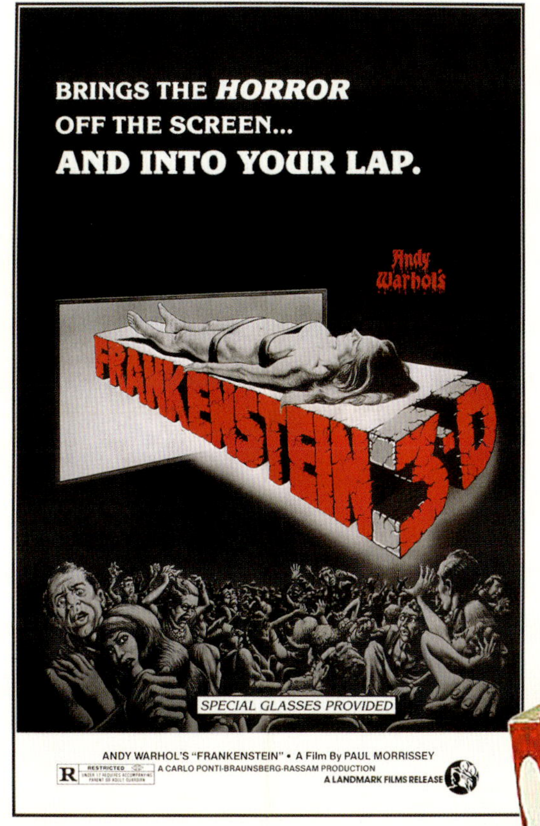

If moving to London ramped up those delightful Grindhouse experiences beyond my wildest dreams, extended trips to Los Angeles and New York during the Disco 1970s was a further earthquake of revelation. Summer night Drive-Ins and neon-drenched 42nd Street, who could ask for anything more? I bravely and valiantly marched into notorious dives to see everything I thought would be denied a certificate back in backward Blighty, such as **Andy Warhol's Frankenstein** (1973) in 3D, **Flesh Gordon** (1974), and a clutch of porno chic items like **The Devil in Miss Jones** (1973) and **Memories Within Miss Aggie** (1974).

On later visits I was lucky to have as my Manhattan guide the incredible Bill Landis, who changed perceptions on Exploitation as Art with his seminal fanzine 'Sleazoid Express'.

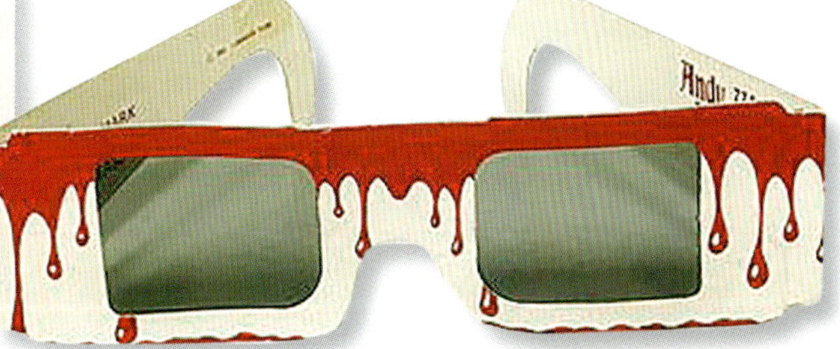

NOT TO BE CONFUSED WITH THE ORIGINAL "FLASH GORDON"
AN OUTRAGEOUS PARODY OF YESTERDAYS' SUPER HEROS!
GRAFFITTI PRODUCTIONS
FLESH GORDON
PETER LOCKE & JIM BUCKLEY
PRESENT
A MAMMOTH FILM RELEASE
STARRING
JASON WILLIAMS / Flesh Gordon
SUZANNE FIELDS / Dale Ardor
JOHN HOYT / Prof. Gordon
Produced By / HOWARD ZIEHM
WILLIAM OSCO
Directed By / HOWARD ZIEHM
MICHAEL BENVENISTE
In Metro Color

His non-stop mantra about 'mainstream' critics assuming they knew better than supposed 'unsophisticated' audiences how to judge a good or bad film was an inspiration to me and his desire to find alternative representations of what constituted guilty pleasure entertainment away from the classic ideal resonated in my professional writing forever after. Together we saw **Ms.45** (1981) twinned with **Amin: The Rise and Fall** (1981) at a particularly rundown 42nd Street cesspit and I soon realised the pimps, pushers and assorted degenerates who were in the auditorium with us were a major part of the theatre of the entire Exploitation experience. They would have their legs draped over the seat in front, excitedly talk back at the screen when not yelling at each other, cheer the brutality, constantly wolfwhistle and make brain-freezingly lewd comments whenever a naked girl or sex scene reared their heads. Totally different to the far more refined British reactions I had come across before. But the one trip with Bill I will never forget is our excursion to a dilapidated Bowery cinema to see a gay porno triple bill, in which he suddenly appeared as a cast member.

Another Times Square expedition highlight was attending the opening day performance (16 February 1976) of the granddaddy of all infamous Grindhouse con tricks, **Snuff** (1976) at the Mann's National. We queued for ages to get in, constantly being harassed by protestors (paid for, as we all subsequently discovered) and handed flyers denouncing the disgusting screening. It cost an outrageous $4 for a ticket, which I eventually came to realise was money well spent, not because of the dire movie's laughable cash-in fakery, but because I have dined out on this Exploitation pinnacle forever after. For I will never forget the palpable wave of shocked expectancy that swept through the jam-packed crowd when the tacked-on gore finale started, only to be deflated by someone yelling, "I want my money back!"

Veteran Exploitation director/producer Roger Corman once explained the required elements needed for his medic and mammary cycle, beginning with **The Student Nurses** (1970):

"Exploitation of the male sexual fantasy, a comedic sub-plot, action and violence, another slightly-to-the-left-of-centre sub-plot, frontal nudity from the waist up, total nudity from behind, no pubic hair and the title in the dialogue somewhere". Still pretty good rules for anyone willing to toe the line in order to prove they are talented enough and ready to step up into 'proper' cinema. For truly gifted filmmakers can grab at a minuscule budget tight schedule, a low-paid, inexperienced/non-union crew, minimal production values, sensational promotion campaigns and saturated bookings aimed at specific demographics to rise above their aggressively marketed competition and shine. Like Martin Scorsese, Robert Towne, Jonathan Demme, Francis Ford Coppola, Joe Dante, Peter Jackson, and so on.

There was also the growing distaff equivalent determining Exploitation items be made for the slowly emerging pro-active female demographic in response to the Women's Lib movement too. They were women, hear them roar, in numbers too big for distributors to ignore! As usual, the Exploitation industry was ahead of the curve in appealing to the fairer sex with subject matters far removed from Doris Day, beach parties and the coy drama of getting to first base. King Leer Russ Meyer probably started it with **Faster, Pussycat! Kill! Kill!** (1965) but it was a few more years until the super-aggressive dominatrix started to come to the fore. So what if **She-Devils on Wheels** (1968), **The Big Doll House** (1971), **The Hot Box** (1972) or **The Doll Squad** (1973) simply did a sexual role reversal, casting forceful women as male mirror images, ones looking at men as mere lust objects and instantly disposable mates. It was during the peak era for Exploitation that women started making the viewing choices rather than leaving it to chance anyway. And that subtle feminist shift would filter into the mainstream pretty quickly, changing it forever.

One from that list of female-skewed movies represents the first time I can recall seeing the word Exploitation used to describe what I had

always thought of as mere B-movie pulp trash. Outside the distributor press books that is, which would always highlight the 'exploitable' aspects of the picture in question. My favourites: "The radio tape for **Ilsa: She Wolf of the SS** (1975) is available in two versions. One, of women screaming, will need to be approved by your local radio station. Or we can supply a more subdued version"; "**The Christine Jorgensen Story** (1970) will be of particular interest to those associated with the medical profession – hospital staff, Nursing Associations, Red Cross Societies, St. John's Ambulance Brigades, etc, so be sure to let them know about the forthcoming presentation". As if!

Released in the UK by the inimitable Master of Hyperbole, producer, director and distributor Antony Balch, Mark Lester's **Truck Stop Women** (1974) garnered contemporary reviews unlike any I'd ever read before. Critics quoting its Greek tragedy underpinnings, understated eccentricities and murderous matriarchal role models positioned it as not only a cult film in the making – which it did indeed become – but also as a prime example of bargain basement Exploitation in raw action. Suddenly it all clicked into place and I realised exactly what the genre was meant to be, plus what it could be when someone with the right mindset tackled it head-on, with no apologies. And like centrefold girls Mamie Van Doren, Tura Satana, Edy Williams and Erica Gavin before her, and Cheri Caffaro and Cheryl/Rainbeaux Smith after, doomed femme fatale Claudia Jennings lit up the screen to become an iconic Grindhouse Girl.

I've had many discussions on this subject over the years with my peers and filmmakers from all across the globe, and experience has led me to break down what I believe are 'The Five Capital T Rules of Exploitation': Tat, Titillation, Trash, Terror and Treasure…

TAT

The completely careless movie made by barely competent filmmakers who either have creativity delusions, or have just thrown something together knowing it will find an audience no matter how bad it is, merely based on the catchy title. Examples: **The Corpse Grinders** (1971), **Blood Orgy of the She-Devils** (1973), **The Mighty Gorga** (1969) and **The Sweet Sound of Death** (1965).

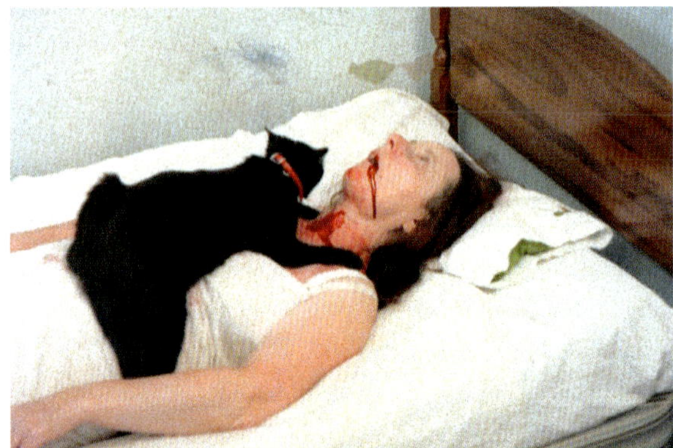

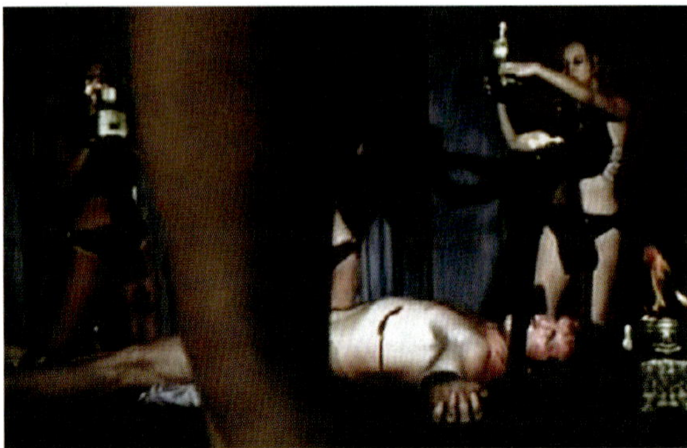

TITILLATION

The cheap erotic thriller/comedy/horror that sacrifices everything, from decent performances and serviceable script to cheap locations and shoddy direction, just as long as the quota of topless and naked backside shots is filled. A few gross *double entendres* don't go amiss either. Examples: **The Naked Hours** (1964), **Girls Come First** (1975) and all films in the peek-a-bush 1970s German **Schulmädchen-Report** series.

TRASH

The blatantly commercial construct that revels in its own kitsch and aura of immediate disposability, dabbling in poor taste, highlighting needless nudity, gratuitous gore and heightened violence. Basically the canny reversal of all acceptable market forces: A-List stars, narrative realism, psychological development and big budget production values. Examples: **Terminal Island** (1973) and **The Arena** (1974).

TERROR

The horror, science fiction fantasy item that doesn't need any stars, proper direction or technical skills, just one or two notable sudden jolts, gruesome moments or prominent monster nonsense to create crucial word-of-mouth. Examples: **The Flesh Eaters** (1964), **Love Me Deadly** (1972) and **Bloodlust** (1976).

TREASURE

The ripe-for-discovery films that show a clear *auteur* sensibility the moment they open and are instantly destined for cult status. Ones cleverly using accepted clichés and the consistent set of Exploitation preoccupations by twisting them for their own political, sexual and cultural ends to create something special. Examples: **Spider Baby** (1967), **The Bell of Hell** (1973), **Jackson County Jail** (1976) and **Alligator** (1980).

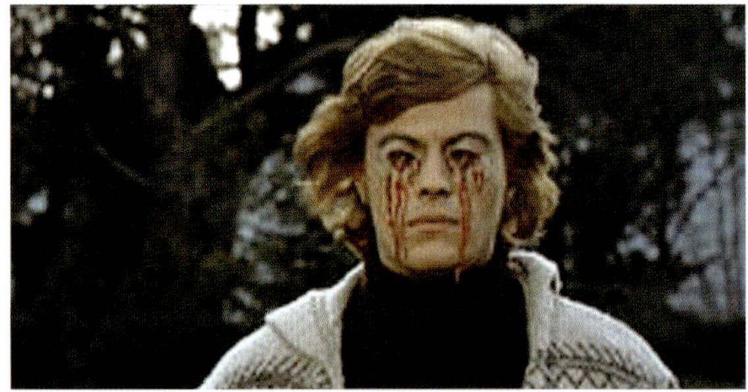

It was always a constant source of irritation to me in my adolescence when scouring 'Castle of Frankenstein' or 'Famous Monsters of Filmland' magazines that the movies illustrated would seem to be so easily accessible to my American counterparts. In Great Britain I wouldn't be able to see any of the choice items being raved about by editors Calvin Beck, Forrest J. Ackerman, and especially contributor-turned-director Joe Dante. I could only yearn to see **The Horror Chamber of Dr. Faustus/Les yeux sans visage** (1960) or **Jack the Ripper** (1959) while those lucky Yanks could just turn up at their local cinema, pay and walk in. The reality wasn't quite as simple as that of course, even though there clearly was a disconnection between the United Kingdom and the United States in terms of cultural differences and the regulatory environment where ratings were concerned.

First there was the poles-apart mindset of the British Board of Film Censors/Classification in Britain and the Motion Picture Association of America. While most everything genre related was slapped with an X certificate by the BBFC in the UK, a G, M or GP rating seemed to suffice in the States, the latter with that MPAA-insisted-upon poster box explanation: 'Parental Guidance Suggested. All Ages Admitted'. Essentially a meaningless certificate if children were allowed entrance no matter what. American friends and acquaintances have told me they barely registered the MPAA ratings, if at all, and were almost never refused admission to see anything unless it contained obvious nudity or a sex scene. **Blood Feast** (1963) at a pay per vehicle Drive-In meant no one was checking the back seats or car boots for stowaways anyway. Even when Mario Bava's **Black Sunday** (1960) touted the producer warning "The picture will shock you like no picture ever has", that it may be "harmful to the young and impressionable" and that it shouldn't be viewed by anyone younger than 14 years of age. Remember how British horror fans had to wait eight years for the badly cut and retitled **Revenge of the Vampire** version to arrive on our shores? At least we didn't have to deal with the Catholic League of Decency though, which condemned anything a bunch of pious hypocrites considered vile and unwholesome. Amazing to think this advisory board could diminish the box office of even the most borderline offensive film.

The 42nd Street environment was a totally separate kettle of fish. There was never any age restriction implemented, not even when pornography started taking over the area. No one ever checked I.D., they just took your money – $1.50 for a horror triple bill usually featuring **The Embalmer** (1965) somewhere in the line-up – and never even asked you to leave the auditorium once the session was over. High volume meant low maintenance and if the place wasn't emptied out within a 24-hour period it saved on housekeeping and cleaning bills. Hence the reason why companies like American International Pictures did so well, as every Exploitation film could still bring in a decent box office return when even clueless children could go through the turnstiles. It was this audience who didn't care about character arcs, plot holes or production values. They just wanted startling action, controversial thrills, bizarre chills and as much bare flesh and racy language as the censors would allow.

It is no coincidence that the most famous incident concerning the effect of Exploitation on American children happened the same year the old ratings system was replaced by a voluntary one. In 1968 Roger Ebert, the celebrated film critic of the

'Chicago Sun-Times' newspaper (and later co-screenwriter of **Beyond the Valley of the Dolls**, 1970) attended a public screening of George A. Romero's epoch-making **Night of the Living Dead** (1968) and was completely shocked, not only by the zombie film itself, but by the large number of children present at the Saturday afternoon matinee. Dumped by their parents, who obviously considered the 40 cent ticket price a baby-sitting bargain, Ebert watched the popcorn-munching kids go from playgroup larking about in the aisles and screaming in fun at the opening Black and White images to crying in unexpected terror and whimpering in shock as the galvanizing true horror of the future classic took hold. His vitriolic diatribe against the censorship system that allowed impressionable children to see such adult content caused a lot of navel-gazing and rethinking about the fast-buck Exploitation business that had many ramifications going forward. Mainly in keeping the adolescent audience out, but also ramping up what was acceptable to exhibitors who couldn't afford to compete with the major studios' slick product. The result was an increase in sick product that Hollywood either could not or would not make. And the rest is Grindhouse history.

Unlike my previous tome, *The FrightFest Guide to Exploitation Movies*, where I felt compelled to cover quite familiar titles to provide the right historical context, *The FrightFest Guide to Grindhouse Movies* delves further beneath the grimy surface to provide a next level, personal depth of understanding of the entire genre. I'm not saying these are the best, worst or most indifferent releases the Drive-In Grindhouse circuit could provide. But I wanted to highlight the very rarely discussed titles that even I was surprised to find tucked away in the dark recesses of my meticulously precise if dusty diaries. Do I regret sitting through some of the films even the most die-hard dreck aficionados might consider an awful chore? Not in the slightest. I deem myself lucky to have lived through what is now seen as a Golden Era for the much criticized genre, and even luckier to have seen everything on the Big Screen as nature always intended. I only hope you take pleasure in what I have spent a stimulating lifetime of compiling for my own enjoyment and now, I trust, yours. Welcome to another peek at the seamy, shocking and scandalous sides of reel life through the deliciously distorted keyhole of an alternative film history.

Right, you've read from what personal angles the following fact-packed reviews are coming, so get ready for yet more in your face excess all areas jaw-dropping thrills, chills and sexcitement that boasts...

You Have Never! Ever! Witnessed Anything Like It!

Now on the screen with every shock and sensation intact!

Actually filmed in the Dark Corners of this Sick World!

A scorching motion picture, everything you knew it had to be!

A story so brutal and horrifying it was kept from the public for over a century!

SEE Incomparable scenes of primitive wonderment!

If you survive this, nothing will scare you again!

He used a camera like most men use a woman!

What is the worst act a woman can be forced to commit... again... and again... and again?

Love Lusts and Blood Lusts that will Shock you out of your seat and mind!

Intrigued? If so join your FrightFest guru of gore and grime to uncover yet more secrets behind the most malicious, malpracticed and murkiest celluloid crimes ever released on an unsuspecting public.

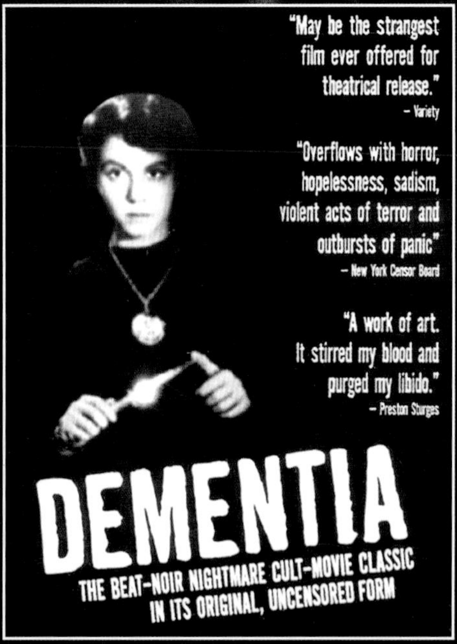

"May be the strangest film ever offered for theatrical release." – Variety

"Overflows with horror, hopelessness, sadism, violent acts of terror and outbursts of panic" – New York Censor Board

"A work of art. It stirred my blood and purged my libido." – Preston Sturges

DEMENTIA

THE BEAT-NOIR NIGHTMARE CULT-MOVIE CLASSIC IN ITS ORIGINAL, UNCENSORED FORM

DEMENTIA

USA, 1953
Directors: John Parker, Bruno VeSota [uncredited].
Producer: John Parker. Screenplay: John Parker.
Music: George Antheil. Cinematography: William C. Thompson.
Cast: Adrienne Barrett, Bruno VeSota, Ben Roseman,
Richard Barron, Ed Hinkle, Lucille Howland.

A cult Exploitation classic that so riled the New York censors after its initial Californian screening that it was banned for two years before getting a delayed release, ironically double-billed with the documentary **Picasso** (1954), only to find a new lease of life thanks to the science fiction blockbuster **The Blob** (1958). Accompanied by a dissonant score by Hollywood veteran George Antheil and sporting no dialogue, director John Parker's unique opus follows 'The Gamin' (Adrienne Barrett), a psychotic young woman on a Freudian nightmare journey through skid row. Encountering tidal waves, wife beating, a circus dwarf, winos and recalling her father killing her mother, she must retrieve a pendant incriminating her in the murder of The Fat Man (Bruno VeSota, associate producer and uncredited co-director). Filmed quickly in the same Venice, California, locations Orson Welles would use for **Touch of Evil** (1958), once past its minuscule initial release, producer Jack H. Harris picked it up, trimmed it down, added a narration by future 'Tonight Show' announcer Ed McMahon and re-titled it **Daughter of Horror**. And by having it play in the famous movie theatre attack scene in Harris's production of **The Blob**, Parker's oddment has endured in the most unusual way.

THE GOLDEN MISTRESS

USA, 1954
Director: Joel Judge [Abner Biberman].
Producers: Richard Kay, Harry Rybnick.
Screenplay: Lee Hewitt, Abner Biberman.
Music: Raoul Kraushaar. Cinematography: William C. Thompson.
Cast: John Agar, Rosemarie Bowe [Rosemarie Stack], Abner Biberman, André Narcisse, Jacques Molant, André Contant.

A perfect example of targeted travelogue functioning as both exotic entertainment and aspirational tourist filler. Throw in a little action and thrills acted out with disinterest by horror staple John Agar (**Tarantula**, 1955) and eye candy Rosemarie Bowe (soon to marry Robert Stack) and the result was an endlessly playable bottom half of a double bill for the boondocks. Abner Biberman directed this jungle horror under the alias Joel Judge, also starring as the villain of the piece. Treasure hunters Agar and Bowe find a valuable idol used in voodoo ceremonies at the bottom of a lake in Haiti.

Biberman steals it but dies of the supposed attached black magic curse so the intrepid duo search out The Untamed lost tribe to return the artefact to its rightful owners. With terrific location photography and vistas of historical sites, the tribal dancing was paid-for performances by the National Folklore Theatre of Haiti, the reason they look so well-choreographed and authentic. On the art reflects life downside, the production hired a local doctor as their on-set physician – Papa 'Doc' François Duvalier, soon to be elected President of Haiti – whose corrupt and murderous government would remain in office until 1971.

THE FLAMING TEENAGE

USA, 1956
Directors: Charles Edwards, Irvin S. Yeaworth Jr.
Producers: Charles Edwards, Irvin S. Yeaworth Jr.
Screenplay: Ethel Barrett, Jean Yeaworth.
Cinematography: John Ayling.
Cast: Noel Reyburn, Ethel Barrett, Jerry Franks, Shirley Holmes, Jan Davis, Jo Warner.

Back in 1945, Charles Edwards directed a short under the title **Twice Convicted**. Even by contemporary standards it was a dated warning about the evils of alcohol, drugs and loose women and remained languishing on the shelf. Until a decade later when the newly minted Teenage Generation began showing increased spending power and laxer attitudes. So Irvin S. Yeaworth Jr., future director of **The Blob** (1958), dusted it off, made it the prologue to a repurposed 'Scare Flick', and helmed additional footage. It begins with an on-screen narrator, sitting behind a desk, and regaling the viewer with the plight of an underage drinker thrown into jail shown the error of his ways by his father taking him to a bar and pointing out all the ruined lives. Then come the Yeaworth appendages, the supposed true-life story of Fred Garland (Noel Reyburn), bored with small town life, who heads for the big city for a showbiz career, hits the bottle, gets hooked on smack and becomes a Born Again Christian when jailed. A time immemorial moral tale blunted into parental propaganda but laced with enough hilarious camp to enjoy, like the crazed boozing sequence straight out of **Reefer Madness** (1936).

NOTHING LIKE HIM HAS HIT THE SCREEN SINCE
JAMES DEAN

TEENAGE WOLFPACK

THINK OF A LAW! ...they've broken it! THINK OF A CRIME! ...they've committed it!

starring
HENRY BOOKHOLT
KAREN BAAL

Directed by GEORG TRESSLER
Produced by WENZEL LUDECKE
Released by DCA

57/595

TEENAGE WOLFPACK

West Germany, 1956
Director: Georg Tressler.
Producer: Wenzel Lüdecke.
Screenplay: Will Tremper, Georg Tressler.
Music: Martin Böttcher.
Cinematography: Heinz Pehlke.
Cast: Horst Buchholz, Karin Baal, Christian Doermer, Jo Herbst, Viktoria von Ballasko, Stanislav Ledinek.

In the aftermath of the **Rebel Without a Cause** (1955) blockbuster acclaim and shocking tragedy, the global film industry was on the lookout for someone they could call the new James Dean. Germany's teen idol answer was Horst Buchholz, or Henry Bookholt as the American posters billed him to disguise its foreign pedigree, in that country's first look at juvenile delinquency. At the time considered incisive and unsentimental enough to win major awards and be considered a post-war classic, it's a tough tale of West Berlin gang violence and robbery arrest as leader of the wolfpack Freddy (Buchholz) plans a mail van raid in order to help his parents pay a massive debt and fulfil his dream of owning a Buick Cabriolet. Redolent with the vibrant atmosphere The Beatles absorbed when they hit Hamburg in their earliest band incarnation, debut director Georg Tressler stayed in the same social ills area with his next movie **Under 18** (1957). Released in the UK as just **Wolfpack** and in America on a double-bill with the British **My Teenage Daughter** (1956) retitled **Teenage Bad Girl**, it made Buchholz an international star who would appear in **Tiger Bay** (1959) and **The Magnificent Seven** (1960).

WHO DONE IT?

UK, 1956
Director: Basil Dearden. Producer: Michael Relph.
Screenplay: T.E.B. Clarke. Music: Philip Green.
Cinematography: Otto Heller.
Cast: Benny Hill, Belinda Lee, David Kossoff, Garry Marsh, George Margo, Ernest Thesiger.

Two decades before he surprisingly took America by storm with his suggestive brand of smutty humour, British comedy star Benny Hill had already snuck into Grindhouses with this slapstick spy caper. One of the Ealing Comedies that rarely gets discussed, scripted by 'Tibby' Clarke (**Passport to Pimlico**, 1949, **The Lavender Hill Mob,** 1951), and directed by Basil Dearden (the **Dead of Night**, 1945, segment 'Hearse Driver'), it was merely a vehicle to consolidate the saucy smirker's showbiz career after making key revue, radio and television inroads with his sometime partner Reg ('On the Buses') Varney. As corny as his future Hill's Angels output, if less risqué, the cheeky chappie plays Hugo Dill, an ice rink janitor who dreams of being a detective. After winning a cash prize and a bloodhound in a magazine sleuthing contest he turns Private Investigator, his first case involving an unfaithful husband and a spy hunt geared around an Iron Curtain scientist and Top Secret weather-creating gizmo. Doomed Fifties sensation Belinda Lee is the romantic sidekick. Mainly reliant for laughs on gag disguises and amusing cameos from the usual comic suspects, it's the high quota of fantasy content that singles this out from the crowd.

THE BLACK SCORPION

USA, 1957
Director: Edward Ludwig.
Producers: Jack Dietz, Frank Melford.
Screenplay: David Duncan, Robert Blees.
Music: Paul Sawtell.
Cinematography: Lionel Lindon.
Cast: Richard Denning, Mara Corday, Carlos Rivas, Mario Navarro, Carlos Múzquiz, Pascual García Peña.

Inspired by **Them!** (1954) and **Tarantula** (1955), this bleak, multi-legged Monsterama might be low budget and the creepy-crawly special effects dimly lit or matted-in poorly but it remains an effectively frightening shocker nevertheless. Especially for arachnophobics, despite the scorpions' faces – using the one large prop sandwiched between fine stop-motion animation – depicted more like a goofy bashed crab! A south-of-the-border volcano eruption unearths a nest of humungous prehistoric scorpions, also home to giant clawed worms and spiders. Wooden geologist hero Richard Denning and local rancher Mara Corday track the last Scorpionida Rex to Mexico City and kill it with an electrified harpoon. **King Kong** (1933) creator Willis O'Brien was the special effects supervisor on this typical for the era B-movie creature feature. Most of the hands-on visuals though were by Pete Peterson who worked with O'Brien on **Mighty Joe Young** (1949) and **The Giant Behemoth** (1959). While plot, script and execution is 1950s bog-standard, the scorpion footage is surprisingly violent, especially the stinger impaling and the train crash. Many claimed the additional insectoid horrors were models from the deleted 'spider pit' sequence in **King Kong**, but O'Brien's protégée Ray Harryhausen never thought so, and he should know!

BOP GIRL GOES CALYPSO

USA, 1957
Director: Howard W. Koch.
Producer: Aubrey Schenck.
Screenplay: Arnold Belgard. Music: Les Baxter.
Cinematography: Carl E. Guthrie.
Cast: Judy Tyler, Bobby Troup, Margo Woode, Lucien Littlefield, Nino Tempo, George O'Hanlon.

Straight after highlighting Rock 'N' Roll as 'the most' in **Untamed Youth** (1957), director Howard W. Koch proclaimed it Deadsville in this bonkers programmer that could only be made by Hollywood squares. College student Robert Hilton – Bobby Troup, writer of the 1946 hit '(Get Your Kicks on) Route 66' – invents an Applause-O-Meter that measures a declining lack of interest in Rock music in such hip clubs as the Downbeat. Predicting a rise in Calypso craziness (seemingly based on Harry Belafonte's chart success), he drags die-hard bop girl Jo Thomas (Judy Tyler) to Club Trinidad to scale the infectious beat. Because, as the crew-cut hep-cat declares, "Tonight I'm going to record the first mass hysteria induced by Calypso!" Merely an excuse to showcase a number of acts as the duo 'make the scene', those featured are Nino Tempo, The Titans, The Mary Kaye Trio and authentic Calypso legend Lord Flea. In truth more Jazz, Do-Wop and Lounge accented, but then Calypso hardly made it out of the Easy Listening bracket – 'There's a Hole in My Bucket' (1961) anyone? Tyler, also the female lead in **Jailhouse Rock** the same year, died in a car crash before either got released.

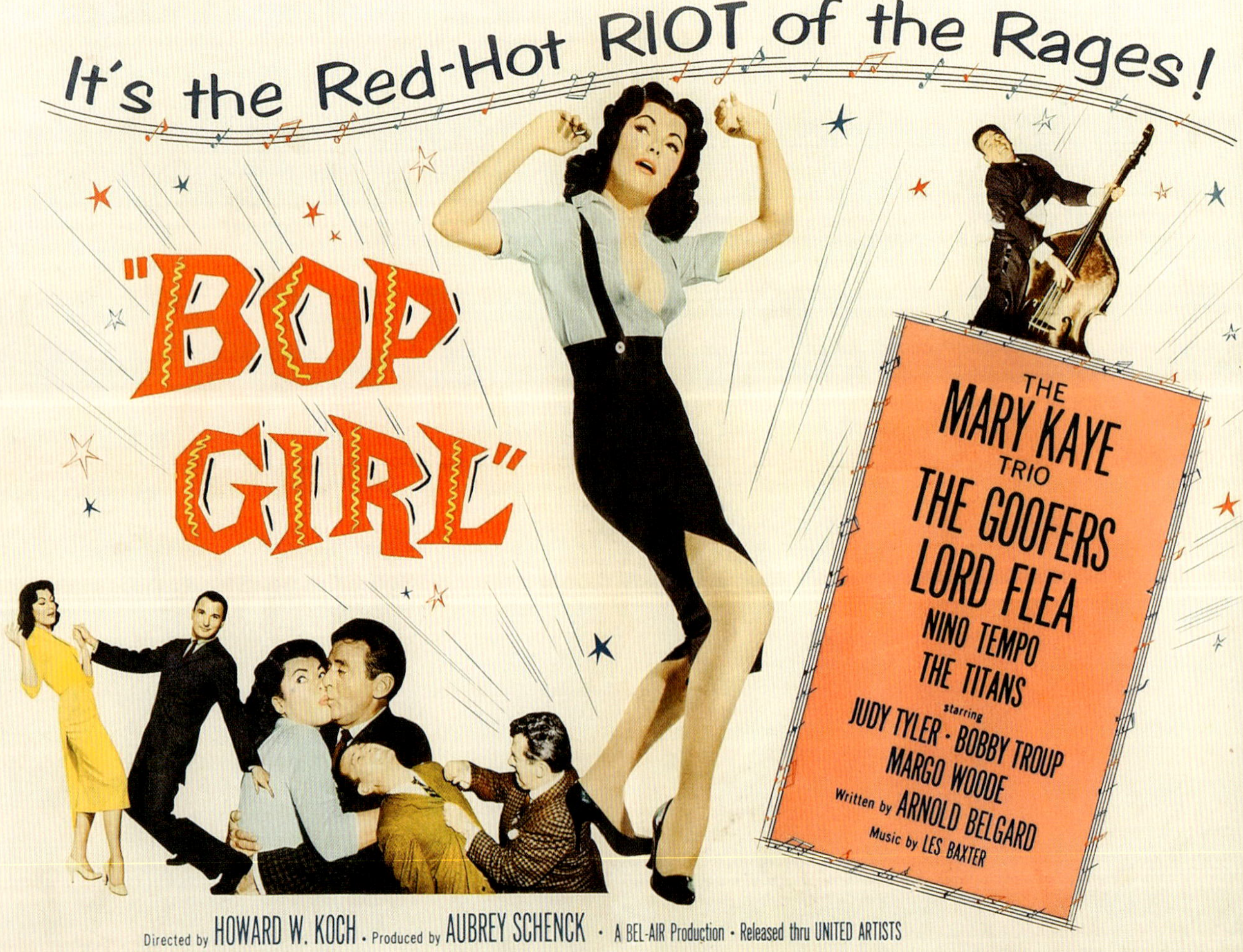

It's the Red-Hot RIOT of the Rages!

"BOP GIRL"

THE MARY KAYE TRIO
THE GOOFERS
LORD FLEA
NINO TEMPO
THE TITANS
starring
JUDY TYLER · BOBBY TROUP
MARGO WOODE
Written by ARNOLD BELGARD
Music by LES BAXTER

Directed by HOWARD W. KOCH · Produced by AUBREY SCHENCK · A BEL-AIR Production · Released thru UNITED ARTISTS

THE GREEN-EYED BLONDE

USA, 1957
Director: Bernard Girard. Producer: Martin Melcher.
Screenplay: Dalton Trumbo. Music: Leith Stevens.
Cinematography: Eddie Fitzgerald.
Cast: Susan Oliver, Linda Plowman [Melinda Casey], Beverly Long, Norma Jean Nilsson, Tommie Moore, Carla Merey, Jean Inness.

The only movie produced by Martin Melcher that didn't headline his megastar wife, Doris Day, is this po-faced 'moral message' movie, incredibly written by the Hollywood 10 blacklisted Dalton Trumbo (**Roman Holiday**, 1953), under the alias Sally Stubblefield. It's an untamed youth melodrama that revolves around illegitimate babies, car theft, promiscuity, drug addiction, dorm riots, murder and death. Despite the title – and who knows if Phyllis's (Susan Oliver) eyes are green or not, considering the black and white photography! – the focus of this unsavoury parable is unwed mother Betsy (Linda Plowman/Melinda Casey), secretly knocked up by her drunk mother's sleazy boyfriend, attempting to hide the baby from the heartless warden, Mrs. Nichols (Jean Inness) at the Martha Washington School for Girls, a Southern California reformatory, where she bonds with the wayward Greeneyes for further mischief. What with talk of naked truths, pent-up fury, kitten-killing and stolen kisses, **The Party Crashers** (1958) director Bernard Girard's basic 'Women In Prison' exploiter sounds exciting. But it hardly even qualifies in the good 'Bad Girls on a Rumble' genre despite the ludicrously explanatory title song crooned by Cornelius Gunter of The Coasters fame, who hit big in 1955 with 'Smokey Joe's Café'.

CASTLE OF THE MONSTERS

Mexico, 1958
Director: Julián Soler.
Producer: Jesús Sotomayor Martínez.
Screenplay: Carlos Orellana. Music: Gustavo César Carrión. Cinematography: Víctor Herrera.
Cast: Antonio Espino, Evangelina Elizondo, Carlos Orellana, Guillermo Orea, Germán Robles, José Wilhelmy.

The Frankenstein Monster, a Mad Scientist, Dracula, the Wolf Man, the Mummy, Dr. Hyde, a Hunchback and the Creature from the Black Lagoon all walk into a creepy castle… Hey, says the gatekeeper, where's the Masked Wrestler? Unusually for a Mexican B-movie nowhere to be seen in this monster mash-up geared around Mexican comic Antonio Espino whose Clavillazo (Great Little Nail) persona schtick – catchphrase "Never do that to me!" – would grace many South of the Border Exploiters, his most famous being **Aladdin and the Marvellous Lamp** (1958). Like that comedy fantasy, this fun fright degustación was directed by Julián Soler and has Dr. Sputnik creating his Universal Monster rip-offs while remaining convinced a local seamstress is destined to be his lover. Luring her to his castle under hypnosis, it's down to Clavillazo, her true intended, to stumble around alligator-infested dungeons and wall-closing panic rooms trying to defeat the evil doctor and his horde of horrors. Famous for his cadaverous-looking Mexican vampire roles, Spanish-born Germán Robles played Dracula, while Santo movie royalty Vicente Lara essayed the Wolf Man. Produced by Producciones Sotomayor, the company would continue to milk this formula with the likes of **The Ship of Monsters** (1960).

CONFESS, DR. CORDA

West Germany, 1958
Director: Josef von Báky. Producer: Artur Brauner. Screenplay: Robert A. Stemmle.
Music: Georg Haentzschel. Cinematography: Göran Strindberg.
Cast: Hardy Krüger, Elisabeth Müller, Lucie Mannheim, Hans Nielsen, Fritz Tillmann, Siegfried Lowitz.

In the mid-Fifties the J. Arthur Rank organisation attempted to groom talented young performers into stars during the post-war Britain movie boom. One was Joan Collins, another Barbara Steele. They also looked to the Continent for up-and-comers, and pounced on handsome German actor Hardy Krüger who they immediately put to work in three pictures practically filmed back-to-back: **The One That Got Away** (1957), **Bachelor of Hearts** (1958) and **Blind Date** (1959). Hence the reason why British Exploitation luminary E(dwin). J. Fancey (of New Realm distributors) snapped up director Josef von Báky's wrong man, place and time thriller starring the former Hitler Youth as the title anaesthetist accused of murdering his mistress in a park. Despite the audience being privy to the bludgeoning by a sex-crazed bicyclist before her lover arrives at their trysting place, von Báky wrings the cringe factor to the maximum as the clueless police pile on the intimidating pressure for him to come clean. Not the first film to posit the notion of trial by popular opinion but one of the clearest in suggesting how the attention spotlight can work against someone's public persona, **Gestehen Sie, Dr. Corda** is an undervalued wages of sin saga.

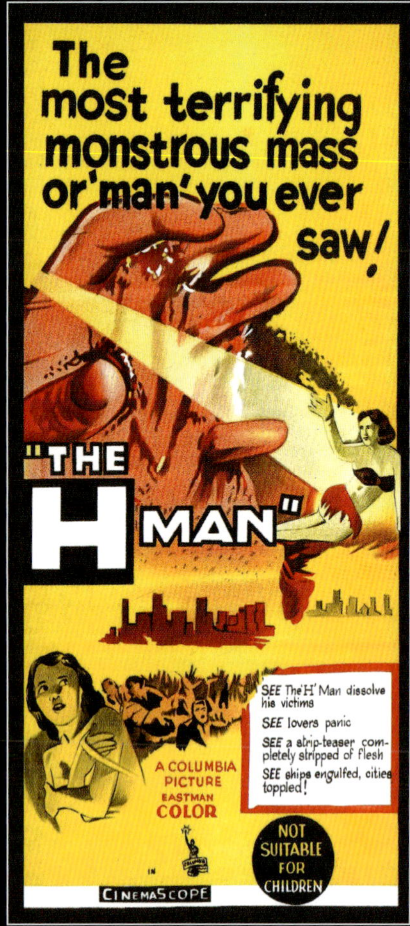

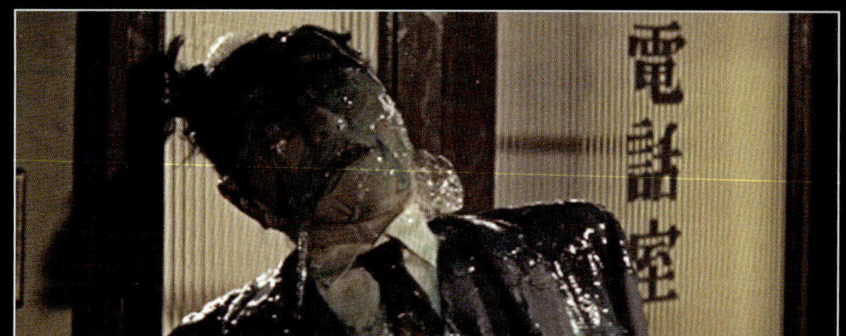

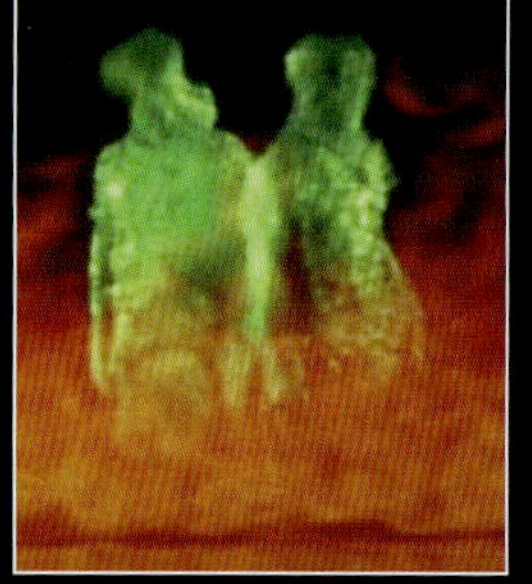

THE H-MAN

Japan, 1958
Director: Ishirô Honda. Producer: Tomoyuki Tanaka.
Screenplay: Takeshi Kimura. Music: Masaru Satô.
Cinematography: Hajime Koizumi.
Cast: Yumi Shirakawa, Kenji Sahara, Akihiko Hirata, Eitarô Ozawa, Koreya Senda, Makoto Satô.

After proving America could cope with Japanese fantasy fare, leading studio Toho Productions, the makers of **Godzilla** (1954), practically took over Drive-Ins in 1959 with **The Mysterians** (1957), **Gigantis** (1959) and this quality Oriental riposte to **The Blob** (1958). Skilfully directed by Ishirô Honda, the one-man monster factory, hydrogen bomb tests in the Pacific Ocean have created radioactive creatures, which can dissolve into a gelatinous mass any other living tissue they touch. Once the authorities believe those who have witnessed the oozing slime in action decimating both heroes and heavies, a man-made holocaust is considered the only action that can stop the viscous threat. Divested of a scantily clad musical number considered too racy for the target audience, Columbia Pictures also withdrew the promotional gimmick of a compressed sponge in the shape of an 'H' that would swell up when wet, as it became clear they were being used as restroom missiles. Instead cinemas had foyer tableaux depicting a melting victim consisting of shoes, shirt, trousers and a toupee piled on top. Visionary Toho special effects genius Eiji Tsuburaya created the impactful dissolving by deflating life-sized rubber humans, filming them in fast-motion, and then running the celluloid at normal speed.

LIFT TO THE SCAFFOLD

France, 1958
Director: Louis Malle. Producer: Jean Thuillier.
Screenplay: Roger Nimier, Louis Malle.
Music: Miles Davis. Cinematography: Henri Decaë.
Cast: Jeanne Moreau, Maurice Ronet, Georges Poujouly,
Yori Bertin, Jean Wall, Elga Andersen.

Ascenseur pour l'échafaud is a stunning exercise in *chic* elegant cool, marking the feature debut of maestro Louis Malle, capturing star Jeanne Moreau in the baby steps of her *Nouvelle Vague* glory, rich in sophisticated Paris atmosphere and showcasing a jazz score by the legendary Miles Davis recorded in one session. But it still could only be sold outside France as Exploitation because of its whiff of sordid sensation. Retitled **Frantic** in English-speaking territories, and based on the novel by Noël Calef, this murder-plot-goes-awry thriller mixes Hitchcock style and Robert Bresson minimalism with effortless aplomb. Former Foreign Legionnaire Julien Tavernier (Maurice Ronet), disgusted by his war-profiteering corporate boss Simon Carala (Jean Wall) embarks on an affair with his wife Florence (Moreau) and then decides to murder him, making it look like suicide. But Julien's best-laid plans are royally scuppered by a chain of ill-fated events when he gets trapped overnight in the office elevator. Quite what the Grindhouses and fleapits made of this artfully crafted *film noir* is anyone's guess. But the opening with Moreau in stark close-up sexily whispering "Je t'aime, je t'aime" over and over to her lover on the phone probably caused punters to stand to attention.

CONFIDENTIAL EXPOSÉ!

The white-hot story of what happens to boys and girls who come to Hollywood... seeking success, and clawing their way to the top!

LOST LONELY AND VICIOUS

starring KEN CLAYTON · BARBARA WILSON and LILYAN CHAUVIN · RICHARD GILDEN

A DRAMATIC SENSATION WITH THE BRIGHTEST STARS OF TOMORROW!

with CAROLE NUGENT · SANDRA GILES

CHARLES CASANELLI · FRANK MYERS · NORMAN GRAHAM · TED AND VINCENT SAIZIS

LOST, LONELY AND VICIOUS

USA, 1958
Director: Frank Myers.
Producer: Charles M. Casinelli.
Screenplay: Norman Graham.
Music: Gil Baumgart, Fredrick David.
Cinematography: Ted Saizis, Vincent Saizis.
Cast: Ken Clayton, Barbara Wilson, Lilyan Chauvin, Richard Gilden, Carol Nugent, Jim Reppert.

Exploiting the tragic death of teen sensation James Dean, director Frank Myers' solo cash-in is really Dull, Talky and Pointless. No mark Ken Clayton plays troubled Johnnie Dennis (J.D., get it?), a rising star whose first major movie, 'Desperate Hours', is about to premiere. Instead of being excited, his rebel without applause depression and obsession with death by drag racing alarms his cougar acting coach (Lilyan Chauvin, in Stella Adler mode). But when he meets innocent drugstore clerk Helen Preacher (Barbara Wilson, a Natalie Wood lookalike), burgeoning romance prompts him to jettison his dark side and truly embrace stardom. An earnest trifle skirting every hot button teenage issue with deathlessly hip dialogue, Myers' slight melodrama does offer a few insights into the fame whore machinations of Fifties Hollywood. The diner where all the wannabe actors congregate is clearly modelled after Schwabs, the famous malt shop where Lana Turner was supposedly discovered. A shame then that so much of the running time is taken up with endless discussions about hot rods, mental anguish and casting directors. Clayton never registers as anything else but an unlikeable moaner with zero mystique, the quality that made his doomed role model such a charismatic charmer.

SCREAMING MIMI

USA, 1958
Director: Gerd Oswald. Producers: Harry Joe Brown, Robert Fellows. Screenplay: Robert Blees.
Cinematography: Burnett Guffey.
Cast: Anita Ekberg, Philip Carey, Gypsy Rose Lee, Harry Townes, Linda Cherney, Romney Brent.

An astoundingly sleazy effort from a major studio (Paramount) circa the late-1950s – no wonder future director of 'The Outer Limits' TV series, Gerd Oswald's curio ended up dumped on a double bill with the problematic art-houser **This Angry Age** (1957). More famous now for mystery author Fredric Brown's 1949 source material somewhat inspiring Dario Argento's script for **The Bird with the Crystal Plumage** (1970), this average psychological *film noir* with slim horror foundations falls short because of **La Dolce Vita** (1960) star Anita Ekberg's low-wattage acting. There truly are moments when you can tell she's trying to remember her lines! Basically, a hard-drinking reporter (Philip Carey, **Monster**, 1980), a schizophrenic stripper (Ekberg), a disgraced psychiatrist (ubiquitous TV series star Harry Townes) and 'The Ripper', a razor-wielding serial killer, collide with deadly reverberations in this tortured chiller circling lesbianism, fetishism and twisted personality syndromes. Throw in the strange Screaming Mimi voodoo statuettes that play a bizarre part in the convoluted proceedings and it's a heady, and heavy-going, mix indeed. Plus points above the well-maintained grubbiness are Ekberg's scene-stealing Great Dane, Devil, and a rare screen appearance by Gypsy Rose Lee as owner of the tawdry El Madhouse strip club.

TOO MUCH, TOO SOON

USA, 1958
Director: Art Napoleon. Producer: Henry Blanke. Screenplay: Art Napoleon, Jo Napoleon.
Music: Ernest Gold. Cinematography: Carl E. Guthrie, Nicholas Musuraca.
Cast: Dorothy Malone, Errol Flynn, Efrem Zimbalist Jr., Ray Danton, Neva Patterson, Murray Hamilton.

Blazing the trail in celebrity tell-all books, Diana Barrymore (daughter of silent movie Hollywood Royalty John Barrymore) sold her scandalous 1957 autobiography to Warner Brothers, who wanted the bestseller to star their **Baby Doll** (1956) sensation Carroll Baker. But when she refused to play another 'nymphomaniac', Dorothy Malone stepped in, thinking it might just be the vehicle to win her second Oscar after **Written on the Wind** (1956). Unfortunately what won out in this rock bottom biopic was dishonest turgid melodrama as failed actress Barrymore attempts to reconnect with her alcoholic father (real-life Barrymore booze-buddy Errol Flynn) but matches his gutter-surfing through barrooms, rehab and failed marriages. Highlights include a reprise of Malone's mad Mambo from her Douglas Sirk classic, a slimy gigolo turn by Ray Danton (future director of **Psychic Killer**, 1975) and first beau Martin Milner's final reveal of baldness, which she astonishingly equates with all the 'dirty tricks' played on her life as a burned-out lush. Despite the upbeat ending, Barrymore died less than two years later from an alleged, but never proven, drug overdose. Exploitation never let a good title slumber: ace-grifter Doris Wishman lampooned it for her male hustler saga **Too Much Too Often!** (1968).

DOROTHY MALONE
as Diana Barrymore
ERROL FLYNN
as her father, John Barrymore

VOICE WITHOUT A SHADOW

Japan, 1958
Director: Seijun Suzuki. Producer: Kaneo Iwai.
Screenplay: Ryuta Akimoto, Susumu Saji.
Music: Hikaru Hayashi. Cinematography: Kazue Nagatsuka.
Cast: Yôko Minamida, Hideaki Nitani, Nobuo Kaneko, Toshio Takahara, Shinsuke Ashida, Jô Shishido.

Japanese director Seijun Suzuki was the prolific Takashi Miike of his day, churning out roughly four films a year until 1967 when his increasingly excessive style caused a falling out with his Nikkatsu Studio bosses. This Hitch-cocktail of pulpy *noir* and OTT imagery is one of his best left-field thrillers, oozing with shadowy lairs, maniacal action, surreal flourishes and seedy characters. A nasty pawnshop robbery homicide has an improbable witness in switchboard operator Asako Takahashi (Yôko Minamida) whose wrong number connection means overhearing the laughing killer in action. But brought in as a police 'ear witness' she can't identify the guilty party and the case goes unsolved. Three years later reporter/ narrator Hiroshi Ishikawa (Hideaki Nitani) joins the cold case when his former employee Asako says she recognizes the culprit's laugh after her husband invited over three clients for a mah-jong game night... Told through Ishikawa's eyes, **Kagenaki koe** (re-titled **Voice Without a Shadow** for English language release) is a solid suspense mystery, perhaps a little far-fetched at times, but always given a seat-edged memorable quality by Suzuki's quirky spin and the soon-to-be familiar cast. There could be no higher praise other than to say this Tokyo-goes-Hollywood crime story might easily have been penned by the author of **Rear Window** (1954), Cornell Woolrich.

BLACK PIT OF DR. M

Mexico, 1959
Director: Fernando Méndez.
Producer: Alfredo Ripstein Jr.
Screenplay: Ramón Obón.
Music: Gustavo César Carrión.
Cinematography: Víctor Herrera.
Cast: Gastón Santos, Rafael Bertrand, Mapita Cortés, Carlos Ancira, Carolina Barret, Luis Aragón, Antonio Raxel.

From the Golden Age of the Mexican Macabre comes this atmospheric chiller also known as **Mysteries from Beyond the Grave**. The follow-up to his two horror classics **El vampiro** (1957) and its quickie sequel **The Vampire's Coffin** (1958), director Fernando Méndez stirs Telenovella soap, mad scientist tropes and a Gothic-laden moody darkness into a lyrical fantasia of ominous afterlife warnings and Faustian pacts. Asylum head Dr. Mazali (Rafael Bertrand) makes a deranged promise with fellow Dr. Aldama (Mexican horror icon Antonio Raxel) agreeing to return from the grave should either die before the other. Indeed, Aldama passes and Mazali conjures up his spirit, which tells him he will reveal all about the hereafter within the next three months. During that time Aldama's wandering ghost looks for his estranged daughter Patricia (Telenovella Queen Mapita Cortés), hoping to talk her into visiting the asylum to learn more about her father. Which she does, only to become the lust object of both Mazali and his handsome assistant, Eduardo (Gastón Santos), leading to the bizarrely touching climax involving an acid attack, false murder charges and a human torch zombie. A stylish low-budget gem with superior design and some memorable shocks.

THE BLOODY BROOD

Canada, 1959
Director: Julian Roffman. Producer: Julian Roffman.
Screenplay: Anne Howard Bailey, Ben Kerner,
Elwood Ullman, Des Hardman. Music: Harry Freedman.
Cinematography: Eugen Schüfftan.
Cast: Peter Falk, Barbara Lord, Jack Betts, Ron Hartmann,
Ron Taylor, Robert Christie.

Sometimes what was devised as a Grindhouse flash-in-the-pan gained a whole new life, playing the circuit for years, when one of the third-billed cast became an overnight star. Before he made **The Mask** (1961), documentarian Julian Roffman directed Peter Falk's second feature film, a mean, moody warm-up for his breakthrough role in **Murder, Inc**. a year later. The future 'Columbo' plays crazed beatnik Nico, a bottom-feeding drug dealer, who watches a man die of a heart attack while hanging out at his local jazz cafe. Fascinated by this experience, he talks a meek TV director pal into killing a stranger with a hamburger containing ground-up glass. When that telegram man dies of intestinal haemorrhaging, his puzzled older brother starts investigating the trail that leads to Nico's murderous mob. Shot in sixteen days in Toronto, Roffman's low-budget wonder hits all the Beat Generation Noir notes with its hip jargon – "He's a salesman, baby... he sells dreams" – and Kerouac-style cod philosophy – "Death... the last great challenge of the collective mind". Even with such splendid support from Barbara Lord and Jack Betts, this shadowy suspense thriller is Falk's showcase – he's knows it and steals every scene as the nervy dope-peddling psychopath.

THE BLOODY BROOD

CURSE OF THE UNDEAD

USA, 1959
Director: Edward Dein. Producer: Joseph Gershenson. Screenplay: Edward Dein, Mildred Dein.
Music: Irving Gertz. Cinematography: Ellis W. Carter.
Cast: Eric Fleming, Michael Pate, Kathleen Crowley, John Hoyt, Bruce Gordon, Edward Binns.

The Horror Western is hardly a crowded field and it's only in more modern times that the hybrid has paid spectacular dividends (**Sundown: The Vampire in Retrea**t, 1989, **Bone Tomahawk**, 2015, **The Pale Door**, 2020). But here is where that sub-genre began, with director Edward (**The Leech Woman**, 1960) Dein's Wild West Vampire novelty item, co-written with his wife Mildred. A border town is being plagued by a series of mysterious deaths where women are found with puncture marks on their necks. The culprit is gunslinger Drake Robey (Western regular Michael Pate), hired to kill ruthless rancher Buffer (Bruce Gordon, 'Peyton Place' TV series regular) by Dolores Carter (Kathleen Crowley) for murdering her father and brother. Drake Robey is cursed to be a roaming vampire after committing suicide and has returned to claim his rightful property inheritance. Robey is seen transforming into a bat and is killed by a bullet carved with a crucifix in the predictable shoot-out climax. For traditional Western fans this was far too way out for the era and wouldn't signify any genre sea change until director William Beaudine's gruesome twosome of **Billy the Kid Versus Dracula** (1966) and **Jesse James Meets Frankenstein's Daughter** (1966).

THE HEAD

West Germany, 1959
Director: Victor Trivas. Producer: Wolf C. Hartwig.
Screenplay: Victor Trivas. Music: Willy Mattes, Jacques Lasry.
Cinematography: Georg Krause.
Cast: Horst Frank, Michel Simon, Karin Kernke, Helmut Schmid, Paul Dahlke, Dieter Eppler, Kurt Müller-Graf.

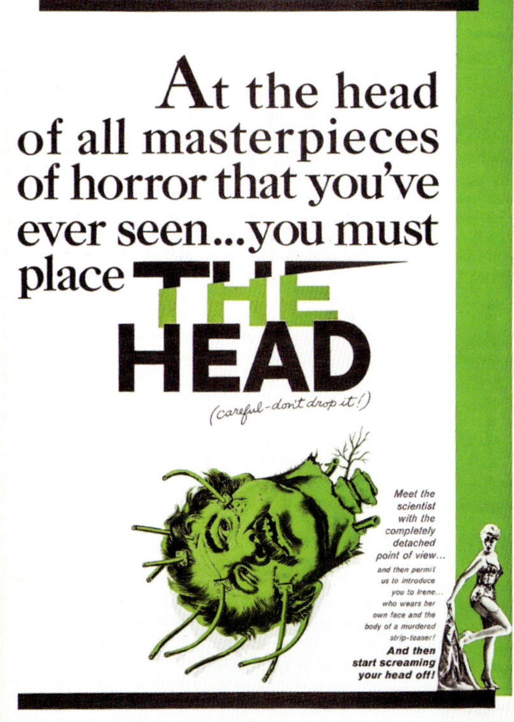

Retitled from **Die Nackte und der Satan** purely so Grindhouse advertising could use 'head' variations, writer/director Victor Trivas was supposedly a Russian émigré who allegedly worked with Sergei Eisenstein and G.W. Pabst but did indeed get Oscar-nominated for writing Orson Welles's **The Stranger** (1946). Clearly slumming it after a 24-year director career gap with this tongue-in-cheek variation on Curt Siodmak's venerable novel 'Donovan's Brain', Trivas nevertheless got his old friend Hermann Warm, designer on the seminal **The Cabinet of Dr. Caligari** (1920), to class up this sleazy oddment. Professor Abel (Michel Simon) invents a serum that keeps a dog's severed head alive. His mad assistant Dr. Ood (Horst Frank, **The Vengeance of Fu Manchu**, 1967) not only uses the serum to keep Abel's own severed head in working order after a failed heart transplant, but also grafts the head of his hunchbacked nurse onto a sexy stripper body to create his ideal woman. Why is most of the dialogue spoken by Abel's head, wired with electrodes on a Bava-esque lit glass sheet, shot from behind? Simon's face had been partially paralyzed by dodgy make-up on a previous film and his vanity forced Trivas to make the necessary adjustment.

TERROR IN THE MIDNIGHT SUN

USA/Sweden, © 1958, first public screening 1959
Director: Virgil W. Vogel. Producer: Bertil Jernberg. Screenplay: Arthur C. Pierce, Robert M. Fresco [uncredited]. Music: Harry Arnold, Allan Johansson. Cinematography: Hilding Bladh.
Cast: Barbara Wilson, Sten Gester, Robert Burton, Bengt Blomgren, Åke Grönberg, John Carradine.

One of those Exploiters that are more fascinating in their back-story than their actual worth, this Swedish/US co-production was directed by Virgil W. Vogel (**The Mole People**, 1956) from a script by Arthur C. Pierce (**The Cosmic Man**, 1959). Local star Sten Gester plays a task force doctor investigating a recently crash-landed meteor in Lapland. Turns out it's really a spaceship and the alien crew have unleashed a giant, furry, Yeti-like creature, causing panic in the nearby villages. Oh, and Gester also romances attractive ice-skater Barbara Wilson, who turns out to be the niece of his tyrant boss.

Thrown together with vague visual culls from **It Came from Outer Space** (1953), **Frankenstein** (1931) and **King Kong** (1933), the most startling sequence has a Wilson body double taking an explicit for the era shower. Minus that controversial nude scene, ace distribution grifter Jerry Warren snapped up the rights, re-edited it, adding extra footage to pad out the already numbing running time, plus an on-screen narration by horror legend John Carradine. Renamed **Invasion of the Animal People**, it finally hit stateside Drive-Ins in 1962 in an incoherent state, double-billed with the Warren-directed jungle jangle **Terror of the Bloodhunters**.

THE DAMNED AND THE DARING

France, 1960
Director: Hervé Bromberger. Producer: Gilbert de Goldschmidt. Screenplay: Hervé Bromberger, Frédéric Grendel. Music: Serge Gainsbourg, Alain Goraguer. Cinematography: Jacques Mercanton. Cast: Jean-Marc Bory, Pascale Roberts, Françoise Dorléac, Jean Babilée, Pierre Mondy, Jean-François Poron, Jacques Moulières.

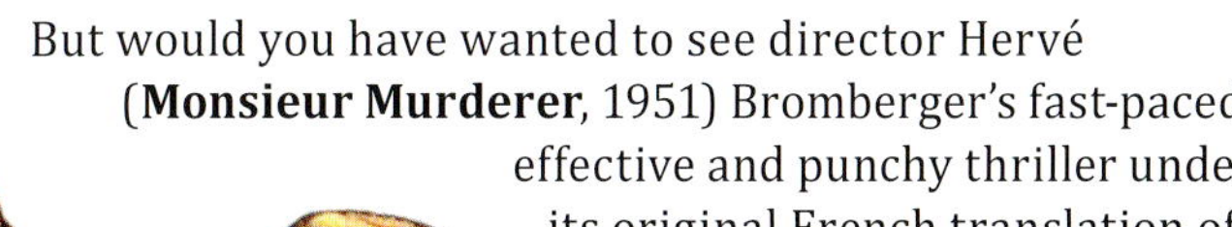

But would you have wanted to see director Hervé (**Monsieur Murderer**, 1951) Bromberger's fast-paced, effective and punchy thriller under its original French translation of **Les loups dans la bergerie** (**The Wolves in the Sheepfold**)? Based on the crime novel by Jean Amila (who, as Jean Meckert, scripted **Le miroir a deux faces**, 1958, remade by Barbra Streisand in 1996 as **The Mirror Has Two Faces**), three thugs on the run from the police hole up in an isolated Alpine reformatory for wayward adolescents, governed by the understanding couple Roger (Jean-Marc Bory) and Irène (Pascale Roberts) who run the institution on an open prison model. Pretty soon the killers take control and hold everyone hostage until the inevitable violent conclusion. However, in the ironic scheme of things, it seems the teen offenders are scared straight by the first-hand actions of the criminals in their midst. **The Desperate Hours** (1955) goes both Method Acting and *Nouvelle Vague* with terrific turns by Bory, Roberts and Françoise Dorléac (the elder, ill-fated sister of French icon Catherine Deneuve). *La glaçage sur le gateau*? The superior mini-score composed by that genius bad boy of cool Gallic pop, Serge Gainsbourg. 'Cha Cha Cha Du Loup' is a mambo must.

ORLAK, THE HELL OF FRANKENSTEIN

Mexico, 1960
Director: Rafael Baledón. Producer: Rafael Baledón.
Screenplay: Alfredo Ruanova, Carlos Enrique Taboada. Music: Jorge Pérez.
Cinematography: Fernando Colín.
Cast: Joaquín Cordero, Andrés Soler, Carlos Ancira, Armando Calvo, Rosa de Castilla, Irma Dorantes, Pedro de Aguillón, David Reynoso.

An enticingly distinctive and solidly successful Mexican interpretation of Mary Shelley's literary creation – the first to do so in this Latino neck of the woods – director Rafael Baledón's deferential take on the monster legend is a chiaroscuro visual delight leaning back to the glory days of German Expressionism. Baledón had found his sure horror feet with **The Man and the Monster** (1958) and **The Swamp of the Lost Monster** (1956) so instantly warmed to the script by screenwriters Alfredo Ruanova and Carlos Enrique Taboada, creators of the aristocratic vampire Nostradamus series. Due to union regulations, it was filmed as a four-part serial on the same sets as **The Curse of Nostradamus** (1961) and then cut together as a feature. Suspected murderer Jamie Rojas (Joaquín Cordero) is completing his sentence for a minor crime and helps Dr. Frankenstein (Andrés Soler) escape from prison. When the mad scientist creates Orlak (Cordero again) out of body parts, Rojas uses the black sombrero and cape-wearing automaton to take revenge on officials and former partners with the help of scarred assistant Eric (Carlos Ancira). More than a few Hammer flourishes grace the agreeably off-kilter atmosphere given by Baledón's cultured and culturally diverse approach.

THE PLAYGIRLS AND THE VAMPIRE

Italy, 1960
Director: Piero Regnoli. Producer: Tiziano Longo.
Screenplay: Piero Regnoli. Music: Aldo Piga.
Cinematography: Aldo Greci.
Cast: Walter Brandi, Lyla Rocco, Maria Giovannini, Alfredo Rizzo, Marisa Quattrini, Leonardo Botta.

A busload of five showgirls, their manager and pianist are forced by bad weather and a collapsed bridge to spend the night in a creepy castle, the home of Count Kernassy (Walter Brandi). Guess what happens? Kernassy notices a striking resemblance between Vera (Lyla Rocco), and Margherita, the great love of his 200-year-old look-alike ancestor who still stalks the premises with blood-dripping fangs at the ready. The first genre movie to show a nude vampire – Maria Giovannini's Katia – writer/director Piero Regnoli landed the job after gaining praise for his scripting duties on **I vampiri/Lust of the Vampire** (1957). Formerly a journalist for a Catholic newspaper, Regnoli's gorgeous-looking Gothic confection was a complete rip-off of Renato Polselli's **The Vampire and the Ballerina** (1960) released six months prior, also starring Brandi, and in addition using the same climax as Hammer's **Dracula** (1958). But it was far sexier and sleazier, even though it too is padded out with endless dance rehearsals and much wandering around dimly-lit corridors in negligees. Regnoli continued with written depravities long after his directing career ended, in such Eurotrash shockers as **Obscene Desire** (1978), **Savana: Violenza Carnale** (1979), **Patrick Still Lives** (1980) and **Satan's Baby Doll** (1982).

SEX KITTENS GO TO COLLEGE

USA, 1960
Director: Albert Zugsmith. Producer: Albert Zugsmith.
Screenplay: Robert Hill. Music: Dean Elliott.
Cinematography: Ellis W. Carter.
Cast: Mamie Van Doren, Tuesday Weld, Mijanou Bardot, Vampira, Jackie Coogan, John Carradine, Conway Twitty, Mickey Shaughnessy, Louis Nye, Pamela Mason.

It's a Grade Z for junk director Albert Zugsmith and this fabulously titled, wretched to watch, all B-movie-star fiasco. Collins College needs a new science department head, so S.A.M. Thinko, the campus computer, is consulted and comes up with high-IQ sexpot Mamie Van Doren. But students and faculty alike are shocked when they discover their teacher used to be a stripper known as the Tallahassee Tassel Tosser. Add in a lame racehorse-fixing gangster subplot, a football jock scared of the opposite sex, a full-figure bra saleswoman, a chimpanzee, and practically every gutter target is hit. Wearing the tight sweaters are Tuesday Weld, Mijanou Bardot (Brigitte's clearly talentless younger sister) and Vampira, with silent era child star Jackie Coogan, John Carradine, two sons of silent comedians Charles Chaplin Jr. and Harold Lloyd Jr., and crooner Conway Twitty singing the song 'Sexpot Goes To College', the original working title. 30 years later Twitty would still be embarrassed to talk about this dud that did at least offer the sight of Carradine dancing the Charleston with Mamie. A Russ Meyer-style seven minutes of topless burlesque was added to the export version, inserted when the robot computer hallucinates after breaking down.

SUSPECT

UK, 1960
Directors: John Boulting, Roy Boulting.
Producers: John Boulting, Roy Boulting.
Screenplay: Nigel Balchin, Roy Boulting, Jeffrey Dell.
Cinematography: Max Greene [Mutz Greenbaum].
Cast: Tony Britton, Virginia Maskell, Thorley Walters, Raymond Huntley, Ian Bannen, Peter Cushing, Spike Milligan.

Responsible for directing and producing a number of British classics – **Brighton Rock** (1948), **Lucky Jim** (1957), **I'm All Right Jack** (1959) – John and Roy Boulting found themselves with three spare weeks of paid Shepperton Studio space. Bet £1,000 they couldn't make another movie in that short space of time, they turned Nigel Balchin's crime novel 'A Sort of Traitors' into this quota quickie, originally titled **The Risk**, with an impressive British cast of horror stalwarts. At the Haughton Research Laboratory in London, scientists under Professor Sewell (Peter Cushing) have developed a cure for bubonic plague. Keen to publish the research, the Ministry of Defence refuse permission in the interests of national security and fear of biological terrorism. But one of their number is so incensed by this Official Secrets Act move, they get drawn into a treasonable act by an enemy foreign power. Initially unfolding more like a television play of the day, with endless scientific talk and stagey monologues, the serviceable spy thriller eventually finds its rhythm to prove engaging even if Spike Milligan as the lab's witless janitor is a comic relief mistake. Not released in the UK until 1962 when it supported Val Guest's whodunit **Jigsaw**.

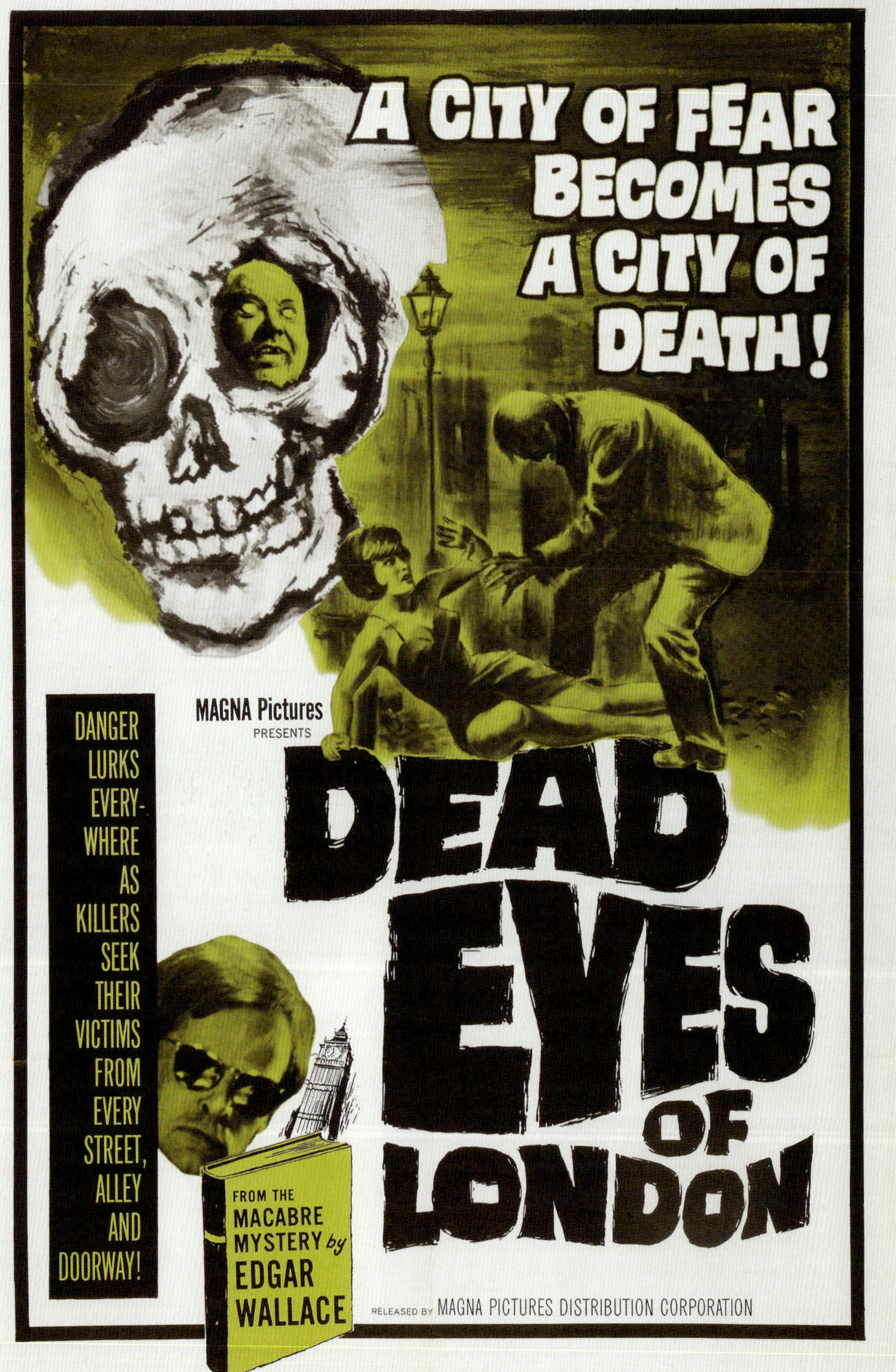
A CITY OF FEAR BECOMES A CITY OF DEATH!
MAGNA Pictures PRESENTS
DEAD EYES OF LONDON
DANGER LURKS EVERY-WHERE AS KILLERS SEEK THEIR VICTIMS FROM EVERY STREET, ALLEY AND DOORWAY!
FROM THE MACABRE MYSTERY by EDGAR WALLACE
RELEASED BY MAGNA PICTURES DISTRIBUTION CORPORATION

DEAD EYES OF LONDON

West Germany, 1961
Director: Alfred Vohrer. Producer: Horst Wendlandt.
Screenplay: Trygve Larsen [Egon Eis], Wolfgang Lukschy.
Music: Heinz Funk. Cinematography: Karl Löb.
Cast: Joachim Fuchsberger, Karin Baal, Dieter Borsche, Wolfgang Lukschy, Eddi Arent, Klaus Kinski, Ann Savo [Anneli Sauli].

That genre melding of *film noir*, whodunit, police procedural, old dark house get-togethers and horror known as the *krimi* in Germany was at its most popular in the early 1960s. And this one, the first of thirteen directed by Alfred Vohrer, the most prolific helmer of them all, was also the first in the Rialto series to feature blood red letter opening credit titles on a black-and-white background, a tradition that would continue until the vogue evaporated and transformed into the *gialli*. Based on the novel 'The Dark Eyes of London', an expanded version of the short story 'The Croakers', by British crime writer icon Edgar Wallace (already filmed in 1939), an unbalanced doctor, the Reverend, orchestrates the murders of wealthy men to benefit from their life insurance policies, using a charity for the blind as a front for his activities. *Krimi* regulars Joachim Fuchsberger and Karin Baal (co-stars in the *giallo* hybrid **What Have You Done to Solange?**, 1972) are intrepid Inspector Larry Holt and braille expert Nora Ward, who team up to investigate the gruesome killings. And Klaus Kinski is on hand, as ever, this time playing a fake blind villain. Talky but entertaining once the puzzle starts to clarify.

FORCE OF IMPULSE

USA, © 1960, first public screening 1961
Director: Saul Swimmer. Producers: Tony Anthony, Peter Gayle.
Screenplay: Francis Swann. Music: Joseph Liebman.
Cinematography: Clifford H. Poland Jr.
Cast: Robert Alda, J. Carrol Naish, Tony Anthony, Teri Hope, Jeff Donnell, Jody McCrea, Bruce Talbot [Brud Talbot], Christina Crawford.

Often when a movie didn't have a clear promotional gimmick, the distributor commissioned a paperback novel based on the screenplay and had it published just prior to release to hopefully engender interest. The most notorious was for **Reptilicus** (1961), which author Dean Owen sexed up to such an extent that potential viewers could only be disappointed. Owen also novelised Hammer's **The Brides of Dracula** (1960) in a clumsy, misspelt, now much sought after tome. But in the case of director Saul Swimmer's teenage class conflict saga, renowned crime and western novelist Marvin H. Albert wrote a respectable tie-in, finessing the basic story of High School football hero Toby Marino (Tony Anthony, future star of the 3D revival adventure **Comin' At Ya!**, 1981) who robs his father's Italian grocery store for money to take posh girl Bunny Reese (Teri Hope) out while ignoring the one who truly loves him. It's all here: beatnik angst, self-absorption, parental concerns, endless sulking and resentment, with cocktail parties and hot-rods an amiable backdrop. 'Charlie Chan' star J. Carrol Naish plays Toby's father, with Robert Alda (Alan's father), Jody McCrea (son of Joel) and Christina Crawford (daughter of Joan and writer of 'Mommie Dearest') rounding out the interesting cult cast.

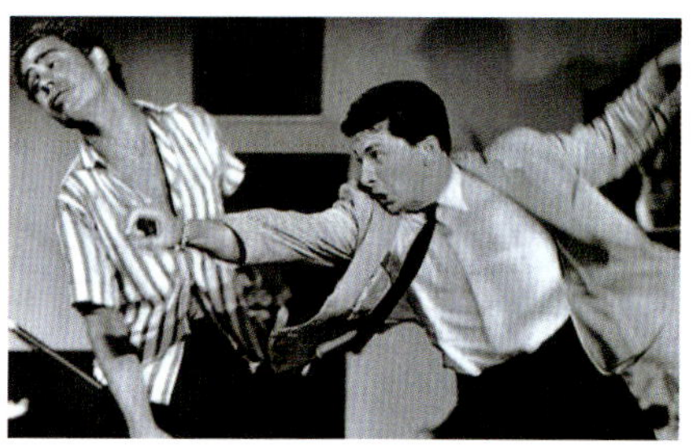

GOLIATH AND THE VAMPIRES

Italy, 1961
Directors: Sergio Corbucci, Giacomo Gentilomo.
Producer: Mario Feliciani.
Screenplay: Sergio Corbucci, Duccio Tessari.
Music: Angelo Francesco Lavagnino, Les Baxter (US version). Cinematography: Alvaro Mancori.
Cast: Gordon Scott, Leonora Ruffo, Jacques Sernas, Gianna Maria Canale, Rocco Vidolazzi, Mario Feliciani, Guido Celano.

Peplum movies were made for international audiences of all ages. But director Giacomo Gentilomo's **Maciste contro il vampiro** was one that earnt the dreaded X certificate in Great Britain, curtailing its 1964 box office potential for Gala Film Distributors. But bolstered by the success of **Sodom and Gomorrah** (1962) with the same rating, Gala put the supernatural sword-and-sandal spectacle, scripted by Sergio Corbucci (**Django**, 1966) and Duccio Tessari (**The Bloodstained Butterfly**, 1971), and co-directed by the former, uncredited, on the Grindhouse circuit for several lucrative months. Gordon Scott's first Italian muscleman epic, after starring in six Tarzan jungle adventures, finds him tracking the raiders who attacked his village and kidnapped all the women, including his fiancé Guja (Leonora Ruffo, **Hercules in the Haunted World**, 1961). The search leads to the island of Salmanak, ruled by Sultan Abdul (Mario Feliciani) himself controlled by Kobrak (Guido Celano), a blood-drinking monster commanding a legion of zombie soldiers. SEE: the torture chamber of the Blue Men, SEE: the holocaust in the cave of fire, etc... An inventive combo of gladiator and gore and superbly photographed by Alvaro Mancori, a master of the genre, this evocative horror seared the memory of many fledging genre buffs.

JOURNEY BENEATH THE DESERT

Italy/France, 1961
Directors: Giuseppe Masini, Edgar G. Ulmer, Frank Borzage [uncredited]. Producers: Luigi Nannerini, Edgar G. Ulmer.
Screenplay: Remigio Del Grosso, Ugo Liberatore, Edgar G. Ulmer.
Music: Carlo Rustichelli. Cinematography: Enzo Serafin.
Cast: Haya Harareet, Jean-Louis Trintignant, Georges Rivière, Rad Fulton [James Westmoreland], Amedeo Nazzari, Giulia Rubini, Gabriele Tinti, Gian Maria Volontè.

Ah, the Exploitation spoiler! Released on European screens at the same time as George Pal's **Atlantis, the Lost Continent** (1961), director Edgar G. Ulmer's compromised fourth adaptation of Pierre Benoit's 1919 novel 'L'Atlantide' was the textbook example of a troubled production. Originally to be directed by Frank Borzage, low-budget pioneer Ulmer took over when the **A Farewell to Arms** (1932) helmer quit after two days due to language problems, the pressures of international co-production and having to share a bogus credit with no-mark Giuseppe Masini because of Italian subsidy rules. Shot as **Antinea, l'amante della città sepolta**, Jean-Louis Trintignant, Georges Rivière, Gabriele Tinti and Gian Maria Volontè are mineral experts forced to crash their helicopter during a storm, only to end up in the underground city of Atlantis where Queen Antinea (**Ben-Hur**, 1959, star Haya Harareet) faces a slave revolution. With lyrical exotic fantasy elbowed out and sand-and-sandal finessing and atomic bombs the main thrust, dodgy matte paintings and tinker-toy special effects sit uneasily with the epic action. Not released in the UK until 1964, and three years after that in America when distributor Joseph E. Levine picked it up to continue his **Hercules** (1958) Italian-sourced market hold.

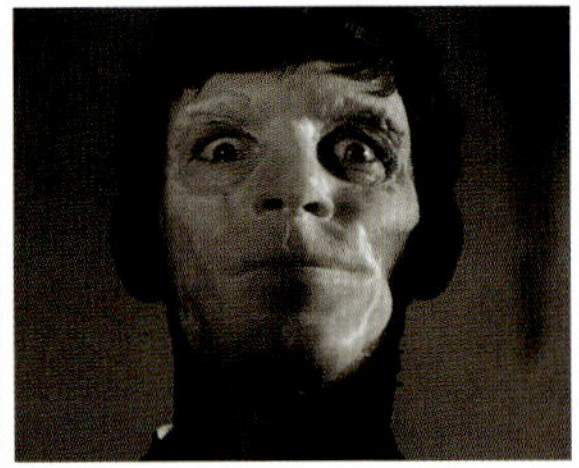

THE MASK

Canada, 1961
Directors: Julian Roffman, Nat Taylor [uncredited]. Producer: Julian Roffman.
Screenplay: Frank Taubes, Sandy Haver, Franklin Delessert, Slavko Vorkapich.
Music: Louis Applebaum.
Cinematography: Herbert S. Alpert.
Cast: Paul Stevens, Claudette Nevins, Bill Walker, Anne Collings, Martin Lavut, Leo Leyden.

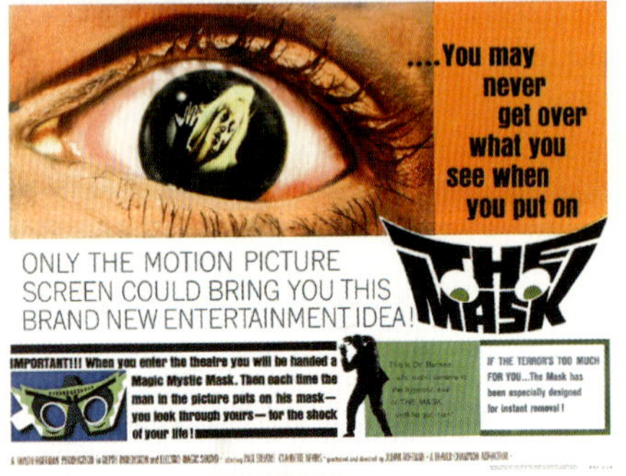

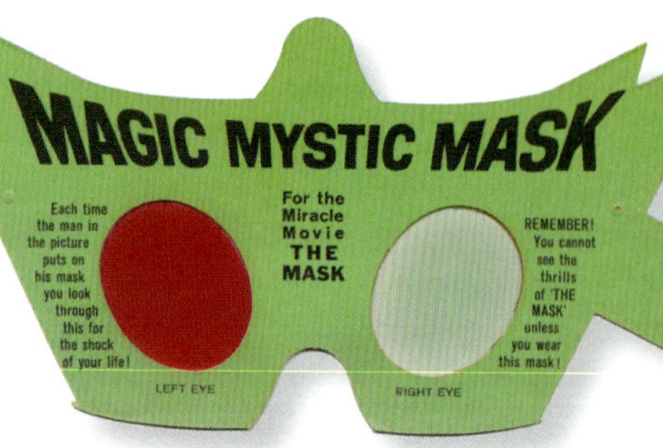

Some genre movies took ages to open outside their own territories. Mario Bava's **Black Sunday/Revenge of the Vampire** (1960) waited eight years for the British censors to get up to speed. Julian Roffman's proto Canadian surrealist horror, retitled **Eyes of Hell**, waited a decade before being shoved on a UK double bill with the three-year delayed Italian thriller **The Young, the Evil and the Savage** (1968). And that was mainly because it was already too late to cash in on the first 1950s 3D wave, but on trend with the late British release of Arch Oboler's **The Bubble** (1966). Psychiatrist Paul Stevens receives a ceremonial tribal mask after archaeologist Martin Lavut's suicide, which apparently makes the wearer commit murder due to possession by evil spirits. Naturally Stevens is curious to see if the curse is true and, along with the audience commanded to put on their 3D glasses, witnesses visions of ghouls making human sacrifice and mist-shrouded boats to the netherworld. The paper-thin plot, full of gaping holes and loose ends, is the barest of pedantic hooks for the flat audience participation gimmick, yet like so many 3D attractions, the film gets released periodically to underline how gullible we once were.

RAG DOLL

UK, 1961
Director: Lance Comfort.
Producer: Tom Blakeley.
Screenplay: Brock Williams, Derry Quinn.
Music: Martin Slavin.
Cinematography: Basil Emmott.
Cast: Jess Conrad, Hermione Baddeley, Kenneth Griffith, Christina Gregg, Patrick Magee, Patrick Jordan.

Poor Lance Comfort; after the disastrous reception to the catastrophic money-loser **Portrait of Clare** (1950), the director got relegated to quickie B-movies, the last of which before his untimely death was the plodding **Devils of Darkness** (1965). But before that he had nurtured the fledgling career of David Hemmings (**Blow-Up**, 1966) with a couple of happy-go-lucky pop star fillers (the best being **Live It Up!**, 1963) and tried to give failed teen idol Jess Conrad ('Cherry Pie', 'This Pullover' his absolute worst singles) a matinee career with this bleak social drama. Hewing close to the cliché of the day, 'the innocent teenager swallowed alive by the Big City', which would reach its apotheosis in **Bitter Harvest** (1963). Here, Carol (Christina Gregg, who ended up in Roger Corman's **The Young Racers**, 1963, based on her performance) heads to London's sleazy Soho after being abused by her drunk stepfather (Patrick Magee) and nearly raped by a diner customer where she falls for wannabe singer/part time burglar Joe Shane (Conrad) and gets pregnant, prompting him to do 'one last job'. Heavy on the seediness while moving at a fair clip (67 minutes only), it was renamed **Young, Willing and Eager** for its American release.

THE SNAKE WOMAN

UK, © 1960, first public screening 1961
Director: Sidney J. Furie.
Producer: George Fowler.
Screenplay: Orville H. Hampton.
Music: Buxton Orr.
Cinematography: Stephen Dade.
Cast: John McCarthy, Susan Travers, Geoffrey Denton, Elsie Wagstaff, Arnold Marlé, John Cazabon.

Just before he broke into the mainstream big-time with the Cliff Richard musical smash **The Young Ones** (1961), the controversial **The Leather Boys** (1964) and the anti-Bond **The Ipcress File** (1965), Sidney J. Furie directed two odd horrors that proved hard to track down on double bills. **Doctor Blood's Coffin** (1961) managed to break through its obscure cult status, but the same can't be said of this infinitely more interesting rare Exploiter. British cop series favourite John Cazabon plays Dr. Adderson (love the snaky surname!). Researching the curative uses of snake venom on mental illness, Adderson experiments on his pregnant wife, who dies giving birth to an eyelid-less cold-blooded daughter. The grown-up Atheris (Susan Travers, the hare-lipped model in **Peeping Tom**, 1960) then stalks the Northumberland moors transfixing her victims as she transforms into a deadly King Cobra. Scripted by Orville H. Hampton of **The Alligator People** (1959) infamy, and over-talky in the dull Scotland Yard investigations, some unique eeriness is lent to the cheap trappings by the opening prelude where Atheris' shed skin is discovered, and the moment a local 'witch' tells the detective to shoot three bullets into a voodoo doll to lift the scaly curse.

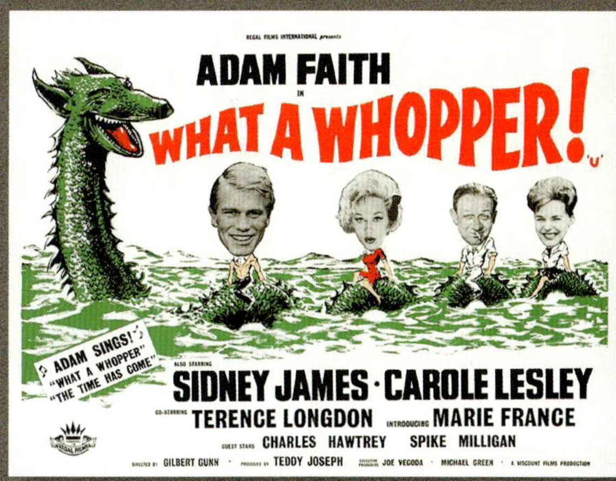

WHAT A WHOPPER

UK, 1961
Director: Gilbert Gunn. Producer: Edward Joseph.
Screenplay: Terry Nation. Music: Laurie Johnson.
Cinematography: Reginald H. Wyer.
Cast: Adam Faith, Sidney James, Charles Hawtrey, Carole Lesley, Terence Longdon, Clive Dunn, Spike Milligan, Wilfrid Brambell, Freddie Frinton.

British teen idol Adam Faith was never out of the pop charts in the early 1960s thanks to his 1959 Number 1 'What Do You Want'. But could he be London's answer to James Dean? That's what the film industry wondered as they cast the blond bombshell in five movies in a row including two eventual cult items, **Beat Girl** (1960) and **What a Carve Up** (1961). This lightweight fantasy farce, co-written by TV acting royalty Trevor Peacock and 'Doctor Who' Dalek creator Terry Nation, directed by Gilbert Gunn of **The Strange World of Planet X** (1958) infamy, stars Faith as an aspiring writer living with Chelsea beatniks (one being Charles Hawtrey!) trying to peddle a book on the Loch Ness Monster for fame and fortune. After being turned down by publishers, the motley crew head to Scotland with a fake photo of a creature they created to kid the locals the legend is genuine. Romantic bedroom complications and other cheerful malarkey repetitiously occurs – aided by Brit comedy treasures Sid James, Spike Milligan, Freddie Frinton and Wilfrid Brambell – before the real monster appears. Faith sings the title theme, written by his personal hitmaker Johnny Worth, arranged by John Barry.

YOUNG AND EAGER

USA, 1961
Director: Gordon Douglas.
Producer: Leonard Freeman.
Screenplay: Leonard Freeman.
Music: Howard Jackson.
Cinematography: Ralph Woolsey.
Cast: Diane McBain, Arthur Kennedy, Will Hutchins, Constance Ford, Claude Akins, Frank Overton.

With upstart AIP and other Exploitation outfits cashing in on the teenage market with bad girls and wild boys, Warner Bros. minted their own sure-fire formula that lasted until beach parties and Beatlemania put them out of fashion. Place their young contract players (Troy Donahue, Connie Stevens, Ty Hardin, Suzanne Pleshette, et al) into provocative adult material, surround them with Hollywood veterans (Claudette Colbert, Rossano Brazzi, etc.) for class and economically gloss them up with solid directors and glamorous backdrops. The most popular were **A Summer Place** (1959), **Parrish** (1961), **Susan Slade** (1961), **Rome Adventure** (1962) and **Palm Springs Weekend** (1963). Based on the 1958 novel 'Claudelle Inglish' by 'Tobacco Road' author Erskine Caldwell, **Young and Eager** stars TV detective series eye candy Diane McBain as the poor white trash Southern girl who remains faithful to handsome rich boyfriend Chad Everett while he is away doing his two-year military service. But when she gets a 'Dear John' letter saying he's in love with another, on goes the tight dress and slutty make up as she becomes the town's good time girl in self-destructive revenge. Ticking every sensationalist and sordid box for the time period, director Gordon (**Them!**, 1954) Douglas's sexy soaper was a Drive-In smash.

THE DEVIL'S MESSENGER

Sweden/USA, © 1961, first public screening 1962
Directors: Herbert L. Strock, Curt Siodmak [uncredited].
Producers: Kenneth Herts [Kenneth Hartford], Gustaf Unger.
Screenplay: Leo Guild, Dory Previn [uncredited], Curt Siodmak [uncredited]. Music: Alfred Gwynn, Lennart Fors [uncredited].
Cinematography: William G. Troiano, Max Wilén [uncredited].
Cast: Lon Chaney Jr., Karen Kadler, Michael Hinn, Ralph Brown, John Crawford, Bert Johnson.

It wasn't just the British or Americans thrilling to 1950s fantasy horror television series like 'Quatermass' or 'Alfred Hitchcock Presents'. Sweden had its own network hit in 1959 with '13 Demon Street', written and directed by Curt Siodmak, and hosted by Lon Chaney Jr., for whom he had written **The Wolf Man** (1941). Chaney Jr. introduced each of the thirteen episodes from his title home, the concept being the chilling crime stories presented are worse than his own unspecified transgression that has doomed him to eternal purgatory. Shot in English but aired with Swedish subtitles, the Herts-Lion International Corporation (the **Carnival of Souls**, 1962, people) saw a marketing opportunity, edited the three 'best' episodes into an anthology and sent Chaney Jr. back to Scandinavia with director Herbert L. Strock (**Teenage Frankenstein**, 1957) to film new framing links. Playing the Devil, Chaney Jr. recruits a suicide victim to help him find suitable Hell inhabitants. One is a photographer using a 'special' camera to kill his models. Another is an anthropologist who pickaxes from ancient frozen ice a prehistoric woman. The third, and most atmospheric, has a man told by a fortune-teller he will die at midnight. A real curio picked up by Tigon.

ESPIRITISMO

Mexico, 1962
Director: Benito Alazraki. Producer: Guillermo Calderón.
Screenplay: Guillermo Calderón, Rafael García Travesi.
Music: Gustavo César Carrión.
Cinematography: Enrique Wallace.
Cast: José Luis Jiménez, Nora Veryán, Carmelita González, Beatriz Aguirre, Alicia Caro, Antonio Bravo, René Cardona Jr.

Every city in America had a Mexican immigrant community. Naturally, Los Angeles had more of an epicentre than most, especially the downtown area, and in 1930 the California Theater at Eighth and Main Streets proclaimed itself to have, "The first all-Spanish program in America". This event ushered in a game-changing period that brought profound change to Latin American cinema and its Hollywood perception via other similar venues, including the Azteca, the Roosevelt, the Mason, Broadway's Million Dollar and the Eléctrico. Large Latino audiences would be attracted by the pairing of films with live entertainment, such as music and appearances by the stars themselves, and Benito Alazraki was one of the many directors who made sure his work was viewed in this keen Exploitation environment. One of seven movies, alongside **Frankenstein el vampiro y compañía** and **Santo vs. the Zombies**, Alazraki made in 1962, **Espiritismo** starred Nora Veryán as a bereaved mother granted three wishes by Satan during a séance. Asking for her dissolute son (future hack director René Cardona Jr.) to be brought back to life causes untold horror in this loose adaptation of the W.W. Jacobs warhorse 'The Monkey's Paw' that accents family disintegration above poor spectral chills.

JULIUS CAESAR AGAINST THE PIRATES

Italy, 1962
Director: Sergio Grieco. Producer: Gastone Guglielmetti. Screenplay: Gino Mangini, Fabio De Agostini, Maria Grazia Borgiotti, Sergio Grieco [uncredited]. Music: Carlo Innocenzi. Cinematography: Vincenzo Seratrice. Cast: Gustavo Rojo, Abbe Lane, Gordon Mitchell, Piero Lulli, Franca Parisi, Susan Terry [Silvana Jachino].

The Italian film industry churned out films in the *peplum* genre relentlessly once **Hercules** (1958) hit worldwide paydirt, and was always on the lookout for different angles on the epic adventure theme. Pirates were a popular adversary – e.g. **The Pirate and the Slave Girl** (1959), **Hercules and the Black Pirates** (1964) – and sleaze merchant director Sergio Grieco (**Beast with a Gun**, 1977) flew the Skull and Crossbones again, after his own **The Pirate of the Black Hawk** (1958), with this entertaining, if minor league spectacle, somewhat ruined by slapdash fight choreography, rubbish mattes and crude miniatures. Based loosely on a true event from the Emperor's early years, Senator Julius Caesar (Gustavo Rojo, **The Valley of Gwangi**, 1969) flees conspiracy-ridden Rome in 75 B.C. and is given refuge by the King of Bithnyia. But en route to sanctuary Caesar is captured by pirates at war with the King and when they demand a gold ransom he vows their eventual destruction. Caesar's love interest Plauzia is played by singer Abbe Lane, one of Latin bandleader Xavier Cugat's many wives, described as "the swingingest sexpot in show business", a moniker that made her a popular femme fatale choice in Italy (see her **Totò** movies).

Julius Caeser
Against
The Pirates

SHERLOCK HOLMES AND THE DEADLY NECKLACE

West Germany/Italy/France, 1962
Director: Terence Fisher. Producer: Artur Brauner.
Screenplay: Curt Siodmak. Music: Martin Slavin.
Cinematography: Richard Angst.
Cast: Christopher Lee, Thorley Walters, Hans Söhnker,
Hans Nielsen, Senta Berger, Ivan Desny, Wolfgang Lukschy.

At the height of his horror fame Christopher Lee was commuting around Europe for pay cheque roles he could play standing on his head. In 1962 he was lured to Germany for roles in such popular *krimis* as **The Devil's Daffodil**, and stayed to make one of his worst movies, incredibly directed by his Hammer stable mate Terence Fisher. After starring in the exemplary **The Hound of the Baskervilles** (1959), this would mark his first outing as Sir Arthur Conan Doyle's super sleuth before appearing as the character again in two 1990s TV movies, and his brother Mycroft in the superb **The Private Life of Sherlock Holmes** (1970). Based supposedly on 'The Valley of Fear', this lame affair finds Holmes and Watson (Thorley Walters) battling Professor Moriarty (Hans Söhnker) for Cleopatra's ancient necklace. With the original script by Universal Monsters icon Curt Siodmak badly rewritten by the German producers, and Lee and Walters' performances ruined by abysmal dubbing, the final fiasco is the worst kind of Eurotrash pudding. Lee barely had a kind word to say about it above the look of Holmes's 221B Baker Street lodgings being entirely correct according to the detailed description in 'The Strand Magazine'.

SLAUGHTER OF THE VAMPIRES

Italy, 1962
Director: Roberto Mauri.
Producer: Dino Sant'Ambrogio.
Screenplay: Roberto Mauri. Music: Aldo Piga.
Cinematography: Ugo Brunelli.
Cast: Walter Brandi, Dieter Eppler, Graziella Granata, Paolo Solvay [Luigi Batzella], Gena Gimmy, Alfredo Rizzo.

Italian actor Walter Brandi/Bigari was having a moment in continental horror in the early 1960s. Following his ace turns in **The Vampire and the Ballerina** (1960) and **The Playgirls and the Vampire** (1960) he starred in this impressive Gothic tale, **La strage dei vampiri**, that took seven years to appear Stateside as **Curse of the Blood-Ghouls** and was dumped onto the bottom of a double bill with the inferior **The Blood Beast Terror/The Vampire Beast Craves Blood** (1968). Torch-bearing peasants drum vampire Dieter Eppler (*krimi* regular) and his mate out of their village, killing her, but allowing him to escape and hide in nobleman Marquis Wolfgang's (Brandi) castle wine cellar. He soon puts Wolfgang's wife Louise (Graziella Granata, **Smog**, 1962) under his blood-sucking spell, a sickness Viennese Dr. Nietzche (Luigi Batzella/Poalo Solvay) instantly recognises and moves to eradicate Van Helsing style. Director Roberto Mauri is scarcely one of the key names when discussing Italy's Golden Age of Horror, his C.V. of scattered *peplum* and Spaghetti Westerns hardly popping with memorable titles (OK, the hilarious **King of Kong Island**, 1968). But while this undead romance is a cut-and-paste Hammer pastiche it sports super production values, great locations and a more coherent plot than most.

SOME PEOPLE

UK, 1962
Director: Clive Donner.
Producer: James Archibald.
Screenplay: John Eldridge.
Music: Ron Grainer.
Cinematography: John Wilcox.
Cast: Kenneth More, Ray Brooks, Annika Wills [Anneke Wills], David Andrews, Angela Douglas, David Hemmings.

Prior to **A Hard Day's Night** (1964), British pop musicals scarcely made any impact Stateside. Here's one, "As gay as a scarlet lipstick" that did because its long-delayed release fraudulently cashed in on Beatlemania and rising star Ray Brooks's Swinging Sixties charisma with **The Knack** (1965). Brooks is one of three Rock 'N' Rollers (alongside David Hemmings and David Andrews) who lose their motorcycle licenses after an accident, and form a band, The Eagles. No, not that one! Great British character actor Kenneth More plays a church organist willing to give the former ton-up boys a fighting chance to succeed using his youth club hall for practice. More had an affair with starlet Angela Douglas while filming in Bristol and although she became his third wife, his career never recovered from the tabloid scandal. Directed leisurely by Clive Donner (**What's New Pussycat**, 1965) with rubbish songs by future 'Doctor Who' composer Ron Grainer – pop princess Carol Deene's version of the title theme barely made the Top 30 – this was astonishingly designed as propaganda to promote the Duke of Edinburgh's Award Scheme, founded by Prince Philip, the 'Good Cause' reason for More's involvement in the first place.

TRAUMA

USA, 1962
Director: Robert Malcolm Young.
Producer: Joe Cranston.
Screenplay: Robert Malcolm Young.
Music: Buddy Collette.
Cinematography: Jacques R. Marquette.
Cast: John Conte, David Garner, Lynn Bari, Lorrie Richards, Bond Blackman, Warren J. Kemmerling.

Fitting into the suspense thriller slot Hammer filled with their **Psycho** (1960) knock-offs **Maniac** (1963), **Paranoiac** (1963), **Nightmare** (1964) and **Hysteria** (1965), Robert Malcolm Young's solo directing credit is a turgidly paced and confused mystery that finally wises up to deliver a modicum of *frisson*. A killer is on the loose in Oakmont town. Emmaline (Lorrie Richards, **The Magic Sword**, 1962) returns home from identifying the body of her murdered friend only to witness her Aunt Helen (B-movie veteran Lynn Bari) being drowned by a shadowy man. Now completely traumatised, she suffers extreme amnesia. But returning home six years later to claim an inheritance, her memory is triggered by events that lead her to figuring out the identity of the unknown murderer. With an overly complicated plot concerning possible gaslighting, a creepy wheelchair, a sinister handyman, a hidden stable chamber and an architect sleuth, there's a lot to grapple with in this unevenly acted low-rent Hitchcocktail. But Jacques R. Marquette's moody B/W photography and Buddy Collette's jazzy score both help to smooth the rocky road to redemption. After scripting **The Crawling Hand** (1963), Young persevered as a very successful TV writer, penning the likes of 'Kojak' and 'Mod Squad'.

AFTER THE FIRES
OF HADES AND THE
SLASHING FRENZY OF
FEROCIOUS BEASTS
THERE REMAINED ONLY
THE VENOM OF
The WITCH'S
CURSE...
The WITCH'S CURSE
starring
KIRK MORRIS/HELENE CHANEL
A MEDALLION PICTURES RELEASE
IN COLOR

THE WITCH'S CURSE

Italy, 1962
Director: Robert Hampton [Riccardo Freda]. Producers: Luigi Carpentieri, Ermanno Donati. Screenplay: Oreste Biancoli, Piero Pierotti. Music: Carlo Franci. Cinematography: Riccardo Pallottini.
Cast: Kirk Morris, Hélène Chanel, Vira Silenti, Angelo Zanolli, Andrea Bosic, Donatella Mauro.

No matter how cobbled together is director Riccardo Freda's tartan sword-and-sandal fantasy, it remains great fun once past the shock of having Maciste (Kirk Morris) turn up in 17th Century Scotland. Owing more to such silent epics as **Cabiria** (1914) and **Faust** (1926) than Mario Bava's **Hercules in the Haunted World** (1961), this action-packed adventure tells the tale of the Loch Laird witch, burnt at the stake for spurning the Mayor's advances. One hundred years later a tree has grown on the spot she was set ablaze and on which young women are compelled to hang themselves. Enter Maciste, in full *peplum* drag, to rip the tree out by its roots and jump into the hole left, leading directly to Hell to reverse the curse. On the journey through the tatty set-designed Hades of Greek mythology (what no Celtic fables?) he sees the damned being tortured and faces a deadly lion (clearly drugged into compliance) before being shown his past deeds by Prometheus in a magic pool. It's here that stock inserts from other Maciste movies – **Monster from the Unknown World** (1961), **Samson and the 7 Miracles** (1961) – are intercut meaning Morris transforms into both Gordon Scott and Gordon Mitchell.

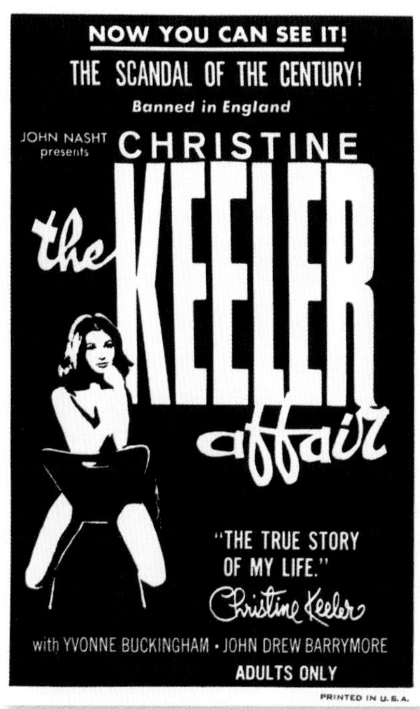

THE CHRISTINE KEELER AFFAIR

UK/Denmark, 1963
Director: Robert Spafford. Producer: John G. Nasht.
Screenplay: Robert Spafford. Music: Roger Bourdin, Roger Connock. Cinematography: Michel Rocca.
Cast: Yvonne Buckingham, John Drew Barrymore, Alicia Brandet, Mel Welles, Peter Prowse, Mimi Heinrich, Christine Keeler.

"Have you been hostessing again?" The headlining Profumo call girl/spy scandal that rocked the Tory Government in 1963 is hilariously trivialised into a Danish-shot, British-banned nudie-cutie romp by director Robert Spafford, one of Italy's top voice dubbers, e.g. **Syndicate Sadists** (1975). Introduced by the notorious and much-maligned naïf Keeler herself before failed starlet Yvonne Buckingham takes over, this hipster classic was filmed on four interchangeable sets – Soho nightspot, basement Notting Hill jazz club, G-Plan mews flat, and a mirrorballed Disco courtroom (the best) – with a staggering minimalism that in its tabloid ineptitude almost becomes Op Art *avant-garde*. When fall guy Stephen Ward (bad movie maven John Drew Barrymore) calls Keeler the camera tracks between two bijou phone tables in a deserted studio, guests at a Jet Set party are all posed window mannequins and, in the startling highlight, a trip to slum landlord Peter Rachman's penthouse has underworld comrades choreographed in time to the discordant beatnik soundtrack. Complete with fleeting poolside nudity, timid hints of homosexuality, Go-Go towel orgies and a five-minute belly-dancing break, it's a turgid mix of fame whore sensation, sleazy surrealism and sledgehammer moralising that is irresistible in its Swinging Sixties gutter surfing.

TOMB OF TORTURE

Italy, 1963
Director: Anthony Kristye [Antonio Boccaci].
Producer: Frank Campitelli [Francesco Campitelli].
Screenplay: Anthony Kristye [Antonio Boccaci], Johnny Seemonell [Giorgio Simonelli].
Music: Armando Sciascia.
Cinematography: William Grace [Francesco Campitelli].
Cast: Annie Albert [Annie Alberti], Thony Maky [Adriano Micantoni], Mark Marian [Marco Marian], Elizabeth Queen [Flora Carosello], William Gray [Antonio Boccaci], Bernard Blay.

A dead countess, her apparent reincarnation (Annie Alberti) and a mutilated ghoul walk into a spooky castle with a subterranean torture chamber... Ah, the Golden Age of early Sixties Italian Gothic where anyone with a creaky script could get a dodgy production company to pony up the lire to excavate the horror export business. Some directors, like Riccardo Freda and Mario Bava, could do wonders with such creepy candle-lit crumble. Others, like one-time Antonio Boccaci, couldn't hack it no matter how hard they tried. For after a quite brutal-for-the-era opening where two girls are abducted, tormented, raped and murdered by the mush-faced monster, an inept whodunit quickly rears its head as it shambles to an obvious villain identity reveal. Sporting the fabulous title **Metempsyco** on spaghetti shores, esteemed genre producer Richard Gordon (**Corridors of Blood**, 1958) acquired the film Stateside, slapped on the **Tomb of Torture** title and Drive-In double-billed it with **Cave of the Living Dead**, his re-cut of the Adrian Hoven starring vampire tale, **Der Fluch der grünen Augen**. As a sign of the terror trove times, the duo was often quadrupled alongside Freda's **The Horrible Dr. Hichcock** and Jess Franco's **The Awful Dr. Orlof** too. Absolute foursome bliss!

TWICE-TOLD TALES

USA, 1963
Director: Sidney Salkow.
Producer: Robert E. Kent. Screenplay: Robert E. Kent.
Music: Richard LaSalle. Cinematography: Ellis W. Carter.
Cast: Vincent Price, Sebastian Cabot, Brett Halsey, Beverly Garland, Richard Denning, Mari Blanchard.

When AIP and Roger Corman hit gold with their Edgar Allan Poe adaptations, others looked to public domain literary properties for horror inspiration. United Artists pounced on Poe contemporary Nathaniel Hawthorne and not only nabbed star Vincent Price, they also followed the portmanteau lead of **Tales of Terror** (1962) with a triple-decker shocker. Price starred in each story, narrating the linking device of a skeleton hand opening a massive compendium book too. In 'Dr. Heidegger's Experiment' he's Alex Medbourne, who discovers a crypt liquid that restores youth. 'Rappacini's Daughter' casts him as Dr. Giacomo Rappacini who makes his daughter poisonous to male touch to keep her sin-free. The final segment finds Price playing Gerald Pyncheon in an adaptation of 'The House of the Seven Gables', but no more faithful to the novel about a family curse than the 1940 movie version, in which he had already co-starred as Clifford Pyncheon. A pretty package that scored big on the Exploitation circuit, despite plodding direction by Sidney Salkow, its debts to Corman's trademark imagery from '**The Facts in the Case of M. Valdemar**' section of **Tales of Terror** and **The Fall of the House of Usher** (1960) are crystal clear.

WINNETOU THE WARRIOR

West Germany/Italy/France, 1963
Director: Harald Reinl. Producer: Horst Wendlandt. Screenplay: Harald G. Petersson. Music: Martin Böttcher. Cinematography: Ernst W. Kalinke.
Cast: Lex Barker, Pierre Brice, Marie Versini, Mario Adorf, Walter Barnes, Chris Howland.

When Austrian director Harald Reinl wasn't making atmospheric *krimis*, he turned his attention to that other rarefied German genre, the Euro Western. **Winnetou 1.Teil/Winnetou the Warrior** (aka **Apache Gold**) was the second film, after **The Treasure of the Silver Lake** (1962) in a ten-plus series, to be based on the Old West novels of Karl May, Europe's most prolific purveyor of the form. Shot in Croatia, where Reinl captured a flawless rendition of the wild frontier, Apache chief Winnetou (Pierre Brice, **Mill of the Stone Women**, 1960) and railway investigator Old Shatterhand (Lex Barker) join forces to foil baddie Mario (**The Bird with the Crystal Plumage**, 1970) Adorf's plan of running a railroad through Indian territories. An action-packed adventure with a supply convoy attack, epic shootouts and a mountain top climax, only the tiresome slapstick antics of a British photographer test the patience. Not that any of that dubious humour made the badly dubbed export cut, which also excised ten minutes of bold vistas and plot. Seen in their full glory these big-budget rivals to gun-fighting American fare are quite something and were huge hits in Germany. Enough to be expertly parodied in 2001 by the wonderful **The Shoe of the Manitou**.

CAVE OF THE LIVING DEAD

West Germany/Yugoslavia, 1964
Director: Akos von Ratony [Ákos Ráthonyi]. Producer: Ákos Ráthonyi.
Screenplay: C.V. Rock [Kurt Roecken]. Music: Herbert Jarczyk.
Cinematography: Hrvoje Saric.
Cast: Adrian Hoven, Erika Remberg, Carl Möhner, Wolfgang Preiss, Karin Field, Emmerich Schrenk.

Double-billed in the USA with the Italian **Tomb of Torture** (1963), distributor Richard Gordon imported this one from Germany (where it was known as **Der Fluch der grünen Augen** – translated as **The Curse of the Green Eyes**) and renamed it **Cave of the Living Dead**. Signifying Austrian matinee idol Adrian Hoven's baby steps into a full-blown horror genre career, first with Jess Franco, leading to his notorious screen violence landmark **Mark of the Devil** (1970), here he's a suave detective assigned to investigate the strange murders of seven nubile young girls in a small village. The deaths always occur just after midnight and during a power outage. But while the doctor says heart failure is the cause, the superstitious locals are convinced vampires are on the loose so Hoven closes in on Professor Wolfgang Preiss (five-time Dr. Mabuse star) who lives in a creepy castle, which is the only place without electricity. While Hammer was forging new Gothic conventions in Great Britain, director Ákos Ráthonyi was content to replay silent movie clichés minted by **Nosferatu** (1922) with little impact. Nevertheless, while a bit of a slog, there is a quirky vibe to the pristinely shot affair with the infrared flashlight vampire detector and melting skull face death. And Herbert Jarczyk's Eurospy-meets-*krimi* score is a groovy gas!

LA CRIPTA E L'INCUBO

CRYPT OF HORROR

Italy/Spain, 1964
Director: Thomas Miller [Camillo Mastrocinque].
Producer: William Mulligan [Marco Mariani].
Screenplay: Robert Bohr [Tonino Valeri], Julian Berry [Ernesto Gastaldi]. Music: Herbert Buckman [Carlo Savina].
Cinematography: Julio Ortas, Giuseppe Aquari.
Cast: Christopher Lee, Audry Amber [Adriana Ambesi], Ursula Davis, José Campos, Véra Valmont, Angel Midlin.

Hammer horror star Christopher Lee was Exploitation gold during the 1960s. His name above the title of any derivative and pointless shocker – you really need examples? – meant Grindhouse profits and this sluggish bore is a prime example. A dull reworking of Mario Bava's classic **Black Sunday** (1960) with a few bits of Joseph Sheridan Le Fanu's Gothic novella 'Carmilla' thrown in, director Camillo (**An Angel for Satan**, 1966) Mastrocinque's plodding potboiler takes the dog-eared clichés of family curses, witches, ornate coaches, musty tombs, crumbling ruins, hunchback pedlars, misty nightmares, haunted bell-ringing and vampires, and does absolutely nothing of inventive note with them. Except modestly highlight the central lesbian relationship between Count Karnstein's (Lee) daughter Laura (Audry Amber/Adriana Ambesi) and passing castle breakdown stranger Ljuba (Ursula Davis). Lee for once plays an upstanding if bewildered lord of the manor, probably the reason it failed to connect with his core audience, along with the protracted thrills continually blunted by Mastrocinque's Italianate heavy-handedness. Filmed atmospherically at the impressive Castello Piccolomini in Balsorano, it would take Hammer another six years before they got round to tackling the same Sapphic subject matter due to British censorship relaxation, with **The Vampire Lovers** (1970).

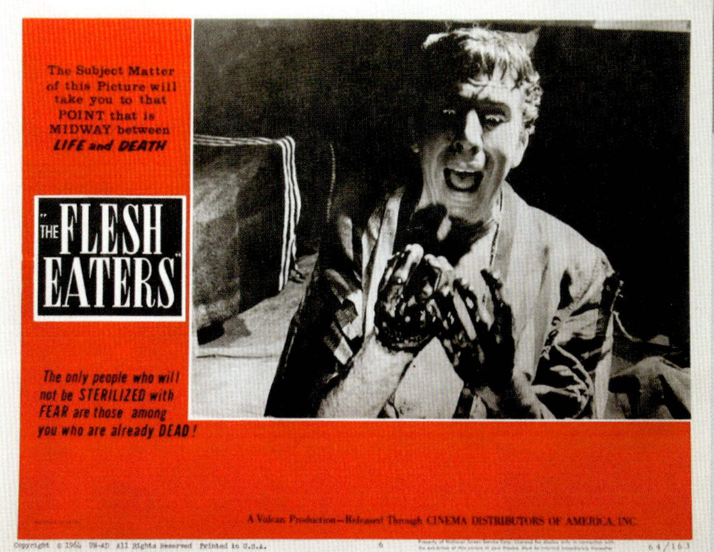

THE FLESH EATERS

USA, © 1962, first public screening 1964
Director: Jack Curtis. Producers: Jack Curtis, Arnold Drake, Terry Curtis [Terry Van Tell]. Screenplay: Arnold Drake. Music: Julian Stein. Cinematography: Carson Davidson.
Cast: Martin Kosleck, Byron Sanders, Barbara Wilkin, Rita Morley, Ray Tudor, Christopher Drake, Darby Nelson, Rita Floyd.

Never given proper due in gore history because of shady production mysteries, the lone directorial effort by cartoon voice artist Jack Curtis remains a fun trashy shocker. Released in Great Britain on a 1968 double bill with **Death Curse of Tartu** (1966), the front-of-house stills were copyrighted 1964, the print 1962, but it was actually shot in 1960, predating **Blood Feast** (1963), the supposed genesis of splatter Exploitation. The first screenplay by Arnold Drake, co-originator of 'Guardians of the Galaxy', the plot is unsurprisingly pure comic strip, as three misfits crash on an island where a crazed marine biologist is cultivating flesh-eating organisms created by twisted Nazis. Funded by Curtis's wife Terry winning $72,000 on a TV quiz show, actress Rita Floyd (she's the radio operator) and dodgy gangsters, extra money came from Curtis filming a hurricane hitting the Montauk location and flogging footage to news stations. With post-synched sound, special effects created by scratching the celluloid emulsion, porridge-mayonnaise stomach explosions and an effective polystyrene monster, it opened in Phoenix, Arizona, Drive-Ins in 1964. By the time of its 1968 re-release a nude Nazi human experiment sequence, added by **Macumba Love** (1960) distributor M.A. Ripps, had been removed and was never seen by British censors.

A GAME OF CRIME

Italy, 1964
Director: Romano Ferrara.
Producer: Ulderico Sciaretta.
Screenplay: Marcello Coscia, Romano Ferrara.
Music: Berto Pisano.
Cast: John Drew Barrymore, Luisa Rivelli, Lisa Gastoni, Jean Claudio, Umberto D'Orsi, Peter Dane.

Many Italian films of the mid-1960s lay claim to being proto-*giallo* items away from the Mario Bava *oeuvre*, like **Sexy Party** (1964), **Libido** (1965) and this cool as a zucchini thriller featuring shimmering black-and-white photography and a super jazzy score by Berto Pisano. Nabbing two stars from **Sexy Party**, John Drew Barrymore and Luisa Rivelli, director Romano Ferrara, whose previous work was the alien invasion sci-fi horror **Hands of a Killer/I pianeti contro di noi** (1962), channels **Double Indemnity** (1944) and Bette Davis melodramas. A web of murder and deceit is spun, involving Barrymore's gambling debts, his boss dying of a suspicious heart attack, his former lover inheriting everything from her husband as long as she stays in the family mansion, and the disfigured, mute, paralysed and deaf brother who screams in torment 24/7. It's a twisted and twisty combo of chills, suspense and Gothic touches, like the old dark house setting and the creepy 'monster' sibling, leading to a memorably bizarre climax in a rat-infested wine cellar. Featured heavily on the *fotobusteri* was popular Italian jazz trumpeter Nini Rosso, who performed the opening song 'Ho bisogno di te'. A year later Rosso hit every European Top 10 with 'Il Silenzio'.

HONEYMOON OF HORROR

USA, 1964
Director: Irwin Meyer. Producer: H.D. Meyer.
Screenplay: Alexander Panas.
Cinematography: Clifford H. Poland Jr.
Cast: Robert Parsons, Abbey Heller,
Alexander Panas, Beverly Lane, Dorothy Farol.

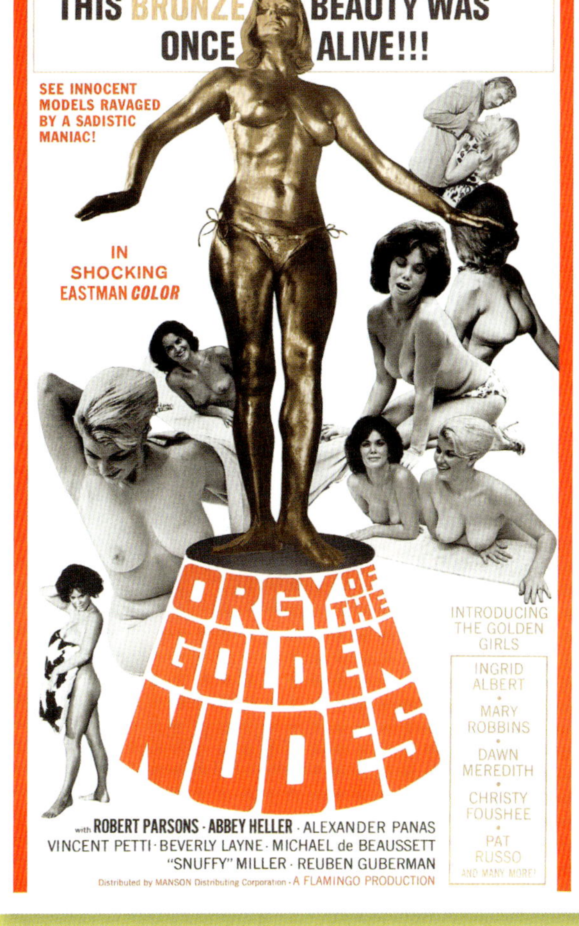

Time and again, as these pages irrefutably confirm, the poster for a cut-price horror was better than anything it supposedly hyped in the actual film itself. This Florida-shot turkey (aka **Orgy of the Golden Nudes**), that lacks even the most rudimentary essentials – actors who can say lines, a coherent script, a cameraman pointing the lens in the right direction, a director with some technical knowledge and an editor able to cut around characters who keep going missing in the narrative – is one for fans of **The Room** (2003). Director Irwin Meyer would endure to produce one halfway decent crime mystery, Larry Cohen's **Deadly Illusion** (1987), but does next-to-nothing with actor/writer Alexander Panas's script, which finds new bride Abbey Heller trapped in a creepy ancient mansion by her crazed artist husband Robert Parsons. Soon she's receiving death threats and narrowly escapes injury in a series of unexplained accidents. Who knew that giant metal globe *objet d'art* suspended above their swimming pool could be so dangerous? There's no shortage of suspects: bonkers Emile himself, his mistress, his sleazy brother (writer Panas), his strange servant and assorted weirdos, beatniks, sculptors and dwarves who populate his bohemian salons. Best line: "Yes, but he's just a minor sex maniac".

KITTEN WITH A WHIP

USA, 1964
Director: Douglas Heyes.
Producer: Harry Keller.
Screenplay: Douglas Heyes.
Cinematography: Joseph F. Biroc.
Cast: Ann-Margret, James Ward [Skip Ward], Richard Anderson, Patricia Barry, John Forsythe, Peter Brown.

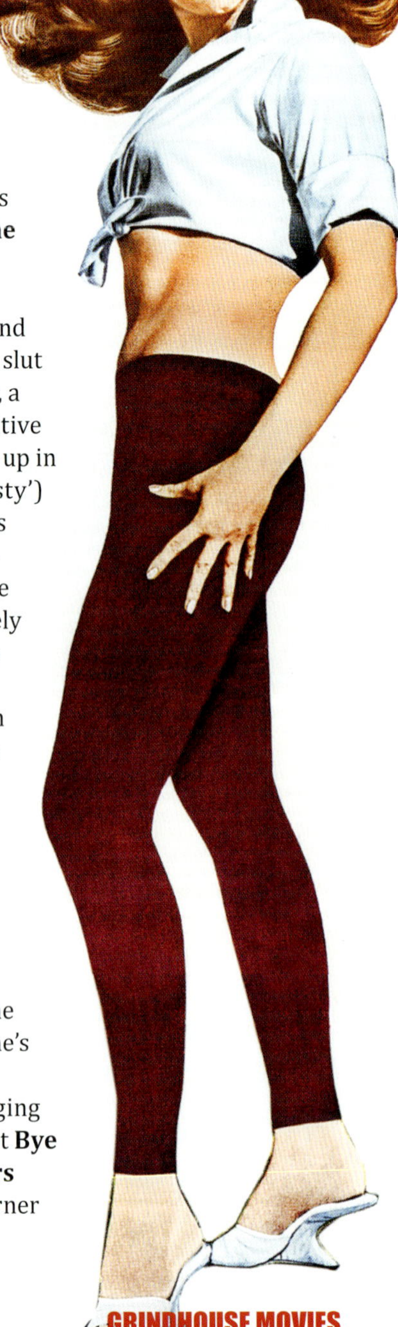

"Why do you think you're such a smoky somethin' when you're nothin' painted blue?" And the runner up in the most quotable camp B-movie stakes after **Beyond the Valley of the Dolls** (1970) is this delicious Juvenile-Delinquent-a-Go-Go trashterpiece starring all-round entertainer Ann-Margret as a slut goddess on wheels. She's Jody, a matron-stabbing, firebug fugitive from reform school who ends up in decent politician John ('Dynasty') Forsythe's bed and blackmails him into helping her two bad-news boyfriends. As one of the thrill-crazy hoods gets severely injured, an enforced road trip to a Tijuana doctor ends this rusty Swinging Sixties hokum on a soap opera downer. (The Tijuana location being the old Bates Motel set from **Psycho**, 1960.) When she's not bumping and grinding around the house, growling out TV stalwart director and co-writer Douglas Heyes's cod-hipster dialogue ("He's the bottle... and then a drop!"), she's smearing lipstick over photo frames and shamelessly mugging to the camera. But hey, the hot **Bye Bye Birdie** (1963) starlet survived this, and junk like **The Pleasure Seekers** (1964), **The Swinger** (1966) and **The Tiger and the Pussycat** (1967) to garner award winning acclaim for **Carnal Knowledge** (1971). Vicious Las Vegas!

KENNETH RIVE Presents
OLIVIA de HAVILLAND
SHE WAS CAGED IN A NIGHTMARE OF GREED, BESTIALITY AND MURDER!
LADY IN A CAGE
ANN SOTHERN as SADE · Written and Produced by LUTHER DAVIS · Directed by WALTER GRAUMAN · A LUTHER DAVIS PRODUCTION · A GALA RELEASE

LADY IN A CAGE

USA, © 1963, first public screening 1964
Director: Walter Grauman. Producer: Luther Davis.
Screenplay: Luther Davis. Music: Paul Glass. Cinematography: Lee Garmes.
Cast: Olivia de Havilland, James Caan, Jennifer Billingsley, Rafael Campos, William Swan, Jeff Corey.

Thanks to **What Ever Happened to Baby Jane?** (1962), every Hollywood diva of a certain Golden Age beat down studio doors to star in ghoulish shockers to revive their careers. Camp icon Joan Crawford was supposed to headline this claustrophobic Walter Grauman directed disturber. But just like with **Hush... Hush, Sweet Charlotte** (1964), Olivia de Havilland replaced Crawford, only this time due to clashing schedules, not feuding with her **Baby Jane** co-star Bette Davis. The **Gone with the Wind** (1939) doyenne plays an invalid poet trapped in her home elevator during a power outage while her house, valuables, courage and soul are upset by an invading gang of teenage hoods fitting the drunk, prostitute, sidekick and moll stereotypes. James Caan, in his first credited feature role, moulded Randall, the leader of the pack, after Marlon Brando in **A Streetcar Named Desire** (1951) and it's he who gets his eyes gouged out by crazed de Havilland. Banned in the UK for three years until it was released on a double bill with a **Them!** (1954) reprise, Grauman brought gritty economy to the stark drama, a powerful statement on the role of war and media bombardment in the numbing of the American psyche.

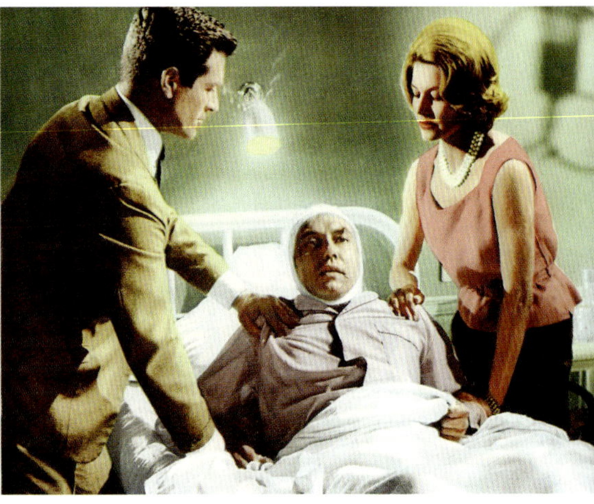

ASSASSINATION IN ROME

Italy/Spain/France, 1965
Director: Silvio Amadio. Producer: Aldo Pomilia. Screenplay: Silvio Amadio, Giovanni Simonelli. Music: Armando Trovadoli [Armando Trovajoli]. Cinematography: Mario Pacheco.
Cast: Cyd Charisse, Hugh O'Brian, Mario Feliciani, Alberto Closas, Juliette Mayniel, Philippe Lemaire, Eleonora Rossi Drago.

With one foot in proto *giallo,* the other in dumb Eurospy shenanigans, **Amuck**! (1972) director Silvio Amadio's convoluted murder mystery does have one thing going for it. And that's a tantalising glimpse behind the Cinecittà scenes to see an unnamed sword-and-sandal feature being shot. That's where hard-nosed, square-jawed Dick Sherman (lacklustre Hugh O'Brian), an American reporter in Rome, has ended up investigating a murder at the famed Trevi Fountains. It turns out the body discovered in that tourist trap has a package of heroin in his pocket, and is somehow connected to the disappearance of the husband of wealthy Shelley North (MGM musical star Cyd Charisse in catatonic mode), by coincidence Dick's old flame. Together they try and find out the truth behind both enigmas while navigating through typically Italian comic relief (a pair of Clouseau style cops), Dick's nosy girlfriend (Eleonora Rossi Drago, **In the Folds of the Flesh**, 1970) who has underworld ties, a detective helper instantly recognisable as doomed collateral damage and a messy reveal that provides a 'didn't see that coming' left-field twist. (Although the original title, **Il segreto del vestito rosso**, which translates as 'The Secret of the Red Dress', seems to give rather more away.)

CALL GIRLS 66

Italy, 1965
Director: Roberto Mauri.
Screenplay: Roberto Mauri, Edoardo Mulargia.
Music: Aldo Piga. Cinematography: Vitaliano Natalucci.
Cast: Alberto Lupo, Marilù Tolo, Lisa Gastoni, Hélène Chanel, Cristina Gaioni, Nerio Bernardi.

The List of Adrian Messenger (1963) clearly impacted on director Roberto Mauri and his co-scripter Edoardo Mulargia. In that John Huston mystery thriller, movie stars hid their famous faces under rubber masks, only revealing their real identities during the final credits. Here a homicidal maniac is using masks of fictitious famous Italian personalities to stalk and kill his prostitute victims, beginning with Hélène Chanel from **The Witch's Curse** (1962). Following a string of similar attacks, Inspector Ferretti (Alberto Lupo, **The Giant of Marathon**, 1959) investigates the call girl operation involving well-connected personalities. Turns out the killer's facial features were destroyed by the Hiroshima bomb blast and he wears masks to get close to his targets without scaring them Phantom of the Opera-style. As much a wonky social satire on fame and fortune, jokey references to Federico Fellini, Pier Paolo Pasolini and Sophia Loren pepper the **La Dolce Vita** (1960) angled plot with slightly off-trend dance floor twisting. The Rome travelogue filler is luminously photographed by Vitaliano Natalucci, and a proto-*giallo noir* atmosphere is well captured. Pitched as a psycho thriller in Italy under the title **Le notti della violenza** (**Night of Violence**), the alternative **Call Girls 66** title put it squarely in the Sexploitation play-off bracket.

OPERATION HURRICANE: FRIDAY NOON

West Germany/France, 1965
Director: Fritz Umgelter. Producer: Gyula Trebitsch.
Screenplay: George Hurdalek. Music: Peter Thomas.
Cinematography: Albert Benitz.
Cast: George Nader, Heinz Weiss, Sylvia Pascal, Helga Schlack, Helmut Förnbacher, Philippe Guégan.

A flat-out Eurospy goodie and first in the German produced Jerry Cotton series, based on the multi-authored series of pulp crime novels, this one an adaptation of 'G-Man Jerry Cotton'. **Robot Monster** (1953) star George Nader found a last gasp Eurotrash career headlining as the FBI agent in all eight 1960s movies after being outed as gay in America by 'Confidential' magazine, a studio trade-off to bury a similar story about his friend Rock Hudson. Here, Cotton is sent undercover to investigate a bowling alley gang involved in a series of interstate gold ingot robberies now progressing to bigger diamond heists. Directed with a devil-may-care élan by TV movie veteran Fritz Umgelter, this appealing mess of James Bond insouciance, 'The Saint' wit and *uber* cheesy special effects – a toy boat exploding like a damp squib caps the 'thrilling' climax, badly executed rear projection turns a truck jumping stunt hilariously surreal – is enjoyable nonsense at its purest and simplest. Superbly scored by *krimi* veteran Peter Thomas, the John Barry of the Cotton series, whose jaunty 'Jerry Cotton March' was a hit signature tune, there was an attempt to revive the beloved franchise in 2010 with Christian Tramitz inheriting the iconic role.

THE POSSESSED

Italy, 1965
Directors: Luigi Bazzoni, Franco Rossellini.
Producer: Manolo Bolognini. Screenplay: Giulio Questi, Luigi Bazzoni, Franco Rossellini. Music: Renzo Rossellini.
Cinematography: Leonida Barboni.
Cast: Peter Baldwin, Virna Lisi, Salvo Randone, Ennio Balbo, Valentina Cortese, Pia Lindström, Pier Giovanni Anchisi.

In between appearing in Riccardo Freda's **The Ghost** (1963) and Michele Lupo's **The Weekend Murders** (1970), and before becoming a go-to US sitcom director ('The Mary Tyler Moore Show', 'The Brady Bunch'), Peter Baldwin starred in this undervalued crime chiller cloaked in ambiguity, the first feature by Luigi Bazzoni (**The Fifth Cord**, 1971, **Footprints on the Moon**, 1975). Based on Giovanni Comisso's novel 'The Lady of the Lake', itself based on real-life 1930/40s murder cases, and adapted by *avant-garde* director Giulio Questi (**Death Laid an Egg**, 1968), Baldwin is novelist Bernard Giovanni, who learns an old flame (future superstar Virna Lisi) has been murdered at a lakeside town. With no physical evidence available due to her body being tossed into the lake, his enquiries lead nowhere as the villagers all remain suspiciously silent. Then another murder occurs, the mystery deepens and Bernard's own life is put in danger. Definitely a mood piece, full of fragmented, unreliable memory and melancholic, unfulfilled romance, Bazzoni's proto-*giallo* is almost a deconstruction of that idiom and a twisted morality fable repeatedly pulling the wool over gimlet eyes. With telling accents on water reflection and secret depths, this haunting transposing of notorious corruption is a must-see rarity.

SECRET AGENT FIREBALL

Italy/France, 1965
Director: Martin Donan [Mino Loy & Luciano Martino].
Producers: Mino Loy, Luciano Martino.
Screenplay: Julian Berry [Ernesto Gastaldi]. Music: Carlo Savina.
Cinematography: Richard Thierry [Riccardo Pallottini].
Cast: Richard Harrison, Dominique Boschero, Wandisa Guida, Alan Collins [Luciano Pigozzi], Jim Clay [Aldo Cecconi], Caroll Brown [Carla Calò].

The first directing credit for Luciano Martino, best known for producing his brother Sergio's sterling output (e.g. **All the Colors of the Dark**, 1972), is the first of a two-picture series featuring Bob Fleming (Spaghetti Western mainstay Richard Harrison) as Agent X117. The second was Antonio Margheriti's **Killers Are Challenged** (1966), where his spy status got changed to the more on-trend 077. Here, rakish Fleming pursues stolen Russian microfilm, spending most time in Beirut chasing evil *femme fatale* Liz Grune (*giallo* star Dominique Boschero), dodging rubber knives and nonsensical fistfights. However, Fleming's love interest Elena, played by Martino's then-wife Wandisa Guida (**Lust of the Vampire**, 1957), does get tortured by everyone's favourite Italian horror support, Luciano Pigozzi/Alan Collins. His Yuri character has a tobacco pipe blowgun and it's in the gadget department that **The Spy Killers**, its alternative title, really shines. Get a load of the pen to detect microwave frequencies, another pen that doubles as a blowtorch, micro-transmitters in aspirin tablets and the matching wristwatch receiver. Best gag is Fleming stealing a helicopter low on fuel and flying to a gas station to fill it up as the pump attendant asks if he'd like his windshield cleaned.

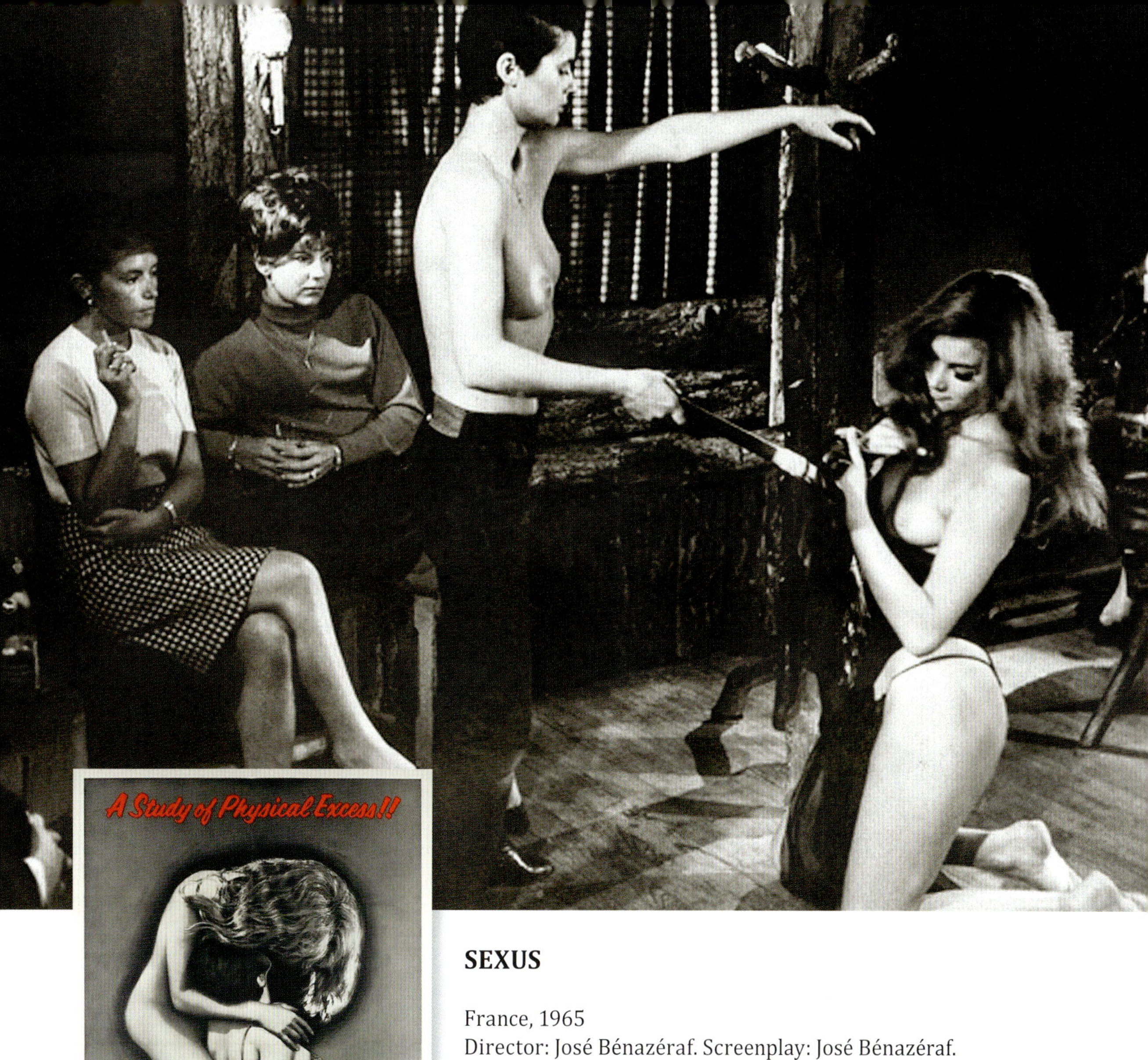

SEXUS

France, 1965
Director: José Bénazéraf. Screenplay: José Bénazéraf.
Music: Chet Baker. Cinematography: Alain Derobe.
Cast: Willy Braque, Yves Duffaut, Annie Josse, Virginia De Solen [Virginie Solenn], Alain Tissier, José Bénazéraf [uncredited].

Or **L'enfer dans la peau/Hell in the Skin**, from pretentious sexploiter José Bénazéraf, director of **Paris Ooh La La** (1963), **Night of Lust** (1963) and the sequel **L'enfer sur la plage/ Hell on the Beach** (1966). The self-proclaimed "erotic poet" carved out a niche in permissive art-house circles with surreal psychodramas designed to create an intimately transgressive climate of sexual desire. And this "Study of Physical Excess" is a prime example, either a disturbing rape fantasy or titillating trash depending on whether you think Godard is merely good or God. Opening with a male narrator informing the audience the entertainment they are about to see features stripping and is therefore only viewable by those aged 18 or over, a beautiful heiress is kidnapped at gunpoint in Paris by two thugs for ransom. Before you can say Stockholm Syndrome, there's an attempted rape, a nightclub excursion to see an S&M lesbian show, attempted murder, lots of tedious banter, arm-wrestling and clock watching, and the lesbian display shown again. With fade-outs, lens warping, repetitious dialogue and swirling camera action meant to disguise the snail pace, and all choreographed to a hip Chet Baker score for 'Ya Ya Twist' heaven. Or hell in the skin!

SUPERSEVEN CALLING CAIRO

Italy/France, 1965
Director: Umberto Lenzi. Producer: Fortunato Misiano. Screenplay: Umberto Lenzi, Piero Pierotti. Music: Angelo Francesco Lavagnino. Cinematography: Augusto Tiezzi. Cast: Roger Browne, Fabienne Dali, Massimo Serato, Rosalba Neri, Andrew Ray [Andrea Aureli], Dina De Santis, Anthony Gradwell [Antonio Gradoli].

Spasmo (1974) director Umberto Lenzi's second Eurospy adventure (the first was **008: Operation Exterminate**, 1965) began a three-picture relationship with *peplum* star Roger Browne, the others being **The Spy Who Loved Flowers** (1966) and **Last Man to Kill** (1966). Here, Browne is the dapper Martin Stevens, aka British Secret Service Agent SuperSeven, searching for stolen Baltonium, a new element 100 times more radioactive than Uranium, fashioned into a movie camera zoom lens by inventor Alex (Massimo Serato, **The Killer Nun**, 1979) and accidentally sold to a tourist. Evil Alex soon joins SuperSeven on the globetrotting race to get to the camera first. Sloppy 007 seconds for sure, and some of the footage is irritatingly reused, but Lenzi's lens saga drags in a groovy disco sequence, a pen gun, an electric shaver transmitter, junkyard go-kart chases and a micro-bomb hidden in SuperSeven's shoe heel. Plus **Lady Frankenstein** (1971) star Rosalba Neri as Faddja, the unwitting pawn of enemy agents, who uses the old Bond "I borrowed your shower" hotel room ploy to infiltrate his emotions. No contest there as it turns out, because SuperSeven's initial main squeeze Denise (Fabienne Dali, **Kill, Baby... Kill!**, 1966) is really a double-crossing Alex stooge...

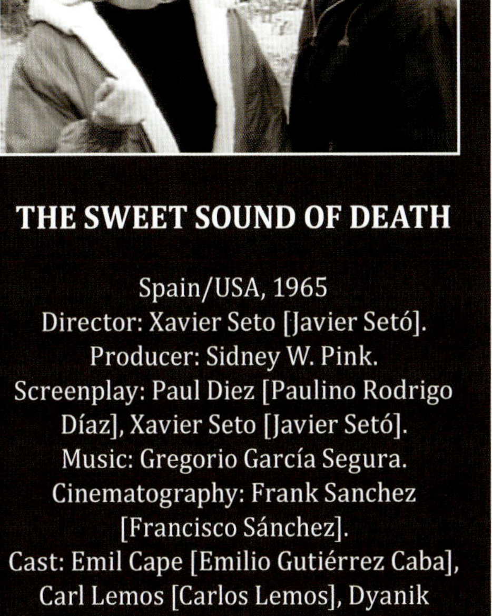

THE SWEET SOUND OF DEATH

Spain/USA, 1965
Director: Xavier Seto [Javier Setó].
Producer: Sidney W. Pink.
Screenplay: Paul Diez [Paulino Rodrigo Díaz], Xavier Seto [Javier Setó].
Music: Gregorio García Segura.
Cinematography: Frank Sanchez [Francisco Sánchez].
Cast: Emil Cape [Emilio Gutiérrez Caba], Carl Lemos [Carlos Lemos], Dyanik Zurakowska, Frank Moran [Paco Morán], Lola Alba [Tota Alba], Daniel Blum, Sun Sanders [Sun De Sanders].

Produced by Sidney Pink, the **Reptilicus** (1961) and **Journey to the Seventh Planet** (1962) man, who blamed its Grindhouse failure on Spanish director Javier Setó's refusal to shoot in colour, **La llamada/The Calling** is important in the Mario Bava-style canon of obsessed Gothic romance. Medical student Pablo (Emilio Gutiérrez Caba) falls in love with classmate Dominique (Dyanik Zurakowska), who takes him to a cemetery to seal their pact that whoever dies first will return to prepare the other for the afterlife. When Dominique does indeed die in a plane crash, Pablo becomes increasingly scared that her ghost is luring him to his death. He must either listen to Professor Urrutia (Carlos Lemos) and his lessons on reality or turn his back on the living and follow his beloved into the netherworld. Strangely compelling and disorientating on an oblique narrative level, the dangers of not letting go of grief is tellingly portrayed through directorial audacity (like Setó's gas-lighter **Macabre**, 1969), sleight-of-hand camerawork, a peculiar jazz score by Gregorio García Segura and subtly complex performances. Devoid of explicit shocks but laden with atmospheric tension that slowly builds to a fittingly eerie climax, this dark fable didn't deserve its Drive-In death.

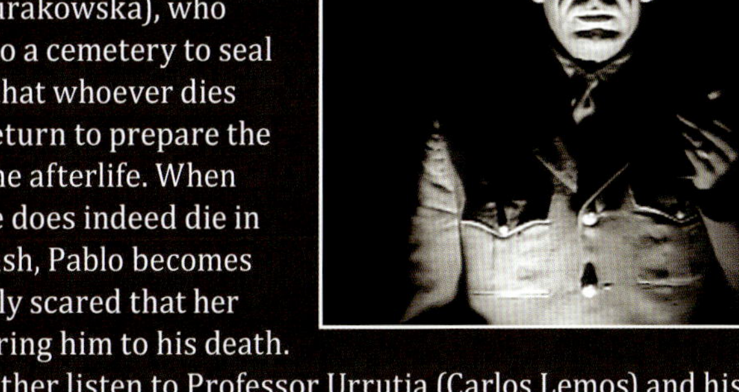

TWO ON A GUILLOTINE

USA, © 1964, first public screening 1965
Director: William Conrad.
Producer: William Conrad.
Screenplay: Henry Slesar, John Kneubuhl.
Music: Max Steiner.
Cinematography: Sam Leavitt.
Cast: Connie Stevens, Dean Jones, Cesar Romero, Virginia Gregg, Connie Gilchrist, Parley Baer.

Warner Bros. had two problems in 1964. What to do with contract star Connie Stevens, coming off successful runs in the TV crime series '77 Sunset Strip' and 'Hawaiian Eye', three hit movies with Troy Donahue and a recording career ('Sixteen Reasons', 'Kookie, Kookie (Lend Me Your Comb)' with Edd Byrnes). And how could they make their expensive sets for **My Fair Lady** (1964) more cost effective? The answer was this harmless haunted house of horror affair, co-written by 'Alfred Hitchcock Hour' and 'Boris Karloff Presents' scripters Henry Slesar and John Kneubuhl, and directed by future 'Cannon' TV star William Conrad. You've heard this one before... When famous magician The Great Duquense, aka Duke (Cesar Romero, The Joker in 'Batman') dies, he bequeaths his entire fortune to estranged daughter Cassie (Stevens), a dead ringer for her mother who mysteriously vanished twenty years before, after rehearsing a guillotine illusion. If Cassie can stay in his creepy mansion for seven days she'll inherit... cue orchestrated bumps in the night threatening to drive her insane and force her to run away screaming. Some okay jolts aside, this quirky oddment boasts the final score from the legendary **Lost Horizon** (1937) composer Max Steiner.

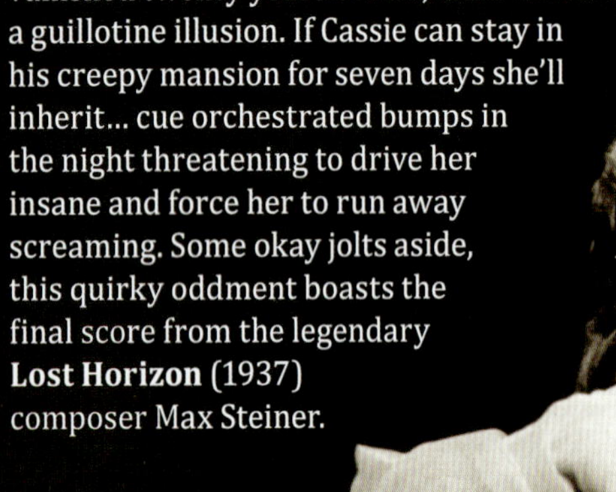

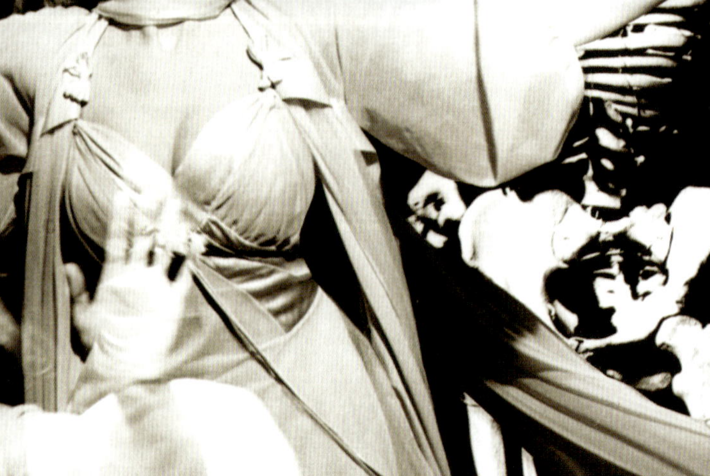

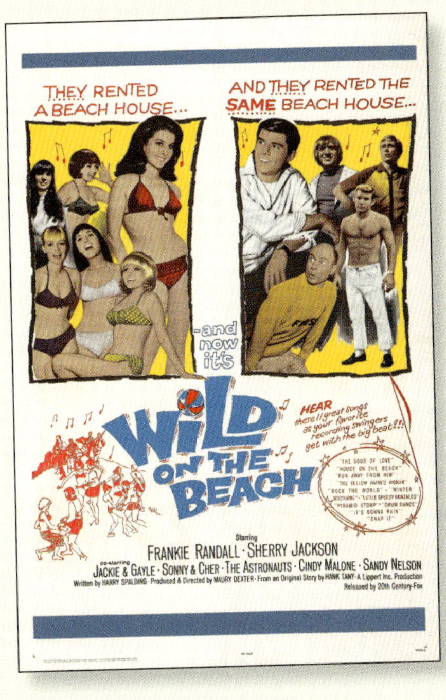

WILD ON THE BEACH

USA, 1965
Director: Maury Dexter. Producer: Maury Dexter.
Screenplay: Harry Spalding. Music: Jimmie Haskell.
Cinematography: Jacques R. Marquette.
Cast: Frankie Randall, Sherry Jackson, Gayle Caldwell, Jackie Miller, Russ Bender, Booth Colman, Justin Smith.

Exploitation outfit American International Pictures hit pay dirt – pay-sand? – when they minted a new teenage genre with **Beach Party** (1963). The copycat surf was up and every distributor tried to cash in on the biceps and bikini combo platforming musical acts of the day. This beach boys and girls affair was directed by Maury Dexter (his second after **The Young Swingers**, 1963) and told the tale of Adam Miller (minor singer Frankie Randall, crooner of the 'Flipper' TV series theme song) and his buddies, forced to share a beach house with Lee Sullivan (Sherry Jackson) and her girlfriends due to accommodation shortages in their seaside college town. Dean Parker (Booth Colman) suspects hanky-panky and forces his clumsy assistant Mort Terwilliger (Justin Smith) to investigate, but the high jinks in this summer holiday were never going to be anything more than super-squeaky-clean. Meanwhile, next-door neighbour and, wouldn't you know it, record producer Shep Kirby (Russ Bender) likes the sounds of The Astronauts wafting past his windows and is eager to sign them up. These low-rent Beach Boys contributed four songs to the soundtrack, along with Sonny and Cher (in their first movie appearance) and drumming legend Sandy Nelson.

BATTLE OF THE MODS

Italy/West Germany, 1966
Director: Franco Montemurro.
Producers: Turi Vasile, Luggi Waldleitner.
Screenplay: Ennio De Concini, Adriano Bolzoni, Michael A. Schreiber [uncredited], Klaus von Wahl.
Music: Udo Jürgens [uncredited], Robby Poitevin [uncredited].
Cinematography: Mario Montuori.
Cast: Joachim Fuchsberger, Ricky Shayne, Elga Andersen, Eleonora Brown, Orchidea De Santis, Jürgen Draeger, Udo Jürgens.

Born in Beirut and raised in France, it wasn't until George Albert Tabbett moved to Italy, learnt to sing and changed his name to Ricky Shayne that he hit the Euro charts with his first single, 'Uno dei Mods' in 1965. Thematically followed up by 'Vi Saluto Amici Mods', it wasn't long before *musicarelli* opportunity knocked and Shayne found himself starring in **The Black Invaders** (1962) director Franco Montemurro's quick-fixer-upper using the tabloid headline sensation of the times, the war between Mods, those Lambretta-riding, dedicated followers of fashion, and Rockers, their greaser biker nemeses. Co-written by *peplum* veteran and Mario Bava's **Black Sunday** (1960) scribe Ennio De Concini, Shayne is Liverpudlian (!) musician Ricky Fuller who, after a bloody gang fight that leaves his girlfriend dead, flees to Rome and has an affair with his father's mistress. Shot in Germany with a cast made up of famous German names – crooner Udo Jürgens, *krimi* star Joachim Fuchsberger and Elga Andersen, Shayne eventually moved there to record one of the very first Giorgio Moroder compositions, 'Ich sprenge alle Ketten' (1968). He remained to have a sizeable Schlager career and in 1971 released his German version of the international hit song 'Mamy Blue'.

BUT YOU WERE DEAD

Italy, 1966
Director: Gianni Vernuccio.
Producer: Gianni Vernuccio.
Screenplay: Enzo Ferrari. Music: Giorgio Gaslini. Cinematography: Gianni Vernuccio.
Cast: Alba Rigazzi, Cristina Gaioni, Walter Pozzi, Alex Morrison [Sandro Pizzochero], Jeanine Falconi, Antonio Bellani.

While it's true that Mario Bava's **Baron Blood** (1972) updated the gloomy Gothic melodrama with all mod cons in mainstream style, a few got there first. Like Gianni Vernuccio's **La lunga notte di Veronique**, which souped up its standard ghost romance with Carnaby Street fashions and sports car chic. When his parents die in a car accident, university student Gianni Bernardi (Sandro Pizzochero/Alex Morrison) goes to stay at his estranged grandfather's villa where he meets the mysteriously ethereal Veronique (Alba Rigazzi) walking the grounds. Turns out she made a suicide pact with his grandfather during the First World War he obviously failed to keep. So she's returned in spirit form to frighten his orphaned grandson into killing himself for hell-hath-no-fury revenge. World War II propaganda documentary filmmaker Vernuccio first directed features in his native Egypt before returning to Italy for the Sabu adventure **Il tesoro del Bengala** (1953), later making a big splash with **Un amore** (1965). Many found the narrative confusing, not helped by Vernuccio's fondness for inserting flashbacks at the oddest intervals. But because it was made at the peak of the Italian horror export business, it found its way to most markets for fast Grindhouse playoff.

DEATH IS NIMBLE, DEATH IS QUICK

Italy/France/Austria, 1966
Directors: Rudolf Zehetgruber, Gianfranco Parolini [uncredited]. Producers: Hans Pflüger, Theo M. Werner [Jacques Willemetz]. Screenplay: Rudolf Zehetgruber. Music: Gino Marinuzzi Jr. Cinematography: Klaus von Rautenfeld. Cast: Tony Kendall, Brad Harris, Ann Smyrner, Dan Vadis, Siegfried Rauch, H.D. Kulatunga.

The second in the successful **Kommissar X** (1965-71) series of seven, and one of the best episodes, reuniting American martial arts expert Captain Tom Rowland (Brad Harris) with his former partner and perpetual nuisance Joe Walker (played by Tony Kendall), better known for his sexual shenanigans than Top Secret operative successes. Here the bickering odd couple go up against The Three Cats (**Drei Gelbe Katzen** being the original German release title), a mysterious Ceylon-based sect formed to battle British colonialism and now involved in more nefarious dealings, in this instance the murder of a special agent after the botched kidnapping of an American millionaire's daughter. Shamelessly lifting a bit of 007 here, cartoon stunts straight out of 'Jonny Quest' there (choreographed by two Italian Hercules, Harris and Dan Vadis) and sporting exotic locations like the villain's Death Lake lair and the usual quota of bodies beautiful, director Rudolf Zehetgruber's Eurospy extravaganza is good-natured fun.

While murderous bellhops overrun the Montevideo Hotel and suite showerheads spray flesh-eating bacteria, the most unusual gadgets are the loud print shirts that block out radiation. Despite their budgets the **Kommissar X** adventures are all wonderfully entertaining, and Rudolf Zehetgruber also directed the fourth film in the series, **Drei grüne Hunde/Three Green Dogs** (1967).

THE GHOST AND MR. CHICKEN

USA, 1966
Director: Alan Rafkin.
Producer: Edward Montagne.
Screenplay: James Fritzell, Everett Greenbaum, Andy Griffith [uncredited]. Music: Vic Mizzy.
Cinematography: William Margulies.
Cast: Don Knotts, Joan Staley, Liam Redmond, Dick Sargent, Skip Homeier, Reta Shaw.

A cornerstone matinee memory for millions of children, especially through double-billing in numerous territories with **Munster, Go Home!** (1966), this huge box-office hit made TV funny man Don Knotts a major movie star. His high-strung fidgety persona had come to the fore in 'The Andy Griffith Show' before being further explored in **The Incredible Mr. Limpet** (1964) part animation family comedy. But it was sit-com director Alan Rafkin who cemented Knotts's laugh-out-loud sex-rattled timidity playing typesetter Luther Heggs, who dreams of becoming a fully-fledged reporter in his small Kansas town. After writing a filler piece about an upcoming anniversary of an unsolved murder at the Old Simmons Place, he's goaded into spending a night alone at the supposed haunted house. The title, a cheeky riff on the 1947 classic **The Ghost and Mrs. Muir**, and filmed next door to the Munster Mansion set on the Universal back lot, this fun-scary comedy full of secret passages, creepy organ music, bleeding portraits and spooky pratfalls is the Stateside answer to **Carry On Screaming!** (1966). So successful was it that Universal put Knotts into several more low-budget comedies, including **The Reluctant Astronaut** (1967) and **The Shakiest Gun in the West** (1968).

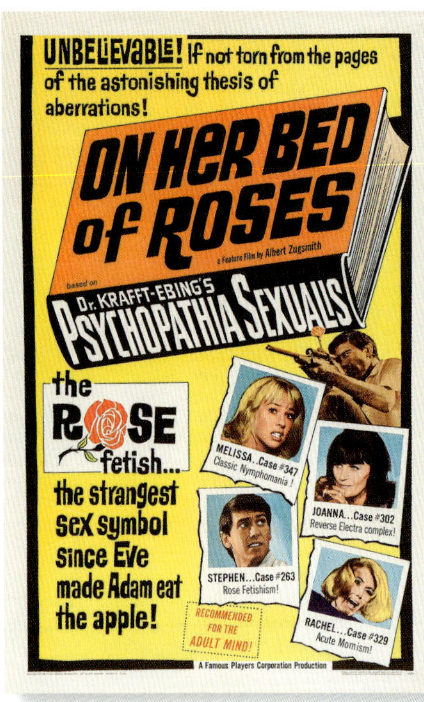

ON HER BED OF ROSES

USA, 1966
Director: Albert Zugsmith [uncredited].
Producer: Robert Caramico.
Screenplay: Albert Zugsmith [uncredited]. Music: Joe Greene.
Cinematography: Robert Caramico.
Cast: Ronald Warren, Sandra Lynn, Barbara Hines,
Lee Gladden, Ric Marlow, Regina Gleason.

From producing the sublime – **The Incredible Shrinking Man** (1957), **Touch of Evil** (1958) – to directing the ridiculous – **The Private Lives of Adam and Eve** (1960), **LSD, I Hate You!** (1966) – mediocre melodramatist Albert Zugsmith scraped the bottom of the Freudian barrel with this overheated sex drama. Not be confused with Joe Sarno's **Red Roses of Passion** (1966), another embarrassment using the thorny flower as an erotic fetish trigger as per the supposed source material, 'Psychopathia Sexualis', the legendary 1886 manual by Dr. Krafft-Ebing that introduced a host of kinks into the public consciousness. It's Melissa Borden (Sandra Lynn) who visits famed psychiatrist Dr. Robert Krafft-Ebing (Lee Gladden) to ascertain why her fiancé has murdered his mother, sniped innocent bystanders and committed suicide. Turns out, after lengthy talky flashbacks, that his repressed upbringing combined with matriarchal domination led to a violent reaction when he couldn't seduce Melissa in a rose garden. Well, at least she beat Lynn Anderson, who sang in 1970 "I beg your pardon (I never promised you a rose garden)". A tortured-soul, cathartic hoot from start to finish, the pounding, evocative jazz soundtrack by Joe (**Tiger by the Tail**, 1970) Greene became a cult vinyl album.

SOUND OF HORROR

Spain, 1966
Director: José Antonio Nieves Conde.
Producer: Gregorio Sacristán de Hoyos.
Screenplay: Sam X. Abarbanel, Gregg G. Tallas, José Antonio Nieves Conde, Gregorio Sacristán de Hoyos. Music: Luis de Pablo.
Cinematography: Manuel Berenguer.
Cast: James Philbrook, Arturo Fernández, Soledad Miranda, José Bódalo, Ingrid Pitt, Lola Gaos.

Ah, the invisible threat genre! From the unseen stalking menace in **Cat People** (1942) and mind-bending doors in **The Haunting** (1963) to the Id monster of **Forbidden Planet** (1956) and the imaginary runic dangers in **Night of the Demon** (1957), suggestion can be a powerful thing as the over-active mind fills in the always infinitely more shocking blanks. Then there's the convenience of having no-cost special effects in the minuscule budgeted end of the Exploitation industry, like the undetectable aliens of **Invisible Invaders** (1959) and the concealed creature in this pot-boiling, mind-numbing nonsense from Spanish writer/director José Antonio Nieves Conde, best known for his erotic thriller **El diablo también llora** (1965). Archaeologists seeking treasure in a valley cave in the Greek mountains uncover a mummified body and are attacked by something invisible that emits an unearthly sound in this turgid talkathon where absolutely nothing happens and the visual effects are beyond laughable. A few howling noises and scraped face moments aside, the most hilarious scenes have claw prints appearing in scattered flour, air embedded axes and a truck roof being torn off. Best remembered now for being the feature debut of apex Hammer Scream Queen, Ingrid Pitt.

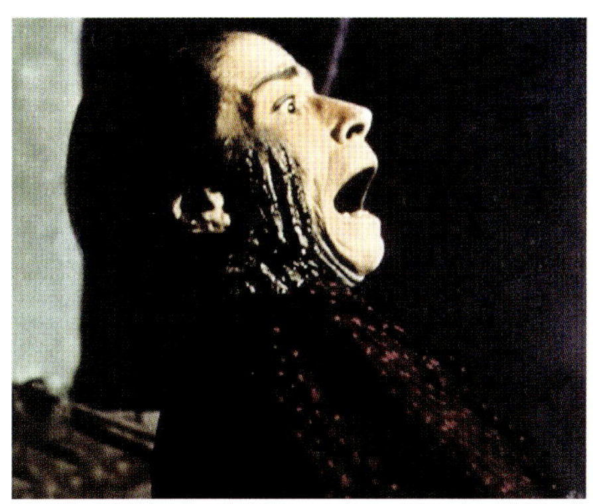

THE THIRD EYE

Italy, 1966
Director: James Warren [Mino Guerrini].
Producer: Louis Mann [Luigi Carpentieri & Ermanno Donati]. Screenplay: James Warren [Mino Guerrini], Dean Craig [Piero Regnoli]. Music: Frank Mason [Francesco De Masi]. Cinematography: Sandy Deaves [Alessandro D'Eva]. Cast: Frank Nero [Franco Nero], Gioia Pascal, Diana Sullivan [Erika Blanc], Olga Sunbeauty [Olga Solbelli], Marina Morgan, Richard Hillock.

Most Italian horror fans know the thinly veiled remake/rip-offs of this Mino Guerrini directed shocker – Emilio Miraglia's **The Night Evelyn Came Out of the Grave** (1971) and Joe D'Amato's **Beyond the Darkness** (1979) – more than the original inspiration itself. Which is a shame as it's a class act all the way even though it pays its own homage by borrowing heavily from **Psycho** (1960). Handsome hunk Franco Nero was on the cusp of **Django** (1966) international fame and becoming Vanessa Redgrave's life partner when he starred as wealthy Count Alberti, who lives alone with his domineering, controlling mother (Olga Solbelli) and their besotted maid Marta (Gioia Pascal). Both women conspire to drive away Mino's fiancée Laura (Erika Blanc) by arranging a fatal car accident, but in an argument after that murder Marta pushes the Countess down the stairs. Losing two key women in his life on the same day causes taxidermy hobbyist Mino to lose his mind and he starts strangling prostitutes and strippers, knowledge Marta uses to blackmail him into marriage. Then Laura's dead-ringer sister arrives and the scene is set for more bloody revenge in a criminally undervalued, perversely twisted and well above average spaghetti thriller.

THE VULTURE

UK/USA/Canada, 1966
Director: Lawrence Huntington.
Producer: Lawrence Huntington.
Screenplay: Lawrence Huntington.
Music: Eric Spear.
Cinematography: Stephen Dade.
Cast: Robert Hutton, Akim Tamiroff, Broderick Crawford, Diane Clare, Philip Friend, Patrick Holt, Annette Carell, Edward Caddick.

British director Lawrence Huntington ended his esteemed quota-quickie career with this arrant nonsense that escaped more than was released, and although filmed in colour was only shown theatrically in black-and white. Fans, if any existed, had to wait for its first TV broadcast to see it the way it was initially filmed with the not-untalented veteran cast – Robert Hutton, Akim Tamiroff, Broderick Crawford – trying to make credible the insane horror hodgepodge about an 18th Century Spanish seaman buried alive with his pet vulture by a venal Cornish squire (Crawford). His brother-in-law (Hutton) finds out the ancient mariner's descendant (Tamiroff) wanting vengeance has atomically fused his body with his ancestor, forgetting about the buried bird, meaning he created a giant feathered creature with a man's face, **The Fly** (1958) style. Old-fashioned direction, ropey, limited special effects and the Cornish setting at odds with the casting, the Paramount press pack suggested dressing up an usher in a half man/half vulture outfit to walk the streets and a 'First Aid Station' in the lobby with 'nurses' offering medical advice to those suffering shock. Shock from being suckered in, more like! **The Oblong Box** (1969) screenplay was Huntington's posthumous film credit.

BARON BRAKOLA

Mexico, 1967
Director: José Díaz Morales. Producer: Luis Enrique Vergara.
Screenplay: José Díaz Morales, Rafael García Travesi, Fernando Osés. Music: Jorge Pérez.
Cinematography: Eduardo Valdés.
Cast: Santo [Rodolfo Guzmán Huerta], Fernando Osés, Mercedes Carreño, Antonio de Hud, Andrea Palma, Ada Carrasco, Susana Robles.

With all the rubber bats, stuffed animals, lap-dissolve transformations, dark decrepit mansions, cobwebbed crypts, mummies, masks and rats you could wish for, famed wrestler El Santo (Rodolfo Guzmán Huerta) battles the vampire Baron Brakola (Fernando Osés) in this brutal action horror given a bizarre spin by *luchador* expert director José Díaz Morales. Back in 1765 – and a good deal of the movie is given over to this colonial Mexico flashback – Santo's ancestor 'Caballero Enmascarado de Plata/Silver Mask' was hired by the parents of the beautiful Rebeca (Susana Robles) to protect her from the rich Brakola's amorous intentions. But resurrected as an ugly vampire after dying in the attempt to kill Silver Mask, Brakola turns Rebeca into a fellow blood-drinker who eventually gets staked by the Zorro-style wrestler. In the present, Brakola has risen from the grave to search for the reincarnation of his lost love and disguises himself as Santo's next opponent to stop history repeating. Let the relentless ringside bashing begin… Shot on the same sets as **Santo vs. the Vampire Women** (1962), and with as many swordfights as rough-and-tumble brawling, this swashbuckling fantasy scores pretty high in the distinctive Santo tag team filmography.

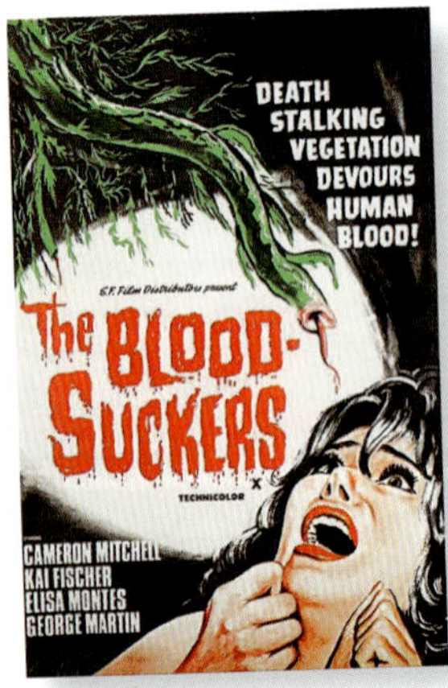

THE BLOODSUCKERS

Spain/West Germany, 1967
Director: Ernst Ritter von Theumer. Producers: George Ferrer, Ernst Ritter von Theumer [uncredited]. Screenplay: Ira Meltcher [Mel Welles], Ernst Ritter von Theumer, Stephen Schmidt [uncredited]. Music: Antón García Abril, José Muñoz Molleda [uncredited]. Cinematography: Cecilio Paniagua, Juan Mariné [uncredited].
Cast: Cameron Mitchell, Elisa Montés, George Martin, Kai Fischer, Rolf von Nauckhoff, Hermann Nehlsen.

Or **Maneater of Hydra**. Only veteran Exploitation maestro and expatriate American Mel Welles (**Lady Frankenstein**, 1971), who played flower shop owner Gravis Mushnick in Roger Corman's classic **The Little Shop of Horrors** (1960), could go on to direct another killer plant movie in the same bonkers vein. Shot in Spain in three weeks and reviewed as "the bloodiest film in the world" by local press, Welles's cheap pseudonymous shocker finds insane Baron von Weser (dubbed Cameron Mitchell) cultivating carnivorous Venus Flytraps that feed on human blood in his island mansion garden. As his upper crust, decadent European guests are murdered one by one (mostly by camera zooms into their terrified faces!) it takes everyone ages to work out what's going on exactly, although it's obvious from the horticultural horror get-go. Also known as **Island of the Doomed**, pitched somewhere between a stereotypical Agatha Christie mystery thriller and a more hilarious **The Day of the Triffids** (1963), **La isla de la muerte** as it was originally titled, opens with fun animated credits and ends with a vine-slurping, branch-bleeding, splatter finale. Mitchell pleading with the fiendish fronds to stop their vampiric nonsense is just one highlight in this twisted Garden of Eden fable that ranks as a late bloomer.

WHAT WAS THE TERRIFYING SECRET
OF THE
VAMPIRE
TREE?
Island
of the
DOOMED
TECHNICOLOR®
TECHNISCOPE®
You'll never
forget...
THE
CLUTCHING
HORROR!
starring CAMERON MITCHELL
Directed by MEL WELLES • An ALLIED ARTISTS Release

A COVENANT WITH DEATH

USA, 1967
Director: Lamont Johnson. Producers: William Conrad, Jimmy Lydon [uncredited]. Screenplay: Saul Levitt, Lawrence B. Marcus. Music: Leonard Rosenman. Cinematography: Robert Burks.
Cast: George Maharis, Laura Devon, Katy Jurado, Earl Holliman, Arthur O'Connell, Sidney Blackmer.

TV director Lamont Johnson earned his big screen chops with this forgotten legal melodrama dealing with thorny issues now the domain of such series as 'Law & Order: Special Victims Unit'. Yet another attempt by Greek hunk George Maharis to turn his 'Route 66' fame into a viable movie career – **Sylvia** (1965), **The Satan Bug** (1965), **The Happening** (1967) all flopped – and peppered with other TV personalities hoping to hitch their wagon to his rising star, including Gene Hackman – "The bristling bestseller comes to angry life" hyped the poster without even mentioning author Stephen Becker's name. When a notorious slut is strangled in the 1920s Southwest, circumstantial evidence convicts her violent husband. It's up to junior judge Maharis to oversee the hanging but the alleged killer freaks out seeing the hood and both he and the hangman fall from the gallows, the latter dying from a head injury. Then the real murderer confesses and commits suicide, leading to the core conundrum – should the now innocent man be tried with the hangman's homicide? Despite getting bogged down in hackneyed romance, Johnson makes it work, but found his feature debut dumped on a double bill with the Italian thriller **Secret Agent Super Dragon** (1966).

DEATH ON THE RUN

Italy/USA, 1967
Director: Sergio Corbucci.
Producers: Clemente Fracassi, William Sachs.
Screenplay: Sergio Corbucci, Frank Ross [Franco Rossetti], Mark Patrick [Massimo Patrizi].
Music: Ivan Vandor, Fiorenzo Carpi [uncredited].
Cinematography: Aiace Parolin.
Cast: Ty Hardin, Michael Rennie, Gordon Mitchell, Paola Pitagora, Vittorio Caprioli, Jamie Silver [Hum Silvers].

One of the grittier cries and thighs hybrid Eurospy thrillers comes from director Sergio Corbucci, the Italian violence action maestro whose hard-hitting influence spread across the entire globe. Was Ty ('Bronco') Hardin's master thief here the inspiration for Leonardo DiCaprio's Rick Dalton in **Once Upon a Time… in Hollywood** (2019)? Could be. The **Berserk** (1967) hero plays Jason who, after escaping Greek justice in Athens, is blackmailed into stealing a dead man's tooth containing microfilm listing important secret agents' identities. No wonder double-crossing British Secret Service Major Clark (Michael Rennie, Klaatu from **The Day the Earth Stood Still**, 1951), The Albanian (*peplum* icon Gordon Mitchell), two ruthless criminal gangs and the cops all want to get their hands on it. Jason's only helpers are best friend Billy 'Pizza' (Vittorio Caprioli) and stripper Greta (Paola Pitagora). Corbucci keeps the pace relentless – one of its alternate titles **Moving Target** couldn't be more appropriate – with non-stop car chases, nasty fisticuffs and gunfights, all pointing to the imminent *poliziotteschi* genre coming down the brutal pike. The big band jazzy score by **Django, Kill!** (1967) composer Ivan Vandor provides a neat counterpoint to all the counter-espionage with a Russian twist at the climax.

THE INCIDENT

USA, 1967
Director: Larry Peerce. Producers: Edward Meadow, Monroe Sachson. Screenplay: Nicholas E. Baehr. Music: Terry Knight. Cinematography: Gerald Hirschfeld.
Cast: Tony Musante, Martin Sheen, Beau Bridges, Brock Peters, Ruby Dee, Jack Gilford.

Still banned in the UK is director Larry ('Batman') Peerce's brilliantly intense subway shocker, which chief censor of the day John Trevelyan called an "even more dangerous film" than **The Wild Angels** (1966). Basically, two violent hoodlums (Tony Musante and Martin Sheen, making his film debut) board a late-night New York subway train from the Bronx to Grand Central Station and terrorise the passengers, something Trevelyan thought was "only too possible", the copycat reason for the outright veto. The sixteen people including a homeless person, army privates, a black couple, a tired teen and elderly Jewish pensioners, fail to collectively face the threat until quiet soldier Beau Bridges steps forward to save the day in the proper – urban – western tradition. With little humour or humanity on show in this tightly-paced melodrama, file this one under too cringe-worthy for its intended art-house audience, hence why it found its way to the Grindhouse circuit. Exteriors were illegally shot using hidden cameras because the NYC Transit Authority would not give the crew permission to film on the subway for obvious incendiary reasons, adding enormous reality to the sometimes theatrical action, with the carriage interiors recreated on a soundstage.

BULLETS
CAN'T KILL IT!
FIRE
CAN'T BURN IT!
WATER
CAN'T DROWN IT!
HOW CAN
WE DESTROY IT
BEFORE IT
DESTROYS
US?

IT

EASTMAN COLOUR

SEVEN ARTS PRODUCTIONS presents "IT" starring RODDY McDOWALL JILL HAWORTH Written, Produced and Directed by HERBERT J. LEDER
A GOLDSTAR PRODUCTION • Released through WARNER-PATHE

IT!

UK, © 1966, first public screening 1967
Director: Herbert J. Leder. Producer: Herbert J. Leder.
Screenplay: Herbert J. Leder. Music: Carlo Martelli.
Cinematography: Davis Boulton.
Cast: Roddy McDowall, Jill Haworth, Paul Maxwell,
Aubrey Richards, Ernest Clark, Oliver Johnston.

Released on a double bill with another dead loss Herbert J. Leder directed production, **The Frozen Dead** (1966), this faux Hammer scream cheese ineffectively purloins 'The Golem' Eastern European myth with an insulting grab-bag larceny. Grown-up Hollywood child star Roddy McDowall slums it as Arthur Pimm, the assistant curator at a musty museum, who discovers an ancient, 8-foot pointy-headed clay figure following a fire at a nearby warehouse. Oh, Pimm also keeps his late mother's corpse for conversation in another nod to the genre's more recent Norman Bates past! Soon Pimm learns the statue will do his murder bidding and when the bodies start piling up, the police drop a nuclear bomb on his house. That's after he decides to destroy London's Hammersmith Bridge, truly the only Hammer allusion of note in Leder's infantile comedy horror combo. Jill Haworth plays Pimm's fantasy love interest, her last job before heading to Broadway to star as Sally Bowles in the landmark musical 'Cabaret'. And it was the movie she and McDowall would eventually refer to as "Sh**It**" that doomed her successful two-year theatre stint to the likes of **The Haunted House of Horror** (1969), **Tower of Evil** (1972) and **The Mutations** (1974).

LSD: HELL FOR A FEW DOLLARS MORE

GUY MADISON
FRANCA POLESELLO
IN
LSD
UNA "ATOMICA,, NEL CERVELLO
EASTMANCOLOR

Italy, 1967
Director: Mike Middleton [Massimo Mida]. Producer: Benito Bertaccini. Screenplay: Bruno Baratti, Odoardo Fiory, Mike Middleton [Massimo Mida]. Music: Egisto Macchi.
Cinematography: Silvano Ippoliti.
Cast: Guy Madison, Franca Polesello, Mario Valgoi, Lucio De Santis, Adriano Micantoni, Karin Skarreso.

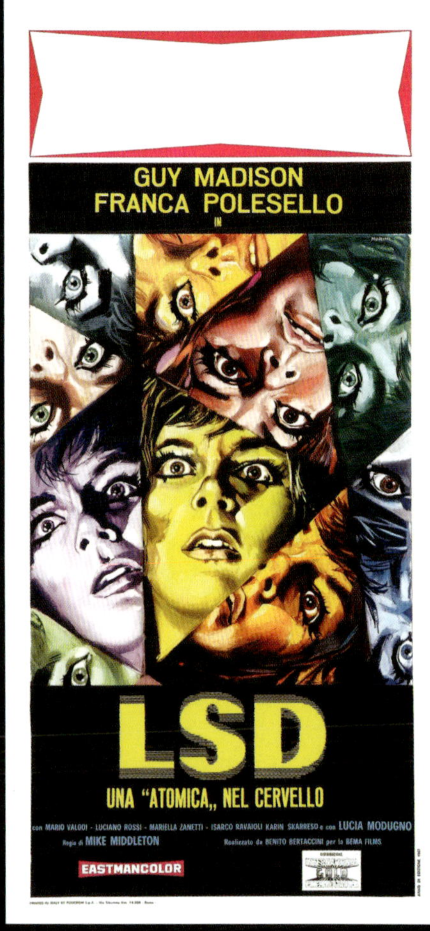

Only the Italians could manufacture a bizarre Eurospy fusion of anti-drug propaganda with a Spaghetti Western hook. After using a toy car to explode two victims and a blowgun to murder another, killer kid Rex Miller grows up to be a top secret agent who uncovers a plot to lace key global nerve centres with potent Acid to create a Utopian world. Rex (Guy Madison, 'Wild Bill Hickok' TV star) has a radio transmitter planted into his neck, infiltrates the ECHO organization behind the deranged scheme, exposes the kingpin Mr. X (Adriano Micantoni) and saves the world from hallucination terrorism. Calling Mike Middleton (Massimo Mida Puccini) a director is pushing it considering the dull and repetitive action but there is much to enjoy in the typical camp aspects of the genre including spur-of-the-moment Go-Go dancing, low-budget gadgetry (lipstick radio, snorkel blowgun, weaponised briefcase, mantel clock communicator, fire-breathing statue) and a Chelsea Girl wardrobe of groovy fashions. There's also hilarious 'documentary' footage of an army platoon secretly given LSD in their morning coffee and freaking out to an exaggerated degree. Violence wise the neck transmitter operation is surprisingly graphic and someone gets ignominiously burnt to a crisp on electrified bars.

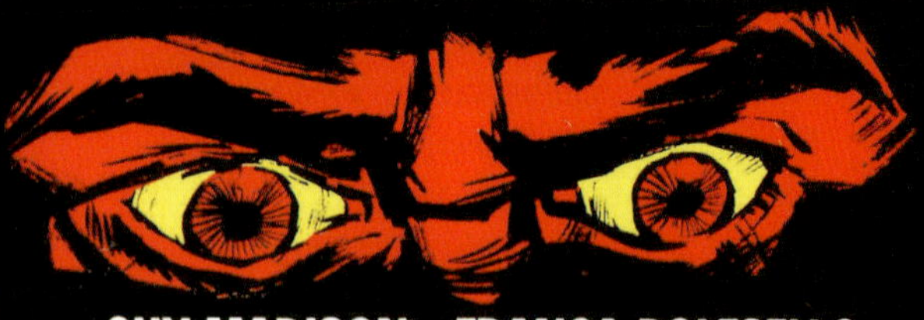

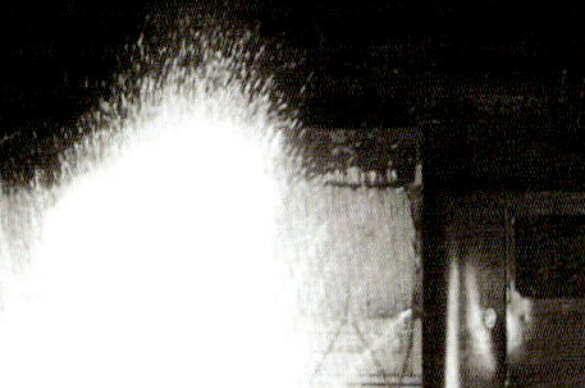

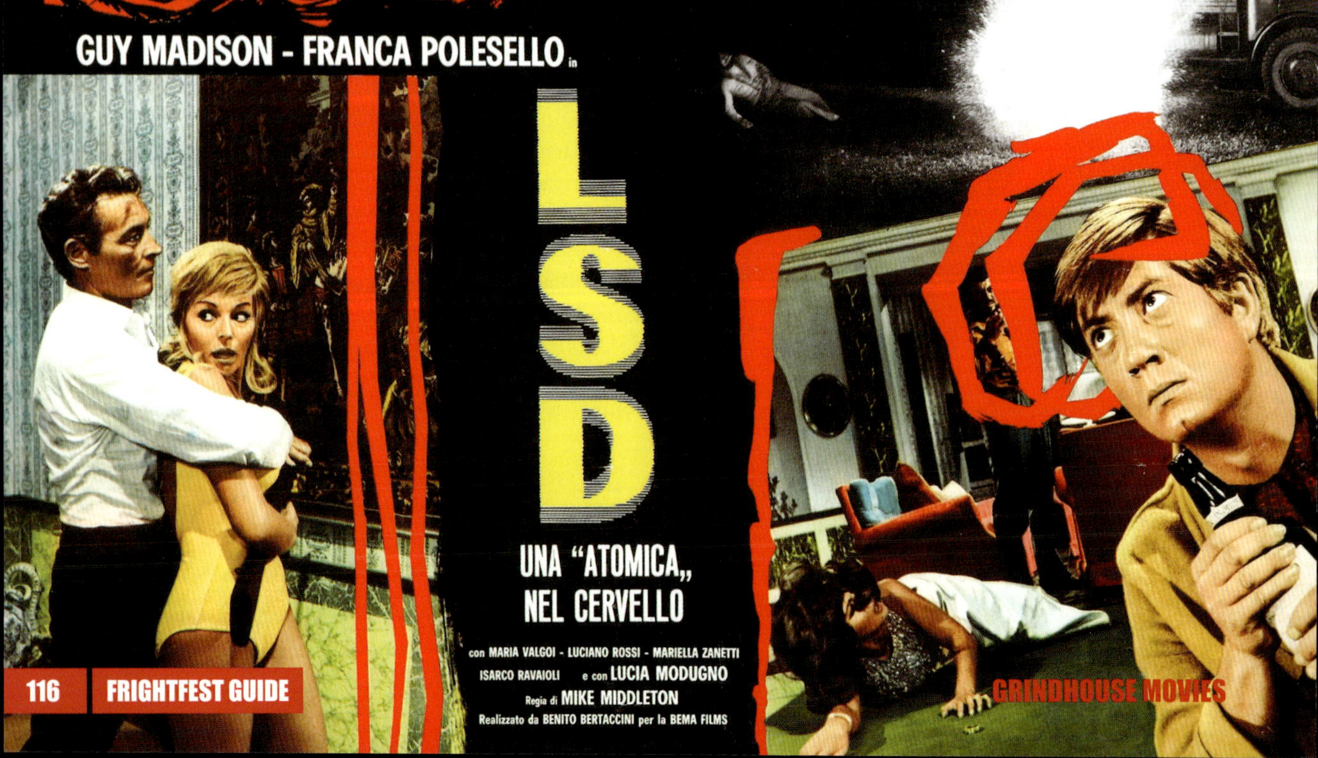
GUY MADISON - FRANCA POLESELLO in
LSD
UNA "ATOMICA,,
NEL CERVELLO
con MARIA VALGOI - LUCIANO ROSSI - MARIELLA ZANETTI
ISARCO RAVAIOLI e con LUCIA MODUGNO
Regia di MIKE MIDDLETON
Realizzato da BENITO BERTACCINI per la BEMA FILMS

MARAT/SADE

UK, © 1966, first public screening 1967
Director: Peter Brook.
Producer: Michael Birkett.
Screenplay: Adrian Mitchell.
Music: Richard Peaslee.
Cinematography: David Watkin.
Cast: Patrick Magee, Ian Richardson, Michael Williams, Clifford Rose, Glenda Jackson, Freddie Jones.

Ever wondered why Amicus-made **The Skull** (1965), what prompted Jess Franco to direct **Justine** (1969) and what caused AIP to finance their enormous flop **De Sade** (1969)? It was all due to one of the most successful theatrical experiences of the Swinging Sixties. From Berlin to London's West End and Broadway, Peter Brook's award-winning and acclaimed production of German-born Peter Weiss's celebrated and disturbing play 'The Persecution and Assassination of Jean-Paul Marat as Performed by the Inmates of the Asylum of Charenton Under the Direction of the Marquis de Sade', as performed by the Royal Shakespeare Company (including Glenda Jackson, Ian Richardson, Freddie Jones and Patrick Magee) took the stage world by storm. Filmed by Brook on a shoestring budget, the truncated movie version – and the long-winded title really is the story encapsulated – offered moviegoers a glimpse into art-house chic and firmly put the name of the notorious Marquis on marquees for the curious. Using the hoary old cliché of a play within a play – the asylum patients are the actors in the play written by inmate De Sade – the foul language and intense subject matter ensured it was booked mistakenly into Grindhouse fleapits the world over.

MASSACRE OF PLEASURE

Luxembourg/France, 1967
Director: Jean-Loup Grosdard [Jean-Pierre Bastid].
Producers: Henry Lange, Gilbert Wolmark.
Screenplay: Christian Sarramia, Chris Pentel.
Music: Glen Buschmann. Cinematography: Jean-Jacques Renon.
Cast: Joël Barbouth, Syd Phyllo [Emilie Benoît], Willy Braque,
Pierre Cabanne, Beatrice Cenci, Robert Dalban.

One of the lesser well-known *enfant terribles* of the French *Nouvelle Vague* was all-round artist, writer and director Jean-Pierre Bastid. He was Jean Cocteau's assistant on **Le testament d'Orphée** (1960), worked with Nicholas Ray and directed several short films before scandalizing censors worldwide, and the Cannes Film Festival, with his first feature originally titled **Massacre pour une orgie**. Banned in the UK for a year until cut to death, and refused release in France until 1973, this erotic thriller filmed in Luxembourg concerned an investigation into three murders leading to a hidden network of white slavery and drug dealing run by a one-eyed thug, a sadist and a fat Greek money launderer, pseudonymously credited to Jean-Loup Grosdard (in homage to Jean-Luc Godard), Bastid staged a fake murder scenario on the Palais du Festival red carpet steps at Cannes to promote what turned into a hot potato for every distributor who touched it, except Olympic International in America, the **House on Bare Mountain** (1963) and **Love Camp 7** (1969) people. Bastid shot back into the spotlight in 2017 thanks to directors Bruno Forzani and Hélène Cattet, who adapted his novel **Let the Corpses Tan** into a terrific art house thriller.

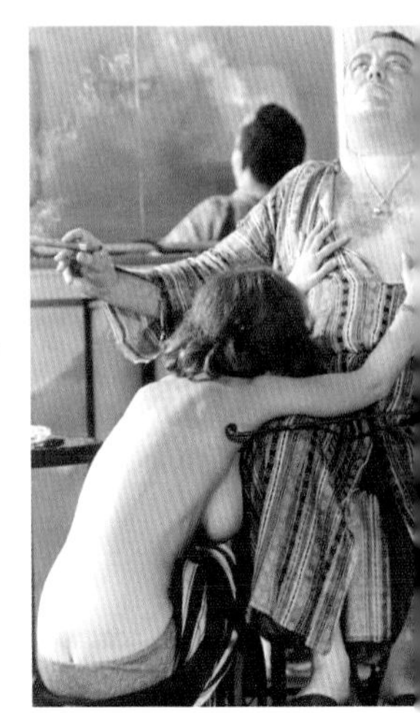

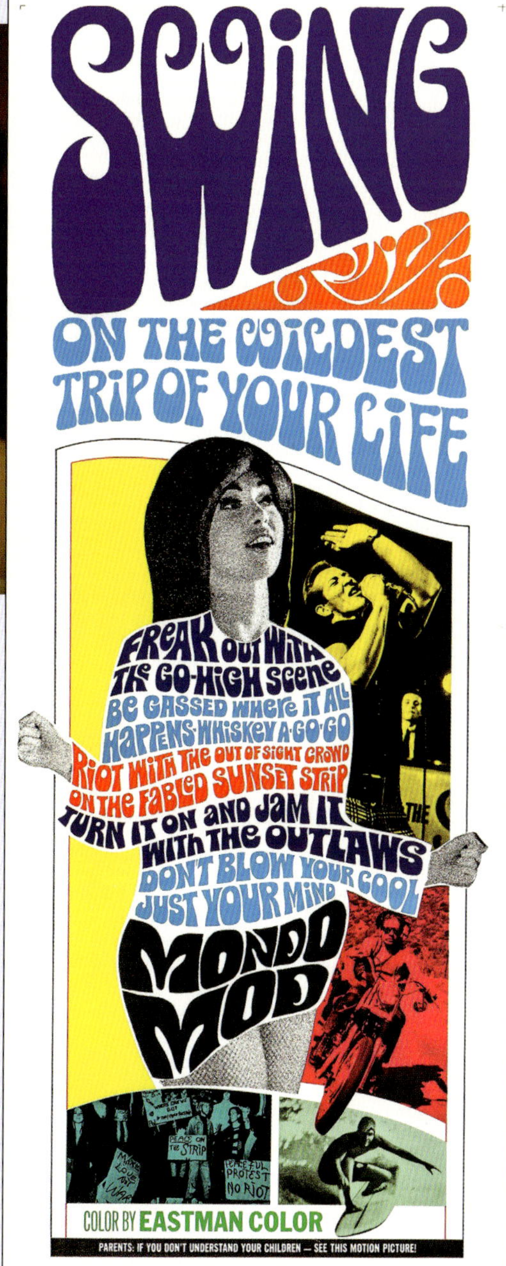

MONDO MOD

USA, 1967
Director: Peter Perry Jr.
Producer: Peter Perry Jr.
Screenplay: Sherman Greene.
Music: The Gretschmen.
Cinematography: Leslie Kovacks [László Kovács], William Zsigmond [Vilmos Zsigmond].
Cast: Humble Harve (narrator), Sam the Soul and the Inspirations, The Group.

It's a Mod, Mod, Mod, Mod World! If you ever wanted to know what your kids were up to in the Swinging Sixties, the last place you'd look for the freak-out facts is the endless array of 'mind-blowing' youth culture Exploiters pretending to tell you where it's at. That director Peter Perry Jr. (aka Seymour Tokus, A.J. Gaylord) was involved in such 'classics' as **The Secret Sex Lives of Romeo and Juliet** (1969), **Knockers Up** (1963) and **The Flesh Merchant** (1956) says everything about this hilarious 'torn from today's headlines' 'Hipness for Dummies' manual, featuring music from The Group and The Gretschmen! From groovy fashions, LSD love-ins and far-out hair-don'ts to pot parties, drugged-out strippers and a look inside Sunset Strip's Whiskey a Go-Go disco, L.A. DJ Humble Harve is your guide to what's hot and what's not on the 'too cool for school' circuit. Quite what go-kart racing, political protest, karate or dirt biking had to do with being Mod who knows, but hey, everything hippie and dippy got thrown in for extra Mondo value. As was often the case with these Drive-In staples, the credits list some future heavyweights; here in the cinematographer department were László Kovács and Vilmos Zsigmond.

THE OLDEST PROFESSION IN THE WORLD

France/West Germany/Italy, 1967
Directors: Claude Autant-Lara, Mauro Bolognini, Philippe de Broca, Jean-Luc Godard, Franco Indovina, Michael Pfleghar. Producers: Joseph Bercholz [uncredited], Horst Wendlandt [uncredited]. Screenplay: Ennio Flaiano, Daniel Boulanger, Georges Tabet, André Tabet, Jean Aurenche, Jean-Luc Godard. Music: Michel Legrand. Cinematography: Pierre Lhomme, Alessandro D'Eva [uncredited], Dario Di Palma [uncredited], Heinz Hölscher [uncredited].
Cast: Michèle Mercier, Elsa Martinelli, Jeanne Moreau, Raquel Welch, Nadia Gray, Marilù Tolo, France Anglade, Anna Karina.

They didn't travel abroad so well, but Italy and France both did good honest box-office in the 1960s with episodic high profile package movies like **Ro.Go.Pa.G.** (1963), Lucio Fulci's **The Maniacs** (1964), and **Four Kinds of Love** (1965). Typically comedies with a socially relevant factor, this better-than-average look at the history of prostitution showcased three French directors – Claude Autant-Lara, Jean-Luc Godard, Philippe de Broca – one German (Michael Pfleghar), and two Italians – Mauro Bolognini and Franco Indovina. It also starred the sexiest actresses of the era: Michèle Mercier, Raquel Welch, Jeanne Moreau, Elsa Martinelli, France Anglade, Nadia Gray, Marilù Tolo, and Anna Karina. Divided into the caveman erotica 'The Prehistoric Era', a 'Roman Nights' fantasy brothel, 'Mademoiselle Mimi' in the French Revolution, a 'La Belle Epoque' courtesan, call girls in 'Paris Today' and 'Anticipation', Godard's futuristic gaze at **Alphaville** (1965) sex robots, it's a well-scripted look at the strengths and weaknesses of the opposing sexes, cultural differences and societal mores. A send-up of the genre appeared with Mauro Ivaldi's **Brigitte, Laura, Ursula, Monica, Raquel, Litz, Florinda, Barbara, Claudia, e Sofia le chiamo tutte... anima mia** (1974) where the Christian names of superstar actresses became the selling point.

THE PENTHOUSE

UK, 1967
Director: Peter Collinson. Producer: Harry Fine. Screenplay: Peter Collinson. Music: Johnny Hawksworth. Cinematography: Arthur Lavis. Cast: Terence Morgan, Suzy Kendall, Tony Beckley, Norman Rodway, Martine Beswick.

Made in just over three weeks for circa £60,000, this is the nudge, nudge, wink, wink shocker, based on Scott Forbes's 1964 play 'The Meter Man', that director Peter Collinson made to serve notice he could be more than a TV series craftsman. It led to **Up the Junction** (1968), **The Italian Job** (1969), **Fright** (1971) and **Straight On Till Morning**, so it worked. But many contemporary critics found the Harold Pinteresque elliptical fantasy via Hitchcockian sleight-of-hand a nauseating home invasion mix. Estate agent Bruce Victor (Terence Morgan, **The Curse of the Mummy's Tomb**, 1964) and his mistress Barbara (Suzy Kendall) spend an illicit night in the penthouse of an unoccupied high-rise. In the morning, therc's a knock at the door and 'meter men' Tom (Tony Beckley) and Dick (Norman Rodway) bust in to drug, sexually abuse and mistreat the self-pitying couple while digging into the psychological motives for their behaviour. Then Harry (Martine Beswick) arrives for more funny games… Get it? Slathering its stagy pretensions with the lip-smacking nastiness Collinson would become Grindhouse famous for, this skilfully made but uncomfortable exposé of unsavoury middle class morality and emotional claustrophobia is the clear harbinger of **Straw Dogs** (1971).

SHANTY TRAMP

USA, 1967
Director: Joseph G. Prieto.
Producer: K. Gordon Murray.
Screenplay: K. Gordon Murray, Reuben Guberman, Joseph G. Prieto. Music: Frank Linales.
Cinematography: J. Rafael Remy [Ralph Remy Jr.].
Cast: Lee Holland [Eleanor Vaill], Kenneth Douglas [Otto Schlessinger], Lewis Galen, Bill Rogers, Lawrence Tobin, Ed Anderson.

From super-tat duo director Joseph G. Prieto (**Miss Leslie's Dolls**, 1973) and producer K. Gordon Murray (**Savages from Hell**, 1968) comes a southern-fried homicide sleaze-o-rama pushing every hot button topic even those further up the grime totem pole were reluctant to broach. Local floozy Emily Stryker (Eleanor Vaill, aka Lee Holland) sashays seductively into a revivalist preacher's tent, inflaming every red-blooded male in attendance. Before long she's caught the collection plate cleric's glad eye, been attacked by leader of the biker pack Savage (Lawrence Tobin) and seduced god-fearing African-American Daniel (Lewis Galen). Discovered in bed with Daniel by her abusive father, Emily cries rape and a lynch mob forms with white supremacist vengeance on their minds. Shot in Florida years before its Grindhouse release, this lip-smacking slice of southern discomfort covers all the steamy bases from holy rolling hypocrisy and **Baby Doll** (1956) immorality to small-town small-mindedness and racial tensions. Vaill, cast due to her willingness to go topless, not her acting ability, underscores its swampy Z-grade potboiling credentials but you do find out what a 'fin' is (a five dollar note) and you'll never hear 'When The Saints Go Marching In' the same gospel way again!

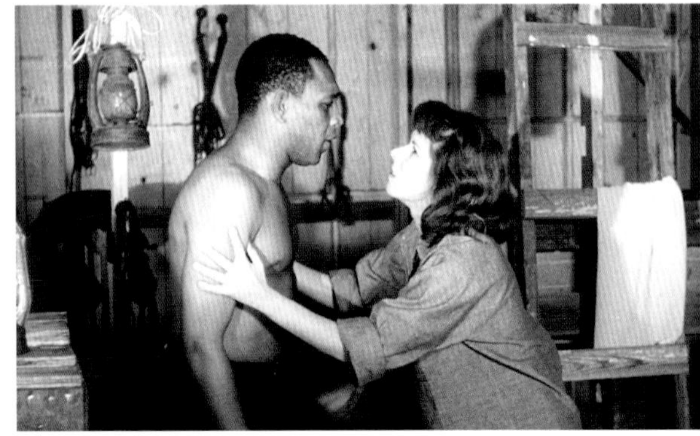

THE SHUTTERED ROOM

UK, © 1966, first public screening 1967
Director: David Greene. Producer: Phillip Hazleton.
Screenplay: D.B. Ledrov, Nat Tanchuck.
Music: Basil Kirchin, Jack Nathan [uncredited].
Cinematography: Ken Hodges.
Cast: Gig Young, Carol Lynley, Oliver Reed, Flora Robson, Judith Arthy, Rick Jones.

Originally earmarked for Ken Russell, who chose **Billion Dollar Brain** (1967) instead, David Greene climbed aboard this project hoping it would unshackle him from being viewed as a mere broadcast director. It didn't, because he was destined to become King of the American TV movie after an average feature film career. But this swirling suspense thriller, easily Greene's most competent chiller, contained some memorable subjective camera jolts for its day despite the constantly rewritten-on-location script. Based on a short story by Arkham House owner August Derleth, who himself based it on story ideas left by H.P. Lovecraft after his death, the 'posthumous collaboration' finds **Bunny Lake Is Missing** (1965) starlet Carol Lynley returning to her New England hometown with husband Gig Young. But the homecoming sparks memories of a past traumatic event, further triggered by bad boy Oliver Reed (in a role not too dissimilar from his turn in **The Damned**, 1962) and a terrible family secret – a disfigured twin sister locked in a shuttered room guarded by dotty Aunt Flora Robson. Superbly appointed in background atmosphere – a craggy coastline filmed in Norfolk and Kent, a wedding-cake lighthouse and a Gothic millhouse ruin – where the highly wrought horror explodes.

GOKÉ, BODY SNATCHER FROM HELL

Japan, 1968
Director: Hajime Satô. Producer: Takashi Inomata [Akira Inomata].
Screenplay: Kyûzô Kobayashi, Susumu Takaku.
Music: Shunsuke Kikuchi. Cinematography: Shizuo Hirase.
Cast: Teruo Yoshida, Tomomi Satô, Eizô Kitamura, Hideo Kô, Kathy Horan, Yûko Kusunoki.

In the wake of the enormous international success of **Godzilla** (1954), Japan's film industry transformed into an assembly line churning out giant monster destruction in sequels, spin-offs and cash-ins. Daiei was the first studio to follow Toho's giant footsteps with the likes of **Warning from Space** (1956) and **Gamera vs. Barugon** (1966), and Shochiku belatedly followed with **The X from Outer Space** (1967), **The Living Skeleton** (1968), **Genocide** (1968) and director Hajime Satô's outrageously entertaining and vibrantly colourful rip-off of **Invasion of the Body Snatchers** (1956). An airplane passes through a mysterious cloud mass and crash-lands in a desert. Everyone seems to survive intact except passenger Hideo Kô, who has been changed into a vampire by the alien mist. It's all part of an intergalactic invasion determined to turn mankind into the blood drinking dead and too late do pilot Teruo Yoshida and stewardess Tomomi Satô realise they are literally the two last humans standing as more flying saucers are on their way. Ignore the terrible acting, purple prose dialogue – "The world's in terrible shape. Trouble between nations grows worse with terrorism breaking out all over the place. Everything's gone crazy!" – and hopeless direction; **Goké** really rules.

THE KILLER LIKES CANDY

Italy/France/West Germany, 1968
Directors: Richard Owens [Federico Chentrens], Maurice Cloche. Producer: Richard Hellman. Screenplay: Maurice Cloche, John Haggarty, Giovanni Simonelli. Music: Gianni Marchetti. Cinematography: Fausto Zuccoli.
Cast: Kerwin Mathews, Marilù Tolo, Gordon Mitchell, Werner Peters, Ann Smyrner, Venantino Venantini, Riccardo Garrone, Bruno Cremer.

Assigned to protect the King of Kafiristan after an assassination attempt, CIA agent Mark Stone (Kerwin Mathews, Harryhausen's Sinbad and Gulliver) journeys to Rome to learn the identity and location of the killer who leaves candy wrappers at the scene of his crimes. Villainous meatpacking CEO Guardino (*krimi* star Werner Peters) gives Stone the most wanted name Oscar Snell (Bruno Cremer) and is rewarded by being doused in petrol and set alight by the sweet-toothed ex-Nazi. Then a second attempt is made on the King's life, with Snell planting a bomb in a hotel elevator and Stone, nicknamed Angel Face, must find out who is behind the dastardly plot or he too will be next in line for the ice bullet no-evidence trick. With Stone's comedy sidekick Costa played by veteran genre actor Venantino Venantini (**The Humanoid**, 1979, **Cannibal Ferox**, 1981), Marilù Tolo the romantic window-dressing and *peplum* icon Gordon Mitchell as bad guy Toni, director Federico Chentrens's soft-edged Eurospy thriller, based on a novel by Adam Saint-Moore, is full of evocative sequences like the gun battles in the Parco dei Mostri in Abruzzi (recognize the sculptures from **Castle of the Living Dead**, 1964?) and the creepy monastery catacombs climax.

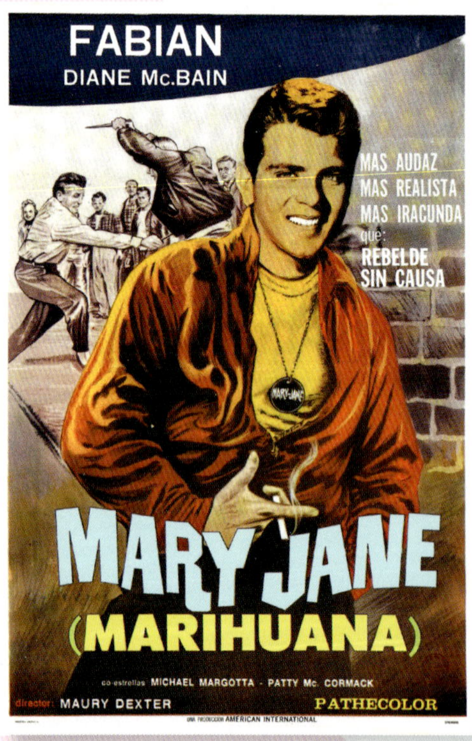

MARYJANE

USA, 1968
Director: Maury Dexter. Producer: Maury Dexter. Screenplay: Dick Gautier, Peter Marshall. Music: Larry Brown, Mike Curb. Cinematography: Richard Moore. Cast: Fabian, Diane McBain, Kevin Coughlin, Michael Margotta, Patty McCormack, Russ Bender.

"AIP – Always timely with the 'Wow' scene" hyped the trade papers over director Maury Dexter's sermonising teen flick about the evils of cannabis. But it was really nothing more than a dopey recycling of the indie Exploitation outfit's delinquent youth clichés from decades past rolled into a joint. High on sensationalism torn from yesterday's headlines more than the title street slang for pot, this old-fashioned reefer madness warning was written by square TV comedian Dick Gautier and game show host Peter Marshall, and couldn't be more dreary and contrived in its social commentary restraint. Star football players at High School USA are heavily into hash and while their cool coach-cum-art teacher Fabian (the **Hound-Dog Man**, 1959, himself) tries to tune in with his turned-on students, he's thrown into jail on a trumped-up charge until it's discovered an on-campus ice cream van man has been selling the weed behind the bleachers. Other main attractions in this hopeless narcotic frolic were Swinging Sixties Bad Girl Diane McBain (**The Mini-Skirt Mob**, 1968), grown-up Patty McCormack, star of **The Bad Seed** (1956) and Michael Margotta, future hippie rebel in right-on movies like **The Strawberry Statement** (1970), here a hilarious abstract painter.

THE POWER

USA, © 1967, first public screening 1968
Director: Byron Haskin. Producer: George Pal. Screenplay: John Gay.
Music: Miklós Rózsa. Cinematography: Ellsworth Fredericks.
Cast: George Hamilton, Suzanne Pleshette, Richard Carlson,
Yvonne De Carlo, Earl Holliman, Gary Merrill.

Producer George Pal and director Byron Haskin teamed together for the last time with this taut para-psychological thriller based on techno sci-fi writer Frank M. Robinson's acclaimed 1956 novel. After the duo's string of popular hits, starting with the classic space invader shocker **The War of the Worlds** (1953) through **Robinson Crusoe on Mars** (1964), MGM wanted out of their contract with Pal and thought, correctly, this deliberately kept-low-budget vanity project would finally sabotage their deal. But Pal, a past master at making the best out of a slim nothing in the special effects department, still delivered the twisting, turning goods in an ingenious and potent package. An elite group of scientists are engaged in human endurance research. When one is killed by a member with telekinetic skills and super-psychic mind control, hero George Hamilton is framed for the murder and undertakes to learn the identity of the real criminal, an alien bent on world domination. Pre-figuring the comic strip blockbuster superhero/supervillain genre by at least thirty years, Haskin's unnerving chiller is a bravura essay in restrained creepiness with one terrific set-piece – Hamilton sheltering in a desert water-hole only to discover it's a US air force bombing target.

in a quiet place she strips
away the structure of his mind and body
...piece by piece.

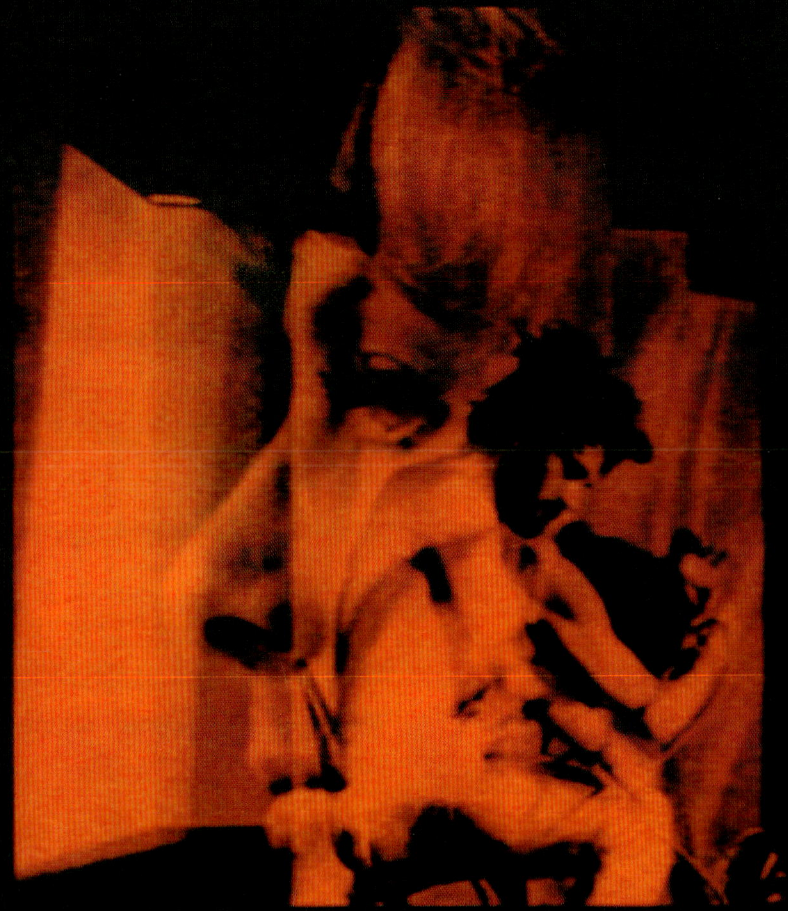

alberto grimaldi presents

vanessa redgrave · franco nero in

a quiet place in the country

with
georges geret · gabriella grimaldi · madeleine damien · rita calderoni

directed by elio petri · screenplay and dialogue by luciano vincenzoni and elio petri

a co-production: pea (produzioni europee associate)-rome les productions artistes associes-paris

R RESTRICTED Under 17 requires accompanying Parent or Adult Guardian

color® United Artists Entertainment from Transamerica Corporation

A QUIET PLACE IN THE COUNTRY

Italy/France, 1968
Director: Elio Petri. Producers: Alberto Grimaldi, Mario Borgognoni Vimercati [uncredited]. Screenplay: Luciano Vincenzoni, Elio Petri. Music: Ennio Morricone. Cinematography: Luigi Kuveiller. Cast: Franco Nero, Vanessa Redgrave, Georges Géret, Gabriella Grimaldi [Gabriella Boccardo], Madeleine Damien, Valerio Ruggeri.

When acclaimed Italian political filmmaker Elio Petri, best known for the Oscar-winning **Investigation of a Citizen Above Suspicion** (1970), tackled genre movies, the result was always remarkable. Arty, pretentious, over-indulgent and sexy to be sure, but they were always an extraordinary trip to the intellectual far side. **The 10th Victim** (1965) is a sci-fi cult classic, and not too far behind should be this *giallo* take on George Oliver Onions's short story 'The Beckoning Fair One', which Mario Bava originally wanted to adapt. Petri swaps Gothic Victoriana for Pop Art psychedelia in this ghost story where avant-garde artist Franco Nero (**Django**, 1966) moves from creatively stifling Milan to a secluded Venetian villa with his agent lover Vanessa Redgrave (**Blow-Up**, 1966). Soon he's being troubled by the presence of a nymphomaniac countess murdered during World War II, who he's convinced is targeting Redgrave via supernatural attack and violent manifestations. A long way from the traditional haunted house of horror, Nero's failure to distinguish between fantasy and reality captures the tortured artist's mentality perfectly. Adding *frisson* to the kinky self-obsession is the fact that Nero and Redgrave were a couple, **Deep Red** (1975) Luigi Kuveiller's cinematography and a fab Ennio Morricone score.

RUN, PSYCHO, RUN

Italy, 1968
Director: Brunello Rondi. Producer: Gaetano Amato. Screenplay: Giuseppe Mangione, Vittoriano Petrilli, Brunello Rondi. Music: Giovanni Fusco. Cinematography: Carlo Bellero.
Cast: Gary Merrill, Elga Andersen, Georges Rivière, Rossella Falk, Margarita Robles, Adriana Asti.

It happens time and again. Writer Brunello Rondi helped Federico Fellini shape his iconic works, including **La Dolce Vita** (1960). But an over-intellectual pretentious approach to his own directing career doomed him from the start and like so many snobby creatives who thought they could contour the clichés of the genre to make something unique, he fell flat on his face. Case in point, this dying days of *La Belle Époque* mystery thriller, which isn't so much of a whodunit as a whybother. It's 1912 and Judge Gary Merrill (Bette Davis's ex-husband) is holidaying with wife Elga Andersen in a Tuscan villa when she's murdered and their son also dies in a related accident. A year later he returns with a lookalike Anderson fiancée to hopefully flush out the killer. Red herrings come and go, talky story threads lead nowhere and creepy organ music emanates from the summerhouse in order to "portray the degeneration of the bourgeoisie with extreme violence", according to a contemporary Rondi interview conducted by a journalist named Dario Argento! So that's why it got a delayed release three years after production, crassly retitled from **Più tardi Claire, più tardi...** and Rondi ended up directing **Black Emmanuelle, White Emmanuelle** (1976).

SIN WITH A STRANGER

France/Italy, 1968
Director: Sergio Gobbi. Producers: Robert Florat, Sergio Gobbi.
Screenplay: Jeanne Cressanges, Sergio Gobbi.
Music: Romuald. Cinematography: Étienne Becker.
Cast: Marie-France Boyer, Pierre Vaneck, Pierre Massimi, Colette Castel, Philippe Ogouz, Jacques Maire.

Titled just **The Stranger/ L'étrangère** in its home country France, **Sex from a Stranger** in the heavily censored British version and **Sin with a Stranger** in America, where it was one of the very first movies to receive an X rating for sexual content, along with Brian De Palma's **Greetings** (1968). And doesn't that just say it all about the mind-set and psyches of each country as the permissive Seventies approached. Singer/actress Marie-France Boyer is the attractive blonde that writer François (Pierre Vaneck) meets on a train and engages in a passionate night of lovemaking. He tells her he's getting a divorce. Barbara tells him she's running away from callous gangsters. But the truth is she's just killed her own child and the police are fast closing in to arrest her. Sergio Gobbi created and directed this sexed-up **Brief Encounter** (1945) containing themes he would return to with films like **A Strange Love Affair** (1971) and **International Prostitution** (1980). Playful, ethereal and absorbing in that typically insouciant French way, this early **Fatal Attraction** (1987) features a gorgeous score by Romuald, composer of **Vertigo for a Killer** (1970). Remade in 2014 by director César Rodríguez as **She, the Stranger.**

THE TOUCHABLES

UK, 1968
Director: Robert Freeman. Producer: John Bryan.
Screenplay: Ian La Frenais. Music: Ken Thorne.
Cinematography: Alan Pudney.
Cast: Judy Huxtable, Ester Anderson, Kathy Simmonds, Marilyn Rickard [Monika Ringwald], David Anthony [Charles Dickens], Ricky Starr.

Youth culture pandering could spell big business but this bizarre Pop Art misfire wasn't so much released as escaped. Note the poster mention of the Fifth Dimension, not as a time/space comparison but as allusion to the group who hit big with the song 'Aquarius' from the Broadway smash musical 'Hair'. Marking the first-time credit for future **Performance** writer/director Donald Cammell, along with producer brother David, while the screenplay was rewritten by Ian La Frenais, from a story by former fashion photographer turned director Robert Freeman (unsurprisingly he only made one other feature, **Secret World**, 1969), the themes are very much of Cammell's calibre. Four rich idle women (one being Judy Huxtable, star of **The Psychopath**, 1966), known as The Vice Squad, kidnap permissive rock star David Anthony (aka real pop star Charles Dickens), use him as a sex slave, playmate and *objet d'art* before staging a mock trial, finding him guilty of wantonness and sentencing him to death. Meanwhile a gay racketeer who hides his criminality behind a pro-wrestler persona plans to ransom the rocker to his frantic managers. Using the fetish imagery of the day – pinball, mini-skirts, Habitat furniture – it's a pretentious car crash and a deliciously untouchable one.

TOWER OF SCREAMING VIRGINS

West Germany/Italy/France, 1968
Directors: François Legrand [Franz Antel], Fritz Umgelter [uncredited]. Producer: Wolf C. Hartwig. Screenplay: Kurt Nachmann. Music: Mario Migliardi. Cinematography: Oberdan Troiani.
Cast: Terry Torday [Teri Tordai], Jean Piat, Véronique Vendell, Uschi Glas, Marie-Ange Aniès, Karlheinz Fiege.

Great Exploitation title, and like so many disguising something else entirely. In this instance a lurid and crass German period drama supposedly based on the 1832 stage play 'La Tour de Nesle', adapted by Alexandre Dumas, creator of 'The Count of Monte Cristo' and 'The Three Musketeers' novels, where the title virgins are all men. Sorry, dirty mac brigade! Director Franz Antel/François Legrand's sexed-up swashbuckler relates the story of Marguerite of Burgundy, Queen of France, (Teri Tordai, star of the **Sexy Susan** franchise) who, as history lip-smackingly recounts, had a predilection for holding orgies in her Tower of Sin with her nubile courtesans while husband King Louis X was away at war, and then having her numerous partners killed by the army to deliberately leave no witnesses to her nocturnal debauchery. Badly choreographed action, vaulted castle interiors with winding staircases to nowhere, super production values, bloody murders in the first reel, plenty of above-the-waist nudity and hilarious erotic coupling, plus *krimi* star Uschi Glas playing a Blanche Dubois! What's not to like? Oh, the British retitling of **Der Turm der verbotenen Liebe** was the even more outlandish **She Lost Her... You Know What?** Er, chastity belt, crown, bri-nylon panties, life...?

THE VIOLENT FOUR

Italy, 1968
Director: Carlo Lizzani. Producer: Dino De Laurentiis.
Screenplay: Massimo De Rita, Carlo Lizzani.
Music: Riz Ortolani.
Cinematography: Giuseppe Ruzzolini, Otello Spila.
Cast: Gian Maria Volontè, Don Backy, Ray Lovelock,
Ezio Sancrotti, Piero Mazzarella, Laura Solari.

The thinking behind double-bill pairings was often suspect. What punter would want to see Carlo Lizzani's Italian hit gangster thriller **The Violent Four/Banditi a Milano** only to then sit through Shirley MacLaine in the fluffy brassiere factory comedy romance **The Bliss of Mrs. Blossom** (1968)? Nevertheless, that was the mismatched duo making the Great British rounds in early 1969 on the ABC circuit. In America, Lizzani's cops and robbers B-movie was one of the first flicks to show excerpts of its most exciting scenes on closed circuit TV screens outside the cinema. Attempting to say something profound about violence in modern society and the growing criminal-as-celebrity vogue, Lizzani's co-written screenplay was based on the true story of four thieves who wreaked havoc in Milan and Turin, robbing banks in 1967. Their *modus operandi* was to shoot vast numbers of innocent bystanders after the heists to distract attention. Told from the narrated points of view of each bandit as they are caught and get sent to prison, Lizzani set in bloodstone the *poliziotteschi* tropes to come with much hanging out the windows of speeding automobiles, fender bender action, screeching car chases and blazing machine-gun warfare.

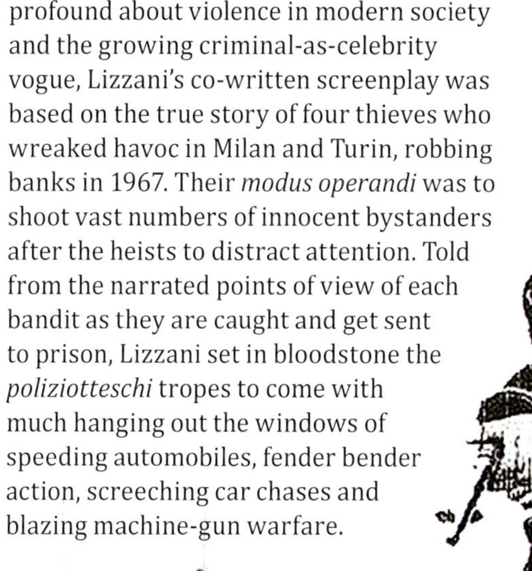

BLIND BEAST

Japan, 1969
Director: Yasuzô Masumura.
Producers: Masaichi Nagata, Kazumasa Nakano. Screenplay: Yoshio Shirasaka.
Music: Hikaru Hayashi. Cinematography: Setsuo Kobayashi.
Cast: Eiji Funakoshi, Mako Midori, Noriko Sengoku.

An off-the-wall *pinku* revolving around magnificent obsessions and weird designs, director Yasuzô Masumura's Japanese take on John Fowles's 1963 novel 'The Collector' sustains an eerie interest despite tumbling into crude masochistic melodrama come the elegantly twisted climax. Blind Tokyo sculptor Michio (Eiji Funakoshi) and his obese mother (Noriko Sengoku) kidnap fashion model Aki (Mako Midori). Keeping her prisoner in a warehouse (**Warehouse** being the unassuming American title) bedecked with his sculptures of giant eyes, mouths and body parts – all recreated from his touch memories of being a professional masseur – Aki soon wises up and realises any hope of escape will only materialise if she pits mother and son against one another. Soon she's manipulated arguments about Michio's virginity and mommy control issues, which ends in orgiastic behaviour on top of a 70-foot reclining rubber nude figure where the ill-matched pair take bites out of each other's flesh and hack off arms and legs. All done tastefully off screen, with subtitles of the "Listen, I have a dandy idea!" variety. Michio's frightening sensitivity is well conveyed by Funakoshi, and the clammy claustrophobia encouraged by his huge darkened studio is blind terror personified as psychosexual dismemberment romance never looked so good.

GIRLS FOR PLEASURE

France, 1969
Director: Jean-Claude Roy. Producer: René Thévenet. Screenplay: Jean-Claude Roy. Music: Jacques Loussier. Cinematography: Claude Saunier.
Cast: Katia Tchenko, Nadia Samir, Béatrice Cardon, Valérie Boisgel, Michel Dacquin, Liane Marelli, Dominique Paturel.

Before becoming a key director in the French pornographic film industry, Jean-Claude Roy (aka Patrick Aubin) learnt his craft in Sexploitation with all manner of seedy apprenticeship titles including **Strip-teaseuses ou ces femmes que l'on croit faciles** (1964), **Erotic Parade** (1968) and **1001 Ways to Love** (1968). Noting the popularity of the Mondo genre, he acquired the rights to Dominique Dallayrac's sensational 1966 bestseller 'Dossier Prostitution', along with producer René Thévenet (**Traitement de choc/The Doctor in the Nude**, 1973) and churned out this 'real-life investigation' into red light districts, streetwalking, brothel organization, police raids, fetish explanations, cross-dressing rent boys, sex film auditions (Tanagra Productions who produced this faux parade daring to actually name themselves), and social workers trying to rehabilitate wavering call girls by teaching them alternative employment. All played to perfection by a roster of rising French stars like Katia Tchenko (**Ronin**, 1998), Valérie Boisgel (**Sex Rally**, 1974) and Dominique Paturel (**La Vie en Rose**, 2007). Typical of the era, it gives the female perspective through the male gaze with quite appalling misogynist attitudes lacking any acceptable empathy. Nevertheless, Roy's anodyne overview of the world's oldest profession can now be seen as historical testimony of the entire proto-permissive era.

盲獣
もうじゅう
カラー作品
撫でる！
嚙む！
えぐる！
血にまみれ、
歓喜の絶頂へ登りつめる
凄まじい興奮！
江戸川乱歩の怪奇の世界を
極限まで描く！
船越英二
緑魔子（東映）
千石規子（東宝）
監督 増村保造
原作 江戸川乱歩
脚本 白坂依志夫
撮影 小林節雄
大映映画
映倫

THE MAD ROOM

USA, 1969
Director: Bernard Girard.
Producer: Norman Maurer.
Screenplay: Bernard Girard, A.Z. Martin [A. Martin Zweiback], Reginald Denham, Garrett Fort.
Music: Dave Grusin.
Cinematography: Harry Stradling Jr.
Cast: Stella Stevens, Shelley Winters, Beverly Garland, Severn Darden, Skip Ward, Carol Cole.

Late in the Maternal Monster day, but undeservedly forgotten, Columbia Pictures dumped this loose horror remake of their 1941 hit **Ladies in Retirement** on a Grindhouse double bill with the Vincent Price western **More Dead Than Alive** (1969) when both failed as A features. In 1957, two children murder their parents, the aftermath witnessed by older sister Stella Stevens, whose testimony gets them committed. Twelve years later the mentally handicapped duo are freed into housekeeper Stevens's care and she asks her employer, wealthy former actress Shelley Winters, if they can all live together. What could possibly go wrong? Directed with an atmospheric flair for the deranged by Bernard Girard, who got this unsubtle reboot assignment for making the crime caper **Dead Heat on a Merry-Go-Round** (1966) a bright and breezy delight, he was less than delighted when it was recut against his wishes, and blamed his career nosedive on its subsequent disastrous box office. Both the ever-engaging Stevens and Oscar-winning Winters are on good form, and elevate the material further despite the former hating working with the latter due to her drunkenness on set. But they had buried the hatchet by the time they co-starred in **The Poseidon Adventure** (1972).

MALENKA

Spain/Italy, 1969
Director: Amando de Ossorio. Producers: Aubrey Ambert, Rosanna Yanni. Screenplay: Amando de Ossorio. Music: Carlo Savina. Cinematography: Fulvio Testi. Cast: Anita Ekberg, John Hamilton [Gianni Medici], Diana Lorys, Adriana Ambesi, Rosanna Yanni, Julián Ugarte.

Famous for being retitled **Fangs of the Living Dead** and dumped on a 1971 Drive-In triple bill with **Curse of the Living Dead** (aka Mario Bava's **Kill, Baby... Kill!**, 1966) and **Revenge of the Living Dead** (**The Murder Clinic**, 1966), director Amando de Ossorio's horror debut showed little of the artistry or style his later genre work, beginning with **Tombs of the Blind Dead** (1972), would become acclaimed for. A landmark Spanish vampire yarn, it was to have starred Boris Karloff as Count Walbrooke, but the horror icon died while in production, and it further condemned Anita Ekberg, the **La Dolce Vita** (1960) blonde bombshell, to nothing but shoddy Exploitation. Playing swimsuit model Sylvia Morel, Ekberg learns she's inherited a castle, a Countess title and knowledge that her grandmother Malenka, for whom she's a dead ringer, was a 17th Century necro-biologist using Black Magic to resurrect the dead. Will she drink Malenka's blood and succumb to the family curse? Not if fiancé Piero (John Hamilton/Gianni Medici) has anything to do with it. Filmed in the same castle as **Frankenstein's Bloody Terror** (1968) and dripping with wasted Gothic atmosphere, the accent is on cleavage and badly dubbed dialogue, with virtually zero blood.

THE MIGHTY GORGA

USA, © 1968, first public screening 1969
Director: David L. Hewitt. Producers: David L. Hewitt, Robert H. O'Neil [Robert Vincent O'Neil].
Screenplay: David Prentiss [David L. Hewitt], Jean Hewitt.
Music: Charles Walden. Cinematography: Gary Graver.
Cast: Anthony Eisley, Megan Timothy, Scott Brady, Kent Taylor, Gary Kent, Greydon Clark.

Director David L. Hewitt dressed up in a ratty gorilla suit as the title primate. A plastic toy dinosaur waved in front of the camera as a special effect. A cave monster spliced in from the Italian *peplum* **Goliath and the Dragon** (1960). Newsreel stock footage of wild animals and volcanic eruptions. Al Adamson repertory actors flubbing their dialogue. Terrible matte lines… The list goes on for this snail-paced adventure fantasy often cited as one of the worst movies ever made. But just like the accepted benchmark **Plan 9 from Outer Space** (1959) it's one you have to see with your own eyes to actually believe it. Nearly bankrupt circus owner Anthony Eisley (**Dracula vs. Frankenstein**, 1971) leads an expedition into darkest Africa hunting for a legendary giant gorilla as a Big Top attraction to turn his fortunes around. Ambushed by natives for human sacrifice, they are saved by the towering Gorga's arrival, forcing them to take shelter in a jewel-encrusted cave. If they can escape Gorga's fury, they could save the circus with the precious gems haul. Everything that can go wrong with this California-shot disaster does, making it an even more shoestring budget **Queen Kong** (1976) must-see.

WHERE ARE YOU GOING ALL NAKED?

Italy, 1969
Director: Pasquale Festa Campanile.
Producer: Mario Cecchi Gori.
Screenplay: Sandro Continenza, Pasquale Festa Campanile, Ottavio Jemma, Luigi Malerba.
Music: Armando Trovajoli.
Cinematography: Roberto Gerardi.
Cast: Tomas Milian, Maria Grazia Buccella, Gastone Moschin, Angela Luce, Lea Lander, Vittorio Gassman.

Most Italian erotic comedies managed to find international distribution mainly because they contained a surprising percentage of nudity or they had the 'Starring Edwige Fenech' seal of approval. But very few of them were actually funny, their crude brand of farcical humour failing to travel. But Pasquale Festa Campanile's hugely enjoyable rip-off of **The Apartment** (1960) by way of countless Carry Ons is an exception to the rule. Comfortable with every genre he tackled, Campanile's nudge-nudge wink-winker stars Tomas Milian as bank clerk Manfredo, who married Tonino (Maria Grazia Buccella, **After the Fox**, 1966) in a state of drunkenness. So waking up next to her in his President's Rome apartment is naturally a major cause for concern. Are they really married? How did he get into the flat? Flooding, blackmail and Buccella's habit of wandering around totally naked, kickstarts a whole raft of mistaken identities, bedroom door slamming and misunderstandings. Perfectly cast with sterling support by Vittorio Gassman, Lea Lander and Gastone Moschin, and outré mod costumes by Luca Sabatelli two years before his **The Cat O'Nine Tails** (1971) designs, this enormous box-office hit was helped by Buccella's pop hit version of the Armando Trovajoli theme song 'Dove vai tutta nuda?'

THE ANCINES WOODS

Spain, 1970
Director: Pedro Olea. Producer: Pedro Olea [uncredited].
Screenplay: Pedro Olea, Juan Antonio Porto.
Music: Antonio Pérez Olea. Cinematography: Aurelio G. Larraya.
Cast: José Luis López Vázquez, Amparo Soler Leal, Antonio Casas, John Steiner, Nuria Torray, María Fernanda Ladrón de Guevara.

Before Paco Plaza directed **Romasanta** (2004), Pedro Olea got there first with the exploits of Manuel Blanco Romasanta, the alleged Werewolf of Allariz, and Spain's first recorded serial killer. In 1853, he admitted to thirteen murders, but claimed he was not responsible because of suffering from the curse of lycanthropy. Although this trial defence was rejected, Queen Isabella II commuted his death sentence to allow doctors to investigate the supposed clinical claim. Now part of Hispanic myth, and also known as The Tallow Man, a nickname earned for rendering his victims' fat into soap, Olea based his beautifully shot, if jerkily paced, festival acclaimed shocker on a novel by Carlos Martínez-Barbeito that added a Galician folk thread to the legend. Popular comedian José Luis López Vázquez wanted to add a dramatic string to his bow and gives a remarkable performance as the epileptic pedlar who lures eleven women into the Ancine woods and is finally caught in a wolf's trap. Former film critic Olea had made a short, **Anabel** (1964), based on the same Marco Denevi story Joseph Losey turned into **Secret Ceremony** (1968), and his knack for mixing history, social issues and magical realism paid off once more.

ANGELS WHO BURN THEIR WINGS

West Germany, 1970
Director: Zbynek Brynych. Producer: Gerald Martell [uncredited]. Screenplay: Herbert Reinecker. Music: Peter Thomas. Cinematography: Josef Vanis. Cast: Nadja Tiller, Susanne Uhlen, Jan Koester, Ellen Umlauf, Harald Baerow, Jochen Busse, Manfred Spies, Siegfried Rauch, Karl-Otto Alberty.

Known for his hard-hitting and critical war dramas in his native Czechoslovakia, director Zbynek Brynych escaped to West Germany only to end up helming their Eurospy adventure equivalents and eventually making his mark on such long running crime series as 'Polizeiinspektion 1' and 'Derrick'. In this lurid thriller, popular Austrian star Nadja Tiller plays Hilde Susmeit, an adulterous wife, whose latest lover is killed by her jealously obsessive son Robert (Jan Koester). This heat-of-the-moment swimming pool murder is witnessed by the mentally disturbed Moni (Susanne Uhlen). Equally obsessed with Robert, Moni hides him in her mother's apartment. Who will find him first in the Munich tower block; the police inspectors (Siegfried Rauch and Karl-Otto Alberty) or his distraught parents? Scripted by Herbert Reinecker, the writer of **The Trapp Family** (1956), that would eventually become the smash hit Broadway musical and roadshow blockbuster **The Sound of Music** (1965), what is striking about Brynych's somewhat surreal thriller – the dance sequences are something else! – is how prescient it is regarding David Cronenberg's **Shivers** in terms of high rise suspense, out-of-control libido, deranged murder and eventual mob rule. Specialist *krimi* composer Peter Thomas provides the brilliant title theme and 'Modern Sex' track.

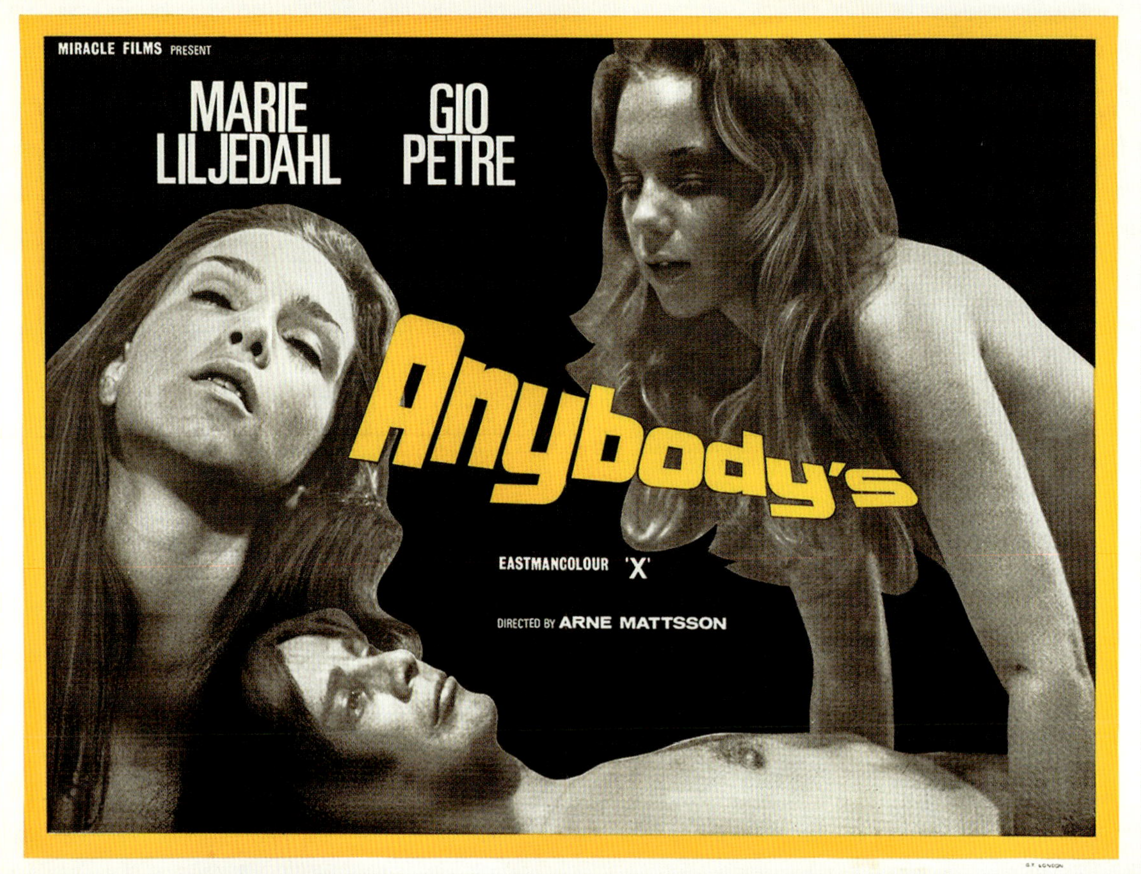

ANYBODY'S

Sweden/Yugoslavia, 1970
Director: Arne Mattsson. Producer: Lennart Berns.
Screenplay: Ernest Hotch. Music: Bengt-Arne Wallin.
Cinematography: Max Wilén.
Cast: Gio Petré, Francisco Rabal, Marie Liljedahl, Julián Mateos, Olivera Vuco [Olivera Katarina], Bozidarka Frajt.

There's nothing like an embittered director taking out his vitriol on film critics who have dissed his prior work and disguising it as Sexploitation in the process. Swedish Arne Mattsson clearly has an axe to grind in **Ann och Eve – de erotiska** – the retitling chiming with what was common slang for a slag back in the permissive days. For what starts out in basic softcore mode with journalist Ann (Gio Petré, **I, a Woman, Part II**, 1968) showing her virgin friend Eve (Marie Liljedahl, **Inga: I Have Lust**, 1968) the delights of bisexual promiscuity before marriage rapidly turns esoteric when they meet famous Italian film director Francesco (Luis Buñuel regular Francisco Rabal) at a party. It transpires Ann is also married to a film director whom she has tried to destroy professionally by organising her fellow writing clique to criticize his work consistently. Things get weirdly surreal – or more ridiculously pretentious depending on whether you came here for the nudity or the incredulity – when Ann follows Francesco to a festival where his latest film is being shown, strangely titled 'The Emperor's New Clothes', just like her husband's last uncompleted work. Methinks the victimized Mattsson protests too much!

THE BALLAD OF TAM LIN

UK, 1970
Director: Roddy McDowall.
Producers: Alan Ladd Jr., Stanley Mann.
Screenplay: William Spier. Music: Stanley Myers.
Cinematography: Billy Williams.
Cast: Ava Gardner, Ian McShane, Richard Wattis, Cyril Cusack, Stephanie Beacham, David Whitman, Joanna Lumley, Madeline Smith, Bruce Robinson.

Want to know the reason why Roddy McDowall didn't reprise his role as Cornelius in **Beneath the Planet of the Apes**, the only one of the five original films from which he is absent? He was deep in the Scottish wilds making his solo directorial effort that would become a misbegotten poisoned chalice of the most peculiar kind. Based on a 16th Century narrative poem by Robert Burns and scripted as a valentine to Hollywood glamourpuss Ava Gardner, the vanity project took the Queen of the Fairies folk tale and plonked it into the middle of dated psychedelia. Ian McShane plays favoured Tom Lynn, who leaves wealthy Gardner's charmed inner circle of lovers and hangers-on to be with the vicar's pregnant daughter Stephanie Beacham. But Gardner is not going to let her latest conquest get away with such a betrayal. With an amazing cast of up-and-comers (Joanna Lumley, Madeline Smith, Bruce Robinson, etc.) and songs by Pentangle underscoring what is essentially vengeful soap opera, the original shoot took place in 1969 and the footage shelved when the production company Commonwealth United went bankrupt. McDowall then did reshoots so AIP could release it under the misrepresentative title **The Devil's Widow**.

DORIAN GRAY

Italy/West Germany, 1970
Director: Massimo Dallamano. Producer: Harry Alan Towers.
Screenplay: Marcello Coscia, Massimo Dallamano, Günter Ebert.
Music: Peppino De Luca, Carlos Pes. Cinematography: Otello Spila.
Cast: Helmut Berger, Richard Todd, Herbert Lom, Marie Liljedahl, Margaret Lee, Maria Rohm.

Notorious libertine Oscar Wilde's archetypal 1890 solo novel went Mod in Exploiter Extraordinaire Harry Alan Towers's flimsy production, weakly directed by Sergio Leone cinematographer-turned-*giallo* specialist Massimo Dallamano. Updating the fable of one man's moral corruption to the more accepting Swinging London values merely dulled down any shock appeal inherent in this over-decorated but under-sexed version of evil being reflected in that infamous portrait in the attic. Pretty boy Helmut Berger, fresh from lover Luchino Visconti's **The Damned** (1969), doesn't really have the acting chops to convey the danger or complex nuances of Wilde's text either. Especially when surprisingly faced with the homosexual tones of Dorian's relationship with Henry Wotton (Herbert Lom) or the tame heterosexual couplings. But his distance and blank 'Dedicated Follower of Fashion' persona often works in spite of itself. Those new to the narrative also might not be quite sure why Dorian stays young while those around him age, no mention of deals with the devil, and the timelines are hopeless conveyed, hardly any years seem to pass at all. Dumped on a double bill with Towers and Jess Franco's **Count Dracula** (1970) – two ruined genre classics for the price of one – it's merely a depraved disaster.

EQUINOX

USA, © 1969, first public screening 1970
Directors: Jack Woods, Dennis Muren [uncredited], Mark Thomas McGee [uncredited]. Producer: Jack H. Harris.
Screenplay: Jack Woods. Music: Jaime Mendoza-Nava [uncredited].
Cinematography: Mike Hoover.
Cast: Edward Connell, Barbara Hewitt, Frank Boers Jr. [Frank Bonner], Robin Christopher, Jack Woods, Jim Phillips [James Phillips].

In 1967, Pasadena City College student Dennis Muren and colleagues rustled up $6,500 and made a 71-minute horror adventure titled **The Equinox... A Journey Into the Supernatural**. Despite the tiny budget Muren, who endured to create special, miniature and optical effects for a number of keynote future classics (**Star Wars**, 1977, **Terminator 2: Judgment Day**, 1991, **Jurassic Park**, 1993), together with luminaries David Allen and Jim Danforth, crafted some great in-camera illusions and stop-motion creatures. The project caught the attention of **The Blob** (1958) man Jack H. Harris, who said he would give it a Drive-In release if an extra 11 minutes of footage could be shot to reshape the plot. The result was a fun and engagingly naïve fantasy that became the primary inspiration for Sam Raimi's **The Evil Dead** (1981). The flimsy scenario finds four unhip teenagers pursued by huge monsters who want an ancient book, bound with human skin, full of ancient Satanic formulas found in a cave by a creepy old scientist. Complete with an invisible boundary to a supernatural netherworld, a disappearing castle and a demonic forest ranger – an attempted rape the only jarring Harris note in what is essentially a good-natured juvenile romp.

FRANKENSTEIN ON CAMPUS

Canada, 1970
Director: Gilbert W. Taylor. Producer: Bill Marshall [William T. Marshall]. Screenplay: David Cobb, Bill Marshall [William T. Marshall], Gilbert W. Taylor. Music: Paul Hoffert. Cinematography: Jackson Samuels. Cast: Robin Ward, Kathleen Sawyer, Austin Willis, Sean Sullivan, Ty Haller, Tony Moffat-Lynch.

Originally titled **Flick** and sometimes known as **Dr. Frankenstein on Campus**, director Gilbert W. Taylor's solo feature is a routine sex-and-horror entry desperate to cash in on the flower power market with an updated youthful riff on the classic Mary Shelley tale. Unjustly expelled from Toronto University after a tabloid drug scandal, mod Viktor Frankenstein (future Canadian TV weatherman Robin Ward) uses his knowledge of the human brain to turn three revolutionary students into remote-controlled zombies to exact revenge. A few unintentionally funny sequences, naked co-ed make-out scenes and offbeat murders later, a stairwell fall reveals Viktor to be the sewn-together monster of old, created by Professor Preston, played by Sean Sullivan, whose role in **2001: A Space Odyssey** (1968) should have been a clue, the real Frankenstein of this curio piece. The first Canuxploitation horror to be funded by the Canadian Film Development Corporation, Taylor's all-too straightforward addition to the multitude of Shelley adaptations led to other directors rushing to the newly created fund. Results included Ivan Reitman's **Cannibal Girls** (1973) and Bob Clark's seminal **Black Christmas** (1974). In the U.K. it was released in 1972 on a double-bill with Harry Kümel's exquisite vampire masterpiece **Daughters of Darkness** (1971).

KILLERS OF THE CASTLE OF BLOOD

Italy/Spain, 1970
Director: José Luis Merino.
Screenplay: Enrico Colombo, José Luis Merino, María del Carmen Martínez Román [uncredited].
Music: Luigi Malatesta.
Cinematography: Emanuele Di Cola.
Cast: Erna Schurer, Carlos Quiney, Agostina Belli, Antonio Jiménez Escribano, Cristiana Galloni, Mariano Vidal Molina.

The unwieldy UK title for an equally dysfunctional gothic muddle – far better are the alternate titles serving the over familiar subject matter best: **Scream of the Demon Lover** (US) – well, there are screams – and **Ivanna** (Spain). For it's biochemist Ivanna (ever topless Eurobabe Erna Schurer) who is hired by the mysterious Baron Janos Dalmar (Carlos Quiney) to research regeneration of burnt flesh techniques. Meanwhile nubile village girls are going missing and the locals suspect the Baron is responsible, feeding their bodies to his two monstrous hounds after ravishment. Flimsy nightgown wanderings with candelabra along gloomy castle corridors, ill-omened servants, strange erotic nightmares, a virgin marriage made in hell, hereditary madness, an evil disfigured twin in the basement, secret torture chambers, spooky organ music, it's all here in director José Luis Merino's stodgy shocker that rarely strays from the well-trodden Euro-pudding path. There is the spiked glove murder weapon upping the ante somewhat and vague plot lifts from 'Jane Eyre' if so inclined to trace a more classical literary bent in a kitsch smoothie for (demon) lovers of such overripe romps through chiller clichés. Shorn of nudity, it got dumped on US Grindhouse circuits with Stephanie Rothman's **The Velvet Vampire** (1971).

HER FIRST MISTAKE WAS GETTING INTO THE CAR!

COLUMBIA PICTURES and LIRA FILMS Present
SAMANTHA EGGAR
OLIVER REED
JOHN McENERY
in an ANATOLE LITVAK Production
The Lady in the Car with glasses and a gun
AA
Co-starring STEPHANE AUDRAN
Screenplay by RICHARD HARRIS and ELEANOR PERRY
Based on the novel by SEBASTIEN JAPRISOT
EDITIONS DENOEL Music by MICHEL LEGRAND
Directed by ANATOLE LITVAK
Produced by RAYMOND DANON and ANATOLE LITVAK
PANAVISION® COLOUR

THE LADY IN THE CAR WITH GLASSES AND A GUN

France, 1970
Director: Anatole Litvak. Producers: Raymond Danon, Anatole Litvak.
Screenplay: Sébastien Japrisot, Anatole Litvak. Music: Michel Legrand. Cinematography: Claude Renoir.
Cast: Samantha Eggar, Oliver Reed, Stéphane Audran, John McEnery, Billie Dixon, André Oumansky.

What an extraordinary body of work sprung from the pen of author Sébastien Japrisot – Costa-Gavras's **The Sleeping Car Murders** (1965), René Clément's **Rider on the Rain** (1970), Just Jaeckin's **Story of O** (1975) and Iain Softley's **Trap for Cinderella** (2013) to name a few. And for his final film **The Snake Pit** (1948) director Anatole Litvak chose this Japrisot novel (adapted again in 1992 and 2015) to turn into a murder mystery à *la mode*. Essentially it's a woman-in-peril warhorse slicked up in decadent chic – or Litvak's square version of it – and jet-set Paris and French Riviera vistas involving a repressed secretary (enchanting Samantha Eggar), a sleek white convertible, a body in the trunk, a sinister hitchhiker (John McEnery), a glacially neurotic but permissive wife (Stéphane Audran) and a daunting advertising agency boss (miscast Oliver Reed). With red herrings aplenty and flashbacks meant to deceive, the final solution raises even more dazedly provocative questions than it answers. With suspense tropes lifted from both the Alfred Hitchcock and Val Lewton textbooks – an Old Dark House and a suspenseful scene staged in a garage complex – it may be Claude Chabrol-lite but this is high-end Eurotrash with one foot in neo *giallo*.

TOOMORROW

UK, 1970
Director: Val Guest.
Producers: Don Kirshner, Harry Saltzman.
Screenplay: Val Guest.
Music: Hugo Montenegro.
Cinematography: Dick Bush.
Cast: Olivia Newton-John, Benny Thomas, Vic Cooper, Karl Chambers, Roy Dotrice, Imogen Hassall.

A decade before making the Disco disaster **Xanadu** (1980), Olivia Newton-John had the misfortune to star in another musical misfire. The misbegotten brainchild of James Bond producer Harry Saltzman and pop legend Don Kirshner, the idea was to launch the title band like the latter previously did with 'The Monkees' TV series. Veteran Val Guest wrote and directed the contrived sci-fi fantasy – he ultimately sued for non-payment – and it was two nightmare years in the making, something that put Newton-John off movies until **Grease** (1978) came along. Even by the poor **Moon Zero Two** (1969) standards of the day, this intergalactic fantasy frolic was flattened froth. Alphoid Roy Dotrice is disguised as a human anthropologist in order to track down a Tonaliser, causing good vibrations on Earth but sterility in Outer Space. Because that instrument was invented by the organist in the skint student Toomorrow combo, the alien whisks them from a pop festival into the galactic space to bring back emotion and soul to the universe. With silly songs composed by Ritchie Adams and Mark Barkan, whom 'Variety' called "tunesmiths in the Bacharach and David league" (!!!) **Toomorrow** was barely released anywhere, even if Newton-John did survive for another day.

WITCHCRAFT '70

Italy, 1970
Directors: Luigi Scattini, Lee Frost [additional sequences, uncredited]. Screenplay: Alberto Bevilacqua, Luigi Scattini. Music: Piero Umiliani. Cinematography: Claudio Racca.
Cast: Alberto Bevilacqua (narrator, Italian language version), Edmund Purdom (narrator, English language version), Anton LaVey, Diane LaVey [uncredited].

Or **Sexy magico** (1963)/**Sweden: Heaven or Hell** (1968) director Luigi Scattini's **Angeli bianchi... angeli neri** bottom scraping of the Mondo barrel. First screened in Italy in 1969, Edmund Purdom narrates this 1970-released English language market alternative edit. It's a mainly faked shockumentary purportedly revealing how Satanism is exerting a grip on the young generation turning to Black Magic for answers in the Age of Aquarius. Demonic rites, erotic prayers and human sacrifice are all illustrated by mainly staged footage. One sequence shows a ritual sin cleansing in Bahia by whipping prostitutes, trance-like dancing and self-mutilation with swords. Then there's a voodoo ceremony in Louisiana hosted by a bad Tina Turner lookalike, a Black Mass held in suburban Bedford and a Church of Satan occult marriage ceremony featuring naked altar girls. Throughout, Purdom plummily informs us that the footage has been acquired at great danger to the filmmakers, without any cooperation of Satanist groups and at great emotional stress cost to the production. If the original Italian version wasn't naff enough, ace American sleaze merchant Lee Frost (aka R.L. Frost, director of **Love Camp 7**, 1969) re-edited the film for the US Grindhouse market and inserted further hippie nonsense to ally it to the post Charles Manson paranoia, and moralistic cop interviews condemning the "unspeakably obscene" practices. Absolutely hilarious.

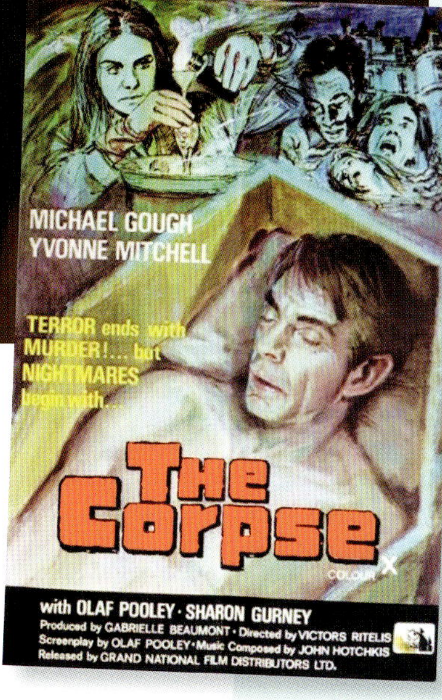

THE CORPSE

UK, 1971
Director: Viktors Ritelis. Producer: Gabrielle Beaumont.
Screenplay: Olaf Pooley. Music: John Hotchkis.
Cinematography: John Mackey.
Cast: Michael Gough, Yvonne Mitchell, Sharon Gurney, Simon Gough, David Butler, Olaf Pooley.

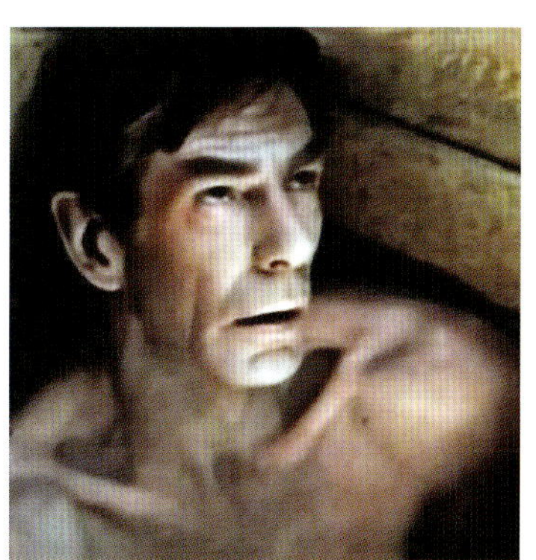

Many directors working in British TV tried parlaying their small screen success to the big one. Despite helming one of the more interesting 'perambulating cadaver' horrors (filmed in the spring of 1969, although not released until 1971), Viktors Ritelis never followed such contemporaries as Peter Sasdy or Don Chaffey into minor genre history. Based on writer (**The Godsend**, 1980) and actor Olaf Pooley's script (he plays the nosy neighbour), Michael Gough slices the ham less thickly than usual as a tyrannical patriarch whose frail wife Yvonne Mitchell and abused daughter Sharon Gurney (**Death Line**, 1972) plot to kill him by faking his suicide. Basic **Diabolique** (1955) knowledge lies at the heart of the plot that leaves Mitchell insane. Strewn with misdirection and neat shock tactics (the crate body nailing is an interesting twist), Ritelis summons up an effectively neo Grand Guignol atmosphere while keeping the intrigue and brooding menace at a premium. Very much a family and friends affair – Gough's own son Simon played his character's son Rupert who was married to Gurney, **The Godsend** director Gabrielle Beaumont produced it for £55,000 – the original title was **The Velvet House**, changed to **Crucible of Horror** in the US and double-billed with **Cauldron of Blood** (1970).

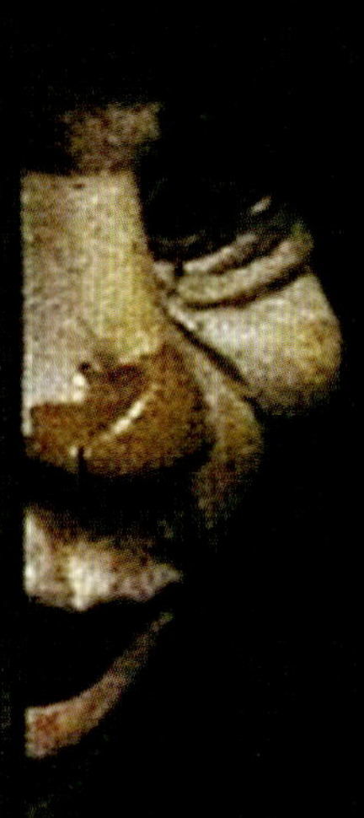

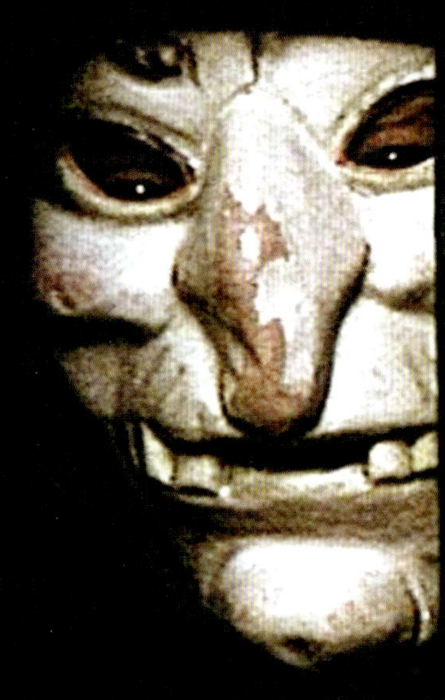

GRAVEYARD OF HORROR

Spain, 1971
Director: Michael Skaife [Miguel Madrid]. Producer: Tony Recoder. Screenplay: Michael Skaife [Miguel Madrid]. Music: Alfonso Santisteban. Cinematography: Alfonso Nieva. Cast: Bill Curran, Catherine Ellison, John Clark, Yocasta Grey [María Paz Madrid], Marisa Shiero, Titania Clement, Beatriz Elorrieta.

A perfect example of how some interesting genre failures were treated by uncaring distributors. **Necrophagus** won the Best Director award for Miguel Madrid/Michael Skaife at the Sitges *Festival de la Cine de Terror* in 1971. Snapped up by Sam Sherman's Independent-International Pictures Corp. for US distribution based on that prize, and because the company had a history of releasing Paul Naschy movies Stateside, its fractured time-jumping narrative, offbeat camerawork, surreal imagery and charnel house theatrics proved alien to test audiences and it was quickly sold to television. Madrid had previously worked with Jess Franco and to be fair his plot is boilerplate but if looked at through a cynical Andy Milliganesque lens it anticipates the cultural Spanish art-quakes to come. Michael Skeffington (Bill Curran) is summoned to his Scottish estate when his wife dies in childbirth. With no one offering any rational explanation for her demise, he exhumes her coffin to find it empty, like others in the cemetery. Then Michael goes missing and his niece Margaret (Beatriz Elorrieta) and a police inspector (Euro-western staple John Clark) begin investigating the Binbrook Castle mystery, unaware they are putting themselves in danger from greedy heirs and, yes, a villainous graveyard horror.

THE HORRIBLE SEXY VAMPIRE

Spain, 1971
Director: José Luis Madrid.
Producer: Al Peppard. Screenplay: José Luis Madrid. Music: Ángel Arteaga.
Cinematography: Francisco J. Madurga.
Cast: Waldemar Wohlfahrt, Patricia Loran, Barta Barry, Joe Campoy, Victor Davis, Adela Tauler.

Note to directors like Spain's José Luis Madrid. If you are going to make a movie where most of the running time is geared around the mystery of what creature the leading killer is, don't put the answer in the title! Both the export title and the original Spanish one – **El vampiro de la autopista** – make it crystal clear before the redundant movie even starts that the often invisible sinister Baron von Winninger is a bloodsucker and not merely a homicidal sadist. But Madrid belabours the point by first honing in on a spate of murders near Stuttgart that seem to occur every 28 years and then switching to Count Oblensky (Waldemar Wohlfahrt) arriving in London to claim his castle inheritance. Said inheritance stipulates that only the Count and his wife can enter the stately pile and must never go down into the dungeons. Cue lots of repetitious attacks on naked women that aren't the least bit sexy and the lacklustre chills from hollow laughter echoing through the corridors that aren't remotely horrible. Correction; the film is indeed horrible. Madrid endured to direct Paul Naschy in the Jack the Ripper *giallo* variant **Seven Murders for Scotland Yard** (1972).

INCENSE FOR THE DAMNED

UK, 1971
Director: Michael Burrowes [Robert Hartford-Davis].
Producer: Graham Harris. Screenplay: Julian More.
Music: Bobby Richards. Cinematography: Desmond Dickinson.
Cast: Patrick Macnee, Peter Cushing, Alexander Davion, Johnny Sekka, Madeleine Hinde, Edward Woodward, Patrick Mower, Imogen Hassall.

Having one of the most tortuous production histories ever, equally mirroring **The Wicker Man** (1973) debacle, ace exploiter Robert Hartford-Davis (**The Black Torment**, 1964, **Gonks Go Beat**, 1965) took his name off his best work when re-edited against his wishes, a narration added (by Alexander Davion, Ted Casablanca in **Valley of the Dolls**, 1967) and turned into an interesting failure. Based on Simon Raven's 1959 novel 'Doctors Wear Scarlet', apparently the first to approach vampirism as a sexual perversion rather than a supernatural affliction, it was a pet project of Hammer director Terence Fisher. When the House of Horror turned the controversial property down, Titan International, the producers of **Corruption** (1968), snapped it up and promptly signed that film's star Peter Cushing and its director. Indeed, all the tinkering does render the final release print an intriguing mess, but a compelling and provocative one nevertheless, as **The Devil Rides Out** (1968) star Patrick Mower plays the Oxford don gone missing on a research mission in Greece. Concerned friends track him to Mykonos where he's wanted by police for his association with a murderous cult led by the 'Countess of Cleavage', British B-movie starlet Imogen Hassall, who committed suicide in 1980.

THE NIGHT DIGGER

UK, 1971
Director: Alastair Reid.
Producers: Alan D. Courtney, Norman S. Powell.
Screenplay: Roald Dahl. Music: Bernard Herrmann.
Cinematography: Alex Thomson.
Cast: Patricia Neal, Pamela Brown, Nicholas Clay, Jean Anderson, Graham Crowden, Yootha Joyce.

Despite being more well known for his dark children's output ('Charlie and the Chocolate Factory', etc.), famed author Roald Dahl continued dabbling with twisted suspense formats between the 'Alfred Hitchcock Presents' (1958) and 'Tales of the Unexpected' (1979) TV series. Here he adapted Joy Cowley's 1967 novel 'Nest in a Falling Tree' but couldn't quite erase its echoes to Emlyn Williams's twice-filmed 1935 play 'Night Must Fall'. A tyrannical blind mother (Pamela Brown) lives in a remote English home with her spinster daughter Maura (Patricia Neal, Dahl's then wife) when their dreary existence is injected with excitement after sexy biker Billy (Nicholas Clay, Lancelot in **Excalibur**, 1981) applies for the position of gardener. But Billy is a travelling rapist murderer who buries his victims in new road works in Dahl's perverse fairytale, turning the main protagonists into an unseeing ogre, an ageing Cinderella and a cursed Prince. Director Alastair Reid's follow-up to the Lolita sexploiter **Baby Love** (1969) turns the familiar screws well and the cast are uniformly excellent. The Hitchcock undercurrent of dark humour cuts through its more unpleasant aspects, and the film is helped enormously by Bernard Herrmann's infamously massacred score, even when 13 minutes was cut from the movie before release.

THE NIGHT VISITOR

USA, © 1970, first public screening 1971
Director: Laslo Benedek. Producer: Mel Ferrer.
Screenplay: Guy Elmes. Music: Henry Mancini.
Cinematography: Henning Kristiansen.
Cast: Max von Sydow, Trevor Howard, Liv Ullmann,
Per Oscarsson, Rupert Davies, Andrew Keir.

Ever wondered what Hammer's early psycho thrillers (**Paranoiac**, 1963, **Hysteria**, 1965, etc.) would have looked like cast with the higher echelons of Ingmar Bergman's rep company? Speculate no more as director Laslo Benedek, whose weird career encompassed everything from **The Wild One** (1953) to **Namu, the Killer Whale** (1966), provides the answer with this curate's egg that figured a refinement makeover would class up the suspense. In fact Christopher Lee was the first choice to play Salem (Max von Sydow, two years from becoming horror royalty in **The Exorcist**, 1973), a Swedish farmer unjustly incarcerated in a lunatic asylum for the axe murder of a hireling. Mentally sharpened by chess games with his guards (a nod to von Sydow's role in Bergman's **The Seventh Seal**, 1957), he sneaks out at night in fascinating **Rififi** (1955) mode to exact a clue-pointing revenge on his brother-in-law (Per Oscarsson), the real guilty party. Despite its lame, ill-conceived ending, the wintry photography evokes the chills of vengeance, the killings are rapid-fire stylish and some effort is made to probe the dark corridors of culpability. But the cast clearly felt the material was beneath them and in detective Trevor Howard's case his performance is phoned in.

TARGET: MURDER

Italy/Spain, 1971
Director: Albert J. Walkner [Bitto Albertini]. Producer: Toni Di Carlo. Screenplay: Ernesto Gastaldi, Eduardo Manzanos Brochero, Luciano Martino. Music: Stelvio Cipriani. Cinematography: Emilio Foriscot. Cast: George Ardisson, Erika Blanc, Alberto de Mendoza, Janine Reynaud, Luciano Pigozzi, Aurora de Alba.

Before putting Laura Gemser on the road to Sexploitation fame with **Black Emanuelle** (1975), director Bitto/Adalberto Albertini was a cinematographer of some note. But dissatisfaction with mid-1960s assignments (**Nudo, crudo e…**, **Secret Agent 777**, both 1965) caused him to jump into directing, with less success. The quality of his output can be crystallized by this workmanlike crime potboiler, aka **L'uomo più velenoso del cobra/The Man More Poisonous Than a Cobra**, or **Human Cobras**. After a masked man stops on-the-run gangster Tony Garden (George Ardisson) mid-whizz around Stockholm, he realises his hiding place has been blown. Worse, Tony's brother Johnny has been killed and he'll have to go back to New York to discover the assassin's identity. With a hitman contract still out on him, Tony attempts to avenge his brother's murder, which becomes more mysterious the more sinister facts he uncovers. With help from Johnny's wife Leslie (Eurotrash royalty Erika Blanc), Tony tries to piece the puzzle together from flashbacks, allowing Ardisson to play his brother too! Co-scripted by Luciano Martino the same year he produced **The Case of the Scorpion's Tail** and **The Strange Vice of Mrs Wardh** for brother Sergio, Stelvio Cipriani's score is a major plus.

THE TODD KILLINGS

USA, © 1970, first public screening 1971
Director: Barry Shear. Producer: Barry Shear.
Screenplay: Dennis Murphy, Joel Oliansky.
Music: Leonard Rosenman.
Cinematography: Harold E. Stine.
Cast: Robert F. Lyons, Richard Thomas,
Belinda Montgomery, Sherry Miles [Sherry E. DeBoer],
Joyce Ames, Holly Near, Barbara Bel Geddes,
Gloria Grahame, Edward Asner, Fay Spain.

Lurid, sordid, galvanising and gripping, director Barry Shear's thrill-killing psychodrama was a 42nd Street sleeper. Like **Truck Stop Women** (1974) and **Jackson County Jail** (1976), a low expectation Exploiter that becomes a surprise success because of its minimal artistic pretension and gung-ho spirit. Based on the true story of mid-1960s multiple murderer Charles Schmid ('The Pied Piper of Tucson'), wannabe rock star Skipper Todd (Robert F. Lyons, **Pendulum**, 1969) is the 23-year-old small Californian town golden boy who charms his way into the pants of high schoolers and then kills them for kicks. The examination of the darker side of downhome America may be a little pat, but Shear, who had his finger on the same pulse in his extraordinary political fantasy **Wild in the Streets** (1968), juxtaposes the psychological and sociological strands of the youthful void conceit with a dynamic technical aplomb. Lyons plays Todd with a cocky, charismatic assurance, Richard Thomas (**Last Summer**, 1969) is terrific as his loyal hanger-on, the naïve Billy Roy, and Barbara Bel Geddes ('Dallas'), Gloria Grahame (**Blood and Lace**, 1971), Edward Asner and Fay Spain give excellent support. **Dead Beat** (1994) and **The Lost** (2006) also used the Schmid case for inspiration.

THE VAMPIRE HAPPENING

West Germany/UK, 1971
Director: Freddie Francis.
Producer: Pier A. Caminneci.
Screenplay: August Rieger. Music: Jerry van Rooyen.
Cinematography: Gérard Vandenberg.
Cast: Ferdy Mayne, Pia Degermark, Thomas Hunter, Yvor Murillo, Ingrid van Bergen, Joachim Kemmer, Oskar Wegrostek.

"Call me Christopher Lee, I'm sure he won't mind", says Ferdy Mayne as Dracula in this extraordinarily feeble farce cash-in of Roman Polanski's **The Fearless Vampire Killers** (1967), which is neither funny nor scary as that classic he starred in as Count Krolock. Directed as if in a coma by Freddie Francis between two of his best ever horrors – **Mumsy, Sonny, Nanny and Girly** (1970) and **Tales from the Crypt** (1972) – this put the first nail in the coffin of star Pia Degermark's movie career after making her spectacular debut in the acclaimed Danish bio-pic **Elvira Madigan** (1967). Blame her husband Pier Andrea Caminneci, friend of controversial German actor Adrian Hoven and producer of Jess Franco's **Sadist Erotica** (1969). There's nothing here Grindhousers hadn't seen a million times before: American actress Betty Williams inherits a Transylvanian castle and accidentally revives her lookalike vampire countess ancestor, Baroness Clarimonde Catani, who unleashes evil on the local village. It ends with the family butler Joseph (Yvor Murillo) and a monk trying to destroy the Baroness but not being able to tell the doppelgangers apart. Joseph says it all when he turns to the camera and says, "Well, I'm getting slightly mixed up!" Indeed.

A.A.A. MASSEUSE, GOOD LOOKING, OFFERS HER SERVICES

Italy, 1972
Director: Demofilo Fidani.
Producer: Demofilo Fidani.
Screenplay: Demofilo Fidani, Mila Vitelli Valenza.
Music: Lallo Gori [Coriolano Gori].
Cinematography: Aldo Giordani.
Cast: Simone Blondel [Simonetta Vitelli], Jerry Colman, Raffaele Curi, Carlo Gentili, Ettore Manni, Hunt Powers [Jack Betts], Paola Senatore, Howard Ross.

Like practically every Italian filmmaker post Dario Argento's **The Bird with the Crystal Plumage** (1970), **Django** dross director Demofilo Fidani entered the *giallo* fray with a competent sex thriller that did little to increase his poor batting average. Still, the vaguely feminist angle was something new for the era, even if that strand increasingly unravels as the script, co-written with Fidani's costume designer wife Mila Vitelli Valenza, indulges in the very Exploitation it condemns. It co-starred the couple's daughter too, Simonetta Vitelli/Simone Blondel, as the best friend of sultry redhead Cristina Graziani (Paola Senatore, **Eaten Alive!**, 1980) who leaves home after constantly clashing with her overbearing father. Placing adverts in the local newspapers – see title – Paola becomes an adept call girl specializing in kinky fetishes. One regular john, Oskar (Howard Ross), becomes her pimp but soon after servicing her up-market clientele, their throats are slit open by a razor-wielding maniac with leather gloves. The cops don't believe she's the killer, but are convinced it's someone close... A modicum of suspense is generated before the strikingly edited, if easily guessed, duo timeline reveal. Mario Bava's **Four Times That Night** (1971) composer Coriolano/Lallo Gori's funky loungecore score fits the finger-snapping bill.

BEWARE! THE BLOB

USA, © 1971, first public screening 1972
Director: Larry Hagman. Producer: Anthony Harris. Screenplay: Jack Woods, Anthony Harris.
Music: Mort Garson. Cinematography: Al Hamm.
Cast: Robert Walker Jr., Gwynne Gilford, Richard Stahl, Richard Webb, Shelley Berman, Godfrey Cambridge.

After geologist Godfrey Cambridge allows an excavated sample of **The Blob** (1958) to thaw, the blood-red slime oozes its way to a bowling alley full of panic-stricken locals. Such is the drawn-out premise of the delayed sequel to producer Jack H. Harris's sci-fi classic, the production history of which is far more interesting than the actual 'ozoner' (i.e. redneck) targeted Exploiter. So often the case! Based on a shelved outline by writer Richard Clair titled 'A Chip Off the Old Blob', Harris's music industry son Anthony wanted to work with his father, dusted off the treatment and, together with **Equinox** (1970) director Jack Woods, concocted this trite alien terror. It turned out that Harris's next-door-neighbour in Malibu was Larry Hagman, star of the successful 'I Dream of Jeannie' sit-com who, when shown the producer's 16mm print of the original, agreed to get together other beach house mates to star in the episodic absorption action, but only if he could direct. The rest is Grindhouse history and would be reissued in 1982 as **Son of Blob** with the tagline "The film that J.R. shot!" after Hagman achieved global fame in the TV supersoap 'Dallas' as J.R. Ewing.

BONNIE'S KIDS

USA, 1972
Director: Arthur Marks. Producer: Charles Stroud.
Screenplay: Arthur Marks. Music: Carson Whitsett.
Cinematography: Robert Charles Wilson.
Cast: Tiffany Bolling, Steve Sandor, Robin Mattson,
Scott Brady, Alex Rocco, Max Showalter, Sharon Gless.

More famous now for inspiring 'The Bonnie Situation' segment in big-fan Quentin Tarantino's **Pulp Fiction** (1994), as far as 1970s Drive-In fare goes this is quintessential babes, boobs and baddies entertainment. 'Perry Mason' TV series alumnus Arthur Marks directed this fast-paced, cleverly plotted, sex crime saga where Ellie (Tiffany Bolling) saves her younger sister Myra (Robin Mattson) from their pervert stepfather by fleeing to their rich crime boss uncle's estate where his lesbian wife also eyes the 15-year-old prize. Uncle wants Ellie involved in a shipment of stolen money, but when she decides to make off with the loot, he sends his two thug bodyguards to track down the fugitives. "You saw seven sensational pages of Tiffany in Playboy magazine", hyped the trailer narration about actress/singer Bolling, who was rapidly becoming Queen of the B's at the time, "Now see 100 sensational minutes (actually 105) of her in **Bonnie's Kids**". Marks's solid direction, loaded with grimy atmosphere and a groovy Carson Whitsett score, make this a lowbrow gem. Marks's secretary during this period was Sharon Gless (future 'Cagney & Lacey' household name), who was so eager to become an actress he cast her in a waitress cameo.

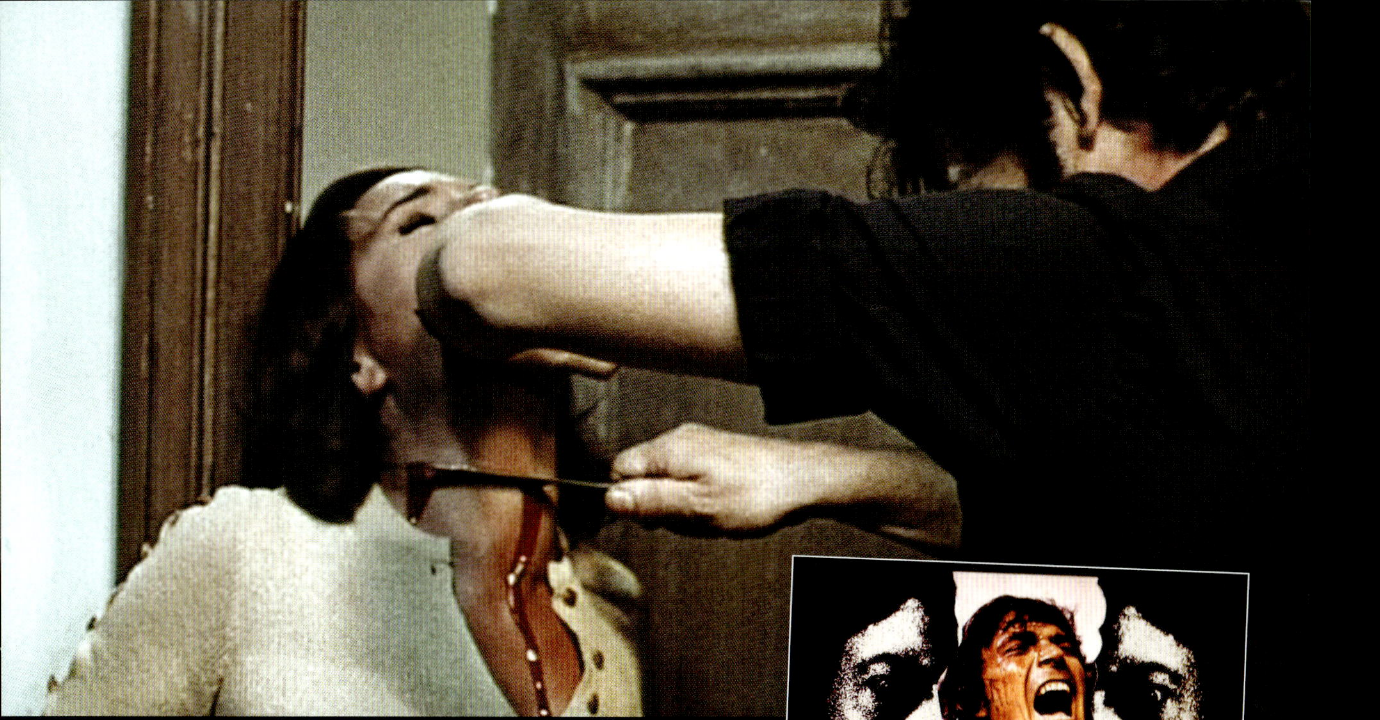

CANNIBAL MAN

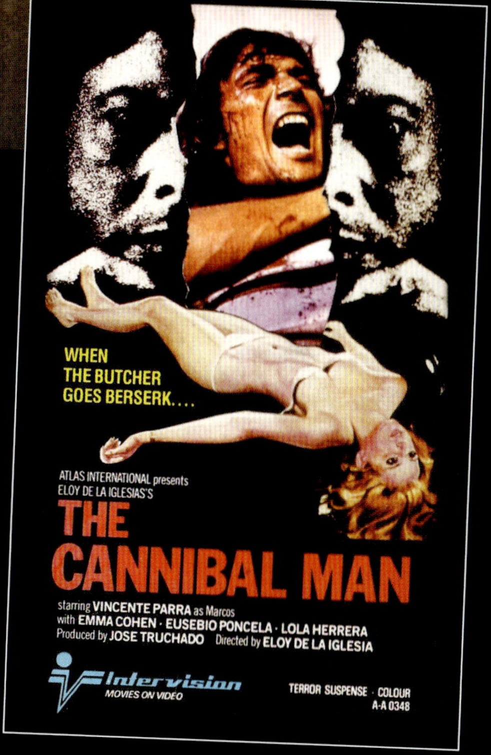

Spain, 1972
Director: Eloy de la Iglesia. Screenplay: Antonio Fos, Eloy de la Iglesia. Music: Fernando García Morcillo. Cinematography: Raúl Artigot.
Cast: Vicente Parra, Emma Cohen, Eusebio Poncela, Charly Bravo, Fernando Sánchez Polack, Goyo Lebrero.

Relatively unknown outside his native Spain, director Eloy de la Iglesia's filmography is an interesting one, taking in quirky horror (**The Glass Ceiling**, 1971), intense thriller (**No One Heard the Scream**, 1973), sci-fi sex (**To Love, Perhaps to Die**, 1973) and gay drama (**Hidden Pleasures**, 1977). Misleadingly retitled from **La semana del asesino** (literally 'The Week of the Killer'), this is a gripping dissertation on urban loneliness as Marcos (Vicente Parra), a Madrid slaughterhouse lackey whose senses have been brutalised by his job, accidentally kills a taxi driver and cuts a swathe through girlfriend and sibling in an effort to cloak his mounting guilt. Meanwhile, he is befriended by the inquisitive gay Nestor (Eusebio Poncela) whose highrise apartment looks down on Marco's hacienda... Designated a British Video Nasty, and therefore instant 'must-see' status, despite the shaky hatchet-in-face moment and genuine slaughterhouse footage, this is not a graphic shocker by any means. It's more in the mental decay **Repulsion** (1965) and reverse **Rear Window** (1954) bracket, with an accent on disaffection and accountability. Released Stateside as **The Apartment on the 13th Floor** and when that failed on a double bill with **The Living Dead at Manchester Morgue** (1974).

DEVIL IN THE BRAIN

Italy/France, 1972
Director: Sergio Sollima. Producer: Maurizio Lodi-Fè.
Screenplay: Suso Cecchi D'Amico, Sergio Sollima.
Music: Ennio Morricone. Cinematography: Aldo Scavarda.
Cast: Stefania Sandrelli, Keir Dullea, Micheline Presle,
Tino Buazzelli, Renato Cestiè, Maurice Ronet.

Sergio Sollima had earned his *auteur* stripes directing the astonishing Lee Van Cleef Spaghetti Western **The Big Gundown** (1966) and the Charles Bronson crime drama **Violent City** (1970). So it was no surprise that when he got around to directing his only *giallo* it would turn out to be a meditative and haunting minor gem, one deserving far wider recognition above its score being yet another masterpiece from composer Ennio Morricone during his most melodically productive period. Stefania Sandrelli (**Black Belly of the Tarantula**, 1971) and Keir Dullea (**De Sade**, 1969) give terrific performances as amnesiac Sandra Graces and concerned Oscar Minno. Attempting to rekindle their old flame after working overseas for many years, Oscar learns Sandra entered her traumatic state because she witnessed her young son Ricky (Renato Cestiè) standing over the dead body of her husband, holding a gun. But is he really the emotionless sociopath his religious reform school psychiatrist has diagnosed? Oscar isn't convinced and is determined to get to the truth even if it means uncomfortable betrayal secrets and conspiracy lies emerging. With Sollima playing on 'truth' themes and refreshing thriller clichés, it's a deliberately measured and sobering mystery with an unexpected twist ending.

DON'T TELL DADDY

West Germany, 1972
Director: Franz Antel. Producer: Fred Zenker. Screenplay: Hans Billian, Gretl Löwinger. Music: Ralf Novy. Cinematography: Ernst W. Kalinke. Cast: Sybil Danning, Eva Garden, Alena [Alena Penz], Christiane Maybach, Claus Tinney, Wolfgang Jansen.

Psst! Want to know the West German idiom for Grindhouse? It's Bahnhofskino, literal translation, Railway Station Cinema, because those seedy fleapit locations were where most Exploitation items gravitated back in the Bonn heyday. And here's a perfect example starring Austrian softcore star turned Scream Queen Sybil Danning (misspelt Sybill on most credits), even if the plot is the age-old aphrodisiac switched with sleeping pills warhorse that provided the basis for many sex comedies of the era. Danning plays Elizabeth, who returns to the family nest after being fired from her job for not 'accommodating' the boss. Sisters Maria (Eva Garden, **Sex Olympics**, 1972) and Christel (Alena Penz, **Salon Kitty**, 1976) are horrified because her prudish nature is bound to curtail their active promiscuity. So they conspire to make sure big sister has sex with every man in town by formulating a potency pill in their father's pharmacy, causing her to be continuously chased by constantly randy locals. Despite the innuendo-laden dialogue, non-stop nudity and eyebrow-raising implied intercourse scenarios, raunch is kept to the tamest level despite the virgin/Viagra narrative. Retitled **Passion Pill Swingers** for Great Britain, **Naughty Nymphs** for American Drive-Ins and, by far the best, '**69 Dalmatians**' in France.

EYE IN THE LABYRINTH

Italy/West Germany, 1972
Director: Mario Caiano. Producer: Nello Santi [Lionello Santi]. Screenplay: Mario Caiano, Antonio Saguera, Horst Hächler. Music: Roberto Nicolosi. Cinematography: Giovanni Ciarlo.
Cast: Rosemary Dexter, Adolfo Celi, Horst Frank, Sybil Danning, Franco Ressel, Michael Maien, Alida Valli.

Bunged on the bottom half of a UK double bill with the sublime **The Bell of Hell** (1973) under the bland title **Blood**, director Mario (**Nightmare Castle**, 1965) Caiano's Alice in Blunderland thriller is a pretty poor show with very little blood worth mentioning. Searching for her missing psychiatrist boyfriend Luca (Horst Frank), troubled Julie (a decent Rosemary Dexter) is led by sleazy gangster Frank (Adolfo Celi) to a seaside villa commune populated by the hippy dippy, arty types and middle-aged swingers seen in such early 1970s Exploitation – druggies, transvestites, nymphos (one being Eurotrash icon Sybil Danning) – overseen by Gerda (Alida Valli). There she learns Luca was a dope-peddling rapist blackmailer and that many people wanted him dead. Turns out, Julie was responsible for his death and trauma has completely blocked it from her memory. The overly complicated plot is indeed labyrinthine and the stabs at Freudian explanations for the textbook neuroses on show are side-splitting when not being toe-curlingly sexist. Fledgling cinematographer Giovanni Ciarlo was obviously still finding his signature style if the shoddy visual distortions are anything to go by, but **Black Sunday** (1960) composer Roberto Nicolosi's Mod score hits the jazzy-trumpet-on-overdrive heights.

FROGS

USA, 1972
Director: George McCowan. Producers: George Edwards, Peter Thomas. Screenplay: Robert Hutchison, Robert Blees. Music: Les Baxter. Cinematography: Mario Tosi.
Cast: Ray Milland, Sam Elliott, Joan Van Ark, Adam Roarke, Judy Pace, Lynn Borden.

One of the first of many nature strikes back eco-horrors that slithered through the 1970s, and still one of the most effective. In spite of the title everything from snakes, spiders, crabs and lizards to alligators, birds, water moccasins and snapping turtles joined in the frenzied fauna assault on the Deep South Crockett family where wheel-chaired Big Daddy Ray Milland (wearing a toupee as creepy as the crawlies) has gathered his bickering clan for birthday and Fourth of July celebrations. Soon the family members, including future 'Knots Landing' mainstay Joan Van Ark and Hells Angels movie stalwart Adam Roarke, meet their tragic environmental fates as the creatures violently assemble. Filmed on location at Florida's Eden State Park, the frog-and-toad wrangler let many amphibians under his watch escape during production, causing its own separate eco crisis. Directed by George McCowan, who shot this back-to-back with **The Magnificent Seven Ride!** (1972) sequel, the bird footage was purloined from nature documentaries and the alligator attack taken from **Bloody Mama** (1970). Based on his shirtless reporter role, Sam Elliott got the lead in **Lifeguard** (1976), his springboard into the Hollywood big time. Stateside AIP double billed it with **Godzilla vs. Hedorah/The Smog Monster** (1971).

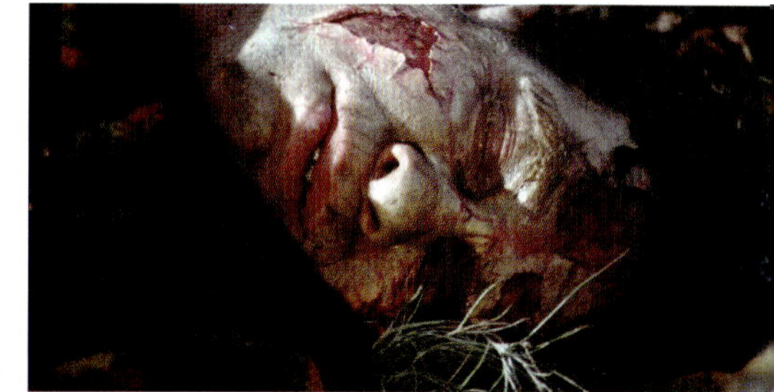

When in Southern California visit Universal Studios
only if you like
gripping suspense,
and surprise endings...
George Peppard
Michael Sarrazin
Christine Belford
We challenge you to guess the ending of...
"The Groundstar Conspiracy"
co-starring Cliff Potts · James Olson Screenplay by MATTHEW HOWARD · Based on "The Alien" by L. P. DAVIES · Directed by LAMONT JOHNSON
Produced by TREVOR WALLACE Executive Producer EARL A. GLICK · A Universal / Hal Roach International Production
TECHNICOLOR® PANAVISION® PG PARENTAL GUIDANCE SUGGESTED SOME MATERIAL MAY NOT BE SUITABLE FOR PRE-TEENAGERS
72/159

THE GROUNDSTAR CONSPIRACY

USA/Canada, 1972
Director: Lamont Johnson.
Producer: Trevor Wallace.
Screenplay: Matthew Howard [Douglas Heyes].
Music: Paul Hoffert. Cinematography: Michael Reed.
Cast: George Peppard, Michael Sarrazin, Christine Belford, Cliff Potts, James Olson, Tim O'Connor.

Leslie P. Davies's novel 'The Alien' (1968) – his previous books 'The Artificial Man' (1965) and 'Psychogeist' (1966) were combined for William Castle's **Project X** (1968) – had originally been optioned by actor Shashi Kapoor and writer/director Satyajit Ray. But when that powerhouse duo couldn't raise the money for an English-language adaptation, Universal Pictures stepped in, hiring dependable **A Gunfight** (1971) director Lamont Johnson to make sense of the bewildering plot. Devolved to basics, cool George Peppard (**Breakfast at Tiffany's**, 1961) is the ruthless government agent assigned to discover why saboteur Michael Sarrazin (**Eye of the Cat**, 1969) blew up the top secret Groundstar Research Complex, incinerating six premier scientists, and stealing national security space probe documents. Spy or pawn, Sarrazin is clueless too as someone has erased his memory. With the help of attractive widow Christine Belford, he starts to piece together the truth about his shocking past. Using superb locations – mainly Simon Fraser University in Vancouver ('Battlestar Galactica' filmed there too) – and having one foot in Cold War espionage, the other in privacy concerns still of keen relevance today, Johnson's persuasive direction lifts the mix of vague sci-fi and mindbender twists and turns well out of any predictable groove.

I WANT WHAT I WANT

UK, © 1971, first public screening 1972
Director: John Dexter. Producer: Raymond Stross.
Screenplay: Gillian Freeman, Gavin Lambert.
Music: Johnny Harris. Cinematography: Gerry Turpin.
Cast: Gavin Lambert, Harry Andrews, Jill Bennett, Paul Rogers, Michael Coles, Sheila Reid, Anne Heywood.

Produced by Raymond Stross (**The Leather Boys**, 1964), starring his Rank charm school wife Anne Heywood between going full Nunsploitation with **The Nun of Monza** (1969) and **The Nun and the Devil** (1973), this dull account of the early transsexual experience is the least interesting of the new snatch batch. Roy (Heywood) can't wait to rush home from the office to swap his business suit for the latest Biba frock. Chucked out by his womanising ex-military father, he takes up lodgings, dresses as a woman and changes his name to Wendy. Another lodger finds Wendy attractive and forces himself on her, leading to humiliation, a self-loathing act of castration and the operating table where he becomes a she for good. Cliché-ridden and pompous, the fault lies completely with director John Dexter, who mistakes Sunday supplement gloss for an artful sympathetic reading of the social issues. Theatrical wunderkind turned **The Virgin Soldiers** (1969) director, Dexter was well known for being a sadistic tyrant to his female leads, so it's no surprise Heywood couldn't man-up at all despite giving an uncanny impression of having a concealed penis. Way too earnest to be exploitative, and that's the bad taste camp problem.

LOVE ME DEADLY

USA, 1972
Director: Jacques Lacerte. Producer: Buck Edwards.
Screenplay: Jacques Lacerte, Buck Edwards [uncredited].
Music: Phil Moody. Cinematography: David Aaron.
Cast: Mary Wilcox, Lyle Waggoner, Christopher Stone, Timothy Scott, Michael Pardue, Dassa Cates.

Movies dealing with necrophilia are few, the best being **The Terror of Dr. Hichcock** (1962) and **Kissed** (1996). Director/lecturer Jacques Lacerte's solo effort puts the sick derangement front and centre for an even more tasteless shock charge that for once delivered on its poster warnings. Mary Wilcox followed her role in **The Beast of the Yellow Night** (1971) with this psychobabbling nonsense as a rich socialite haunted by erotic memories of her late father who can only sublimate sexual impulses with corpses. Checking the obituary columns every day for open casket funerals she can interrupt to steal kissing time with the cadavers, she meets a homosexual mortician (Timothy Scott) who cruises Los Angeles for hustlers to embalm while they are alive. Does she want to join his Satanic cult of like-minded necrophiliacs? (This plot thread was grafted on to pad out the running time and give it a more palatably horrific explanation!) Lyle Waggoner of 'Wonder Woman' TV fame plays Wilcox's new husband, who may hold the key to her 'problem'. Not for the faint-hearted, it was renamed **Secrets of the Death Room** for a double bill with the farming melodrama **November Children** (1972), itself retitled **Nightmare of Death**.

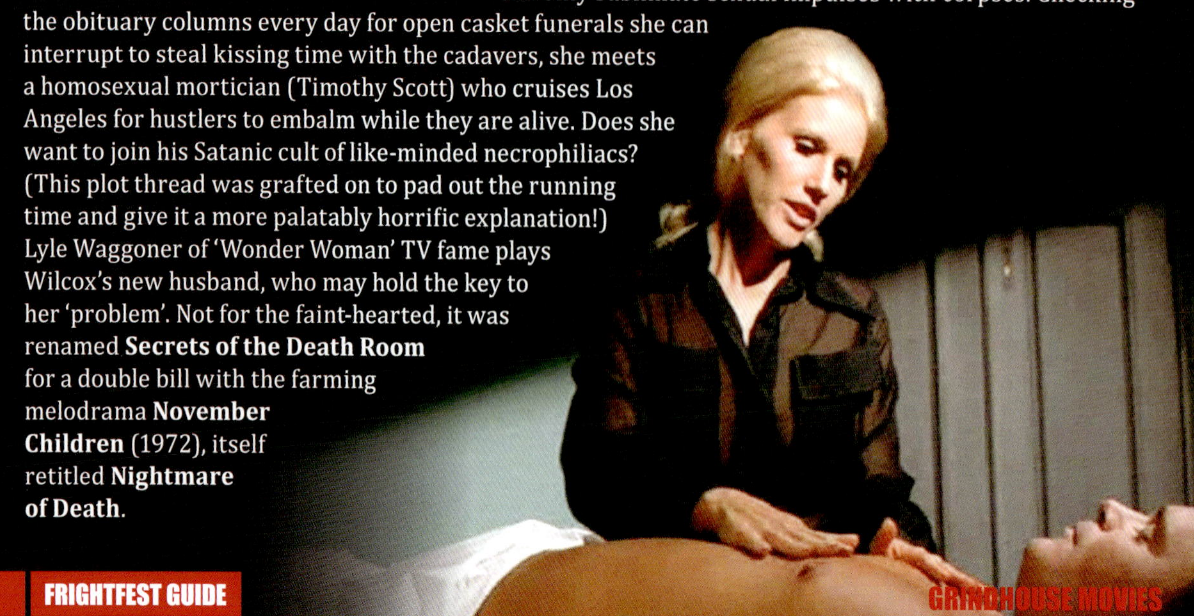

MOONCHILD

USA, 1972
Director: Alan Gadney.
Producer: Patrick Alexander.
Screenplay: Alan Gadney.
Music: Billy Byers, Patrick Williams.
Cinematography: Emmett Alston.
Cast: Victor Buono, John Carradine, William Challee, Janet Landgard, Pat Renella, Mark Travis.

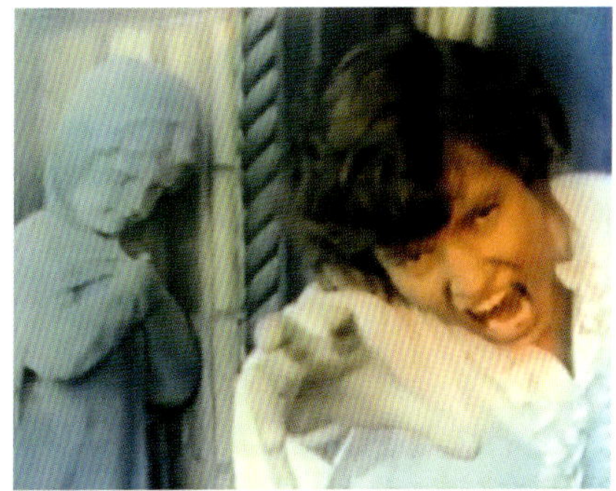

Master's thesis student films turned into viable theatrical properties were a Big Thing in the early 1970s. George Lucas went that route with **THX 1138** (1971). So too did Jack Woods with **Equinox** (1970) and John Carpenter **Dark Star** (1974). But here's one that fell through the cracks despite having a name cast and a trendy storyline about a Jesus-type protagonist undertaking a mystical journey featuring trials by ordeal to uncover a universal truth (think **El Topo**, 1970, **Brother John**, 1971). One-shot Alan Gadney filmed his tribute to American clairvoyant Edgar Cayce, who claimed to channel his own higher self in trance states, under the working title 'Full Moon'; it concerned the pursuit of artistic perfection by student Mark Travis. Drawn to a desert inn, the Keeper of the Words (John Carradine) introduces Travis to a sullen group of guests (including Victor Buono) who engage in a battle for his immortal soul in a spiritual inquisition. Thinking they had the next counterculture hit on their hands, American Films Ltd. were shocked when reviews called Gadney's Cayce history pretentious claptrap. Swiftly repackaged with the currently all-important 'Exorcism' word splashed on the poster, **Moonchild** died another death again on the Grindhouse circuit.

NECROMANCY

USA, 1972
Director: Bert I. Gordon.
Producers: Gail March, Bert I. Gordon [uncredited], Jeffrey M. Sneller [uncredited].
Screenplay: Bert I. Gordon, Gail March. Music: Fred Karger. Cinematography: Winton C. Hoch.
Cast: Orson Welles, Pamela Franklin, Lee Purcell, Michael Ontkean, Harvey Jason, Lisa James.

Size mattered to veteran filmmaker Bert I. Gordon in the 1950s with his fondue set of cheesy sci-fi from **The Amazing Colossal Man** (1957) to **Attack of the Puppet People** (1958). Mr. B.I.G. was still at it in the 1970s in this incompetent witchcraft tale showing in stark relief his deficiencies as both writer and director. But not producer, because he did manage to secure the services of Orson Welles, false nose and all, who was probably still trying to raise funds for his assorted shelved projects. Welles plays Lilith town toy manufacturer Mr. Cato, who is also the leader of a witches' coven trying to restore his dead son. Michael Ontkean and **The Legend of Hell House** (1973) Scream Queen Pamela Franklin are the recently miscarried newcomers who become part of his evil plans. Shot on location at Los Gatos, California, bringing a nice atmosphere to the minuscule budgeted production, there's little surprise or suspense in the edited-with-a-trowel proceedings where an over-abundance of zoom shots doom Franklin's endless visions of Cato's toys being used as occult instruments. **And Soon the Darkness** (1970) star Franklin met husband Harvey Jason on this movie, so something good did come out of it.

THE NIGHT OF A THOUSAND CATS

Mexico, 1972
Director: René Cardona Jr. Producer: Mario A. Zacarías. Screenplay: René Cardona Jr., Mario Marzac [Mario A. Zacarías]. Music: Raúl Lavista. Cinematography: Alex Phillips. Cast: Anjanette Comer, Hugo Stiglitz, Zulma Faiad, Christa Linder, Tere Velázquez, Barbara Angely, Gerardo Cepada.

Did anyone actually count the cats in this feeble feline frightener to see if the title contravened the Trades Descriptions Act? Doubtful, especially as Mexican hack René Cardona Jr. (**Guyana: Cult of the Damned**, 1979) clearly didn't care about the killer kitties' safety either – SEE: The serial scumbag chuck a white pussy over a high wall! Hugo Stiglitz (Cardona's handsome leading man in many of his movies – is there something you want to tell us, René?) is the millionaire playboy who stalks beautiful women in his helicopter, invites them back to his Acapulco castle, murders them with the help of his Tor Johnson lookalike manservant (Gerardo Cepada), cuts off their rubber heads to keep in pickle jars and feeds the leftover flesh to a pit of ravenous cats.

B-movie starlet Anjanette Comer (**The Baby**, 1973) pops up in the schlocky shambles, which ends – spoiler alert! – with Hugo being eaten alive by his furry pets. So he didn't have nine lives either! Clearly the helicopter cost a fortune to hire, the reason for its incessant use to fill up the running time, even though 20 minutes was cut for its US release. Praise Garfield and pass the kitty litter.

STANLEY

USA, 1972
Director: William Grefé. Producer: William Grefé.
Screenplay: Gary Crutcher. Music: William Loose.
Cinematography: Clifford H. Poland Jr.
Cast: Chris Robinson, Alex Rocco, Steve Alaimo, Susan Carroll, Mark Harris, Rey Baumel.

Every bad movie director has to make one film that's better than their average and in William Grefé's case –of the double billed stinkers **Death Curse of Tartu** (1966) and **Sting of Death** (1966) infamy – he had the good sense to steal the **Willard** (1971) nature vs. man concept, substituting rats for rattlesnakes. While this Grefé family and friends affair (his daughters and secretary were extras, he used locations owned by associates) was his dream idea, it was scriptwriter Gary Crutcher who took speed in order to write the entire screenplay over a weekend in time for the hastily scheduled 20-day shoot. Chris Robinson is great as the damaged Vietnam veteran of Seminole Indian descent who withdraws to a shack in the Florida Everglades to breed a snake empire with his pet rattler Stanley and mate Hazel. When snakeskin apparel manufacturer Alex Rocco (**Slither**, 1973!) offers to buy his nest of vipers for raw material and is rebuffed, a psycho hit man is hired to sway the deal. Cue the scaly fight back. Gross and unsettling, with scant attention paid to animal welfare, especially in the startling nightclub act, 'Stanley in Miami' was the intended sequel that sadly never got made.

TOYS ARE NOT FOR CHILDREN

USA, 1972
Director: Stanley H. Brassloff. Producers: Stanley H. Brassloff, Samuel M. Chartock.
Screenplay: Macs McAree. Music: Cathy Lynn, Jacques Urbont. Cinematography: Rolph Laube.
Cast: Marcia Forbes, Harlan Cary Poe, Evelyn Kingsley, Luis Arroyo, Fran Warren, Peter Lightstone.

Director/co-writer Stanley H. Brassloff's wrenching soap opera is the **Grey Gardens** (1975) of Sexploitation. Quite what the dirty raincoat brigade must have thought when they rocked up for a skin flick, only to have a riveting psychodrama thrust in their faces, is a moot point. But whichever way you slice it, **Virgin Doll**, as it was retitled in the UK after a five-year release delay (dumped on the lower half of a double bill with **Seven Women for Satan**, 1976) is a minor gem lurking under wholesale misrepresentation. Marcia Forbes (the wife of Cannon Films president Chris Dewey giving a haunting performance) is Jamie, a toy store shop assistant, whose obsession with childhood playthings stems from her father's guilt buying her presents for being serial unfaithful to his wife, who eventually gives him his marching orders. Her own frigid marriage failing, Jamie meets a hooker who says she knows her father's whereabouts, and before you can say Urban Barbie, has agreed to meet clients to fill her paternal vacuum. Then her father does indeed come calling... A gripping and well-acted drama, with a surprisingly erudite script, the sex and nudity may be minimal but the blistering soul baring isn't.

"toys are not for children"

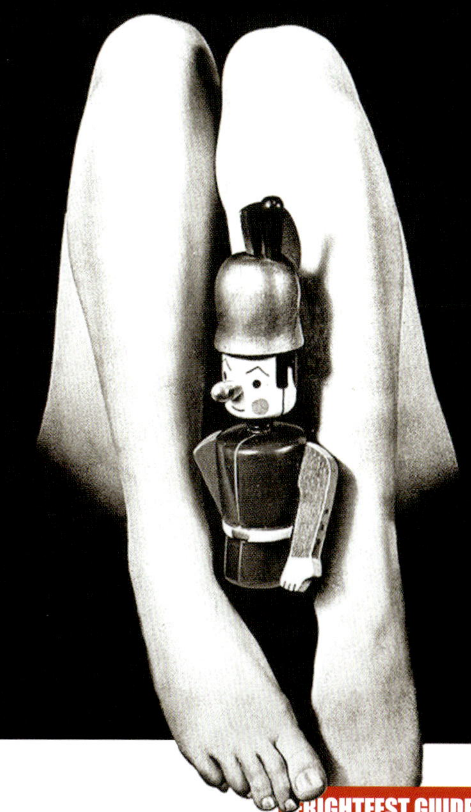

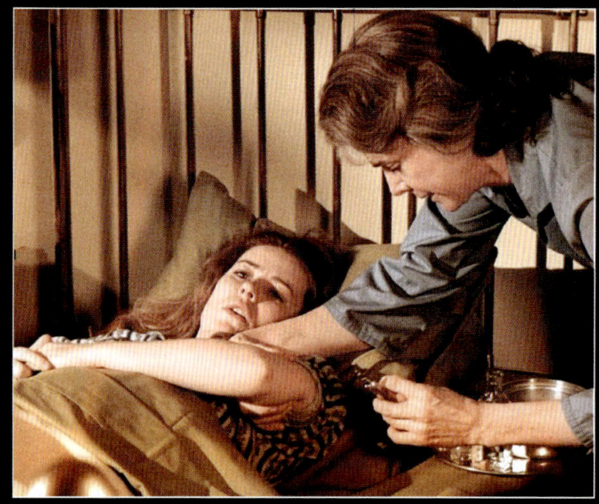

YOU'LL LIKE MY MOTHER

USA, 1972
Director: Lamont Johnson.
Producer: Mort Briskin.
Screenplay: Jo Heims. Music: Gil Mellé.
Cinematography: Jack A. Marta, Vincent Saizis.
Cast: Patty Duke, Rosemary Murphy,
Richard Thomas, Sian Barbara Allen,
Dennis Rucker, Harold Congdon.

Former actor-turned-director Lamont Johnson was a dependable all-rounder who always delivered on style and entertainment values (**The McKenzie Break**, 1970, **Lipstick**, 1976). This refreshing low-key chiller with plenty to scare but enough to also make you care is one of his best, reuniting him with Patty Duke, star of his TV movie **My Sweet Charlie** (1970) for which she won an Emmy Award. The **Valley of the Dolls** (1967) icon plays pregnant Francesca Kinsolving who, after her husband is killed in Vietnam, travels to remote Minnesota to meet the family she's never met. Her mother-in-law (Rosemary Murphy) couldn't be less inviting and, stranded by a blizzard, Francesca starts uncovering the skeletons in her closet, including mentally-retarded Kathleen (Sian Barbara Allen), an inheritance swindle, possible infanticide and a psychotic son (Richard Thomas trading on his All-American good looks) shacked up in the basement after escaping a lunatic asylum. Slipping subtly from classic suspense tones into more expressionist darkness, Johnson serves the material well, blending fears with tears (Duke's birth scene is quite shattering) for a more finessed psycho-geographic workout. Filmed at the Congdon Mansion in Duluth, Minnesota, where in 1977 the owner and heiress Elisabeth Congdon was actually murdered.

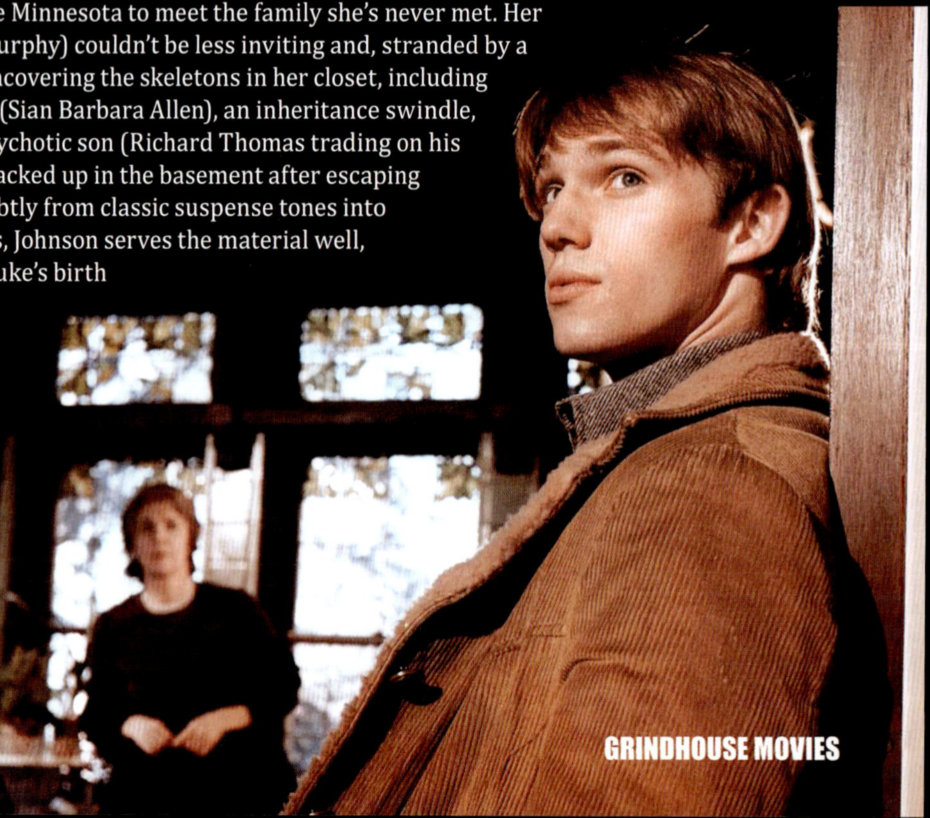

Z.P.G.

USA, 1972
Director: Michael Campus.
Producer: Thomas F. Madigan [Tom Madigan].
Screenplay: Max Ehrlich, Frank De Felitta.
Music: Jonathan Hodge.
Cinematography: Michael Reed.
Cast: Oliver Reed, Geraldine Chaplin, Don Gordon, Diane Cilento, David Markham, Bill Nagy.

Frank De Felitta's novels would in due course make fine movies – **Audrey Rose** (1977), **The Entity** (1982). But the radio thriller writer's feature career started badly with this scripting assignment partnered with Max Ehrlich, **The Reincarnation of Peter Proud** (1975) author who incredibly turned this lousy screenplay into the bestseller 'The Edict'. Standing for Zero Population Growth, (contemporary pundits pointed out the same initials summed up its box-office prospects), Oliver Reed and Geraldine Chaplin are the married couple defying the totalitarian government ban to have a real baby rather than adopt a Cyborg substitute. Neighbours Diane Cilento and Don Gordon threaten to rat them out unless they can toddler-share, until endless squabbling over childcare means they do indeed squeal, forcing the devoted parents now on a Death List to take their chances in the supposed polluted world beyond the city walls. Surprise, surprise, the smog-bound sewer existence they were expecting is instead a blue-sky fantasy island. Directed by Michael Campus, who would helm one of the best Blaxploitation entries, **The Mack** (1973), this dreary dystopian dreck, with a dirge soundtrack by Jonathan (**Villain**, 1971) Hodge, astonishingly won a very detached Chaplin the Best Actress Award at the 1972 Sitges Festival.

ZPG
"ZERO POPULATION GROWTH"

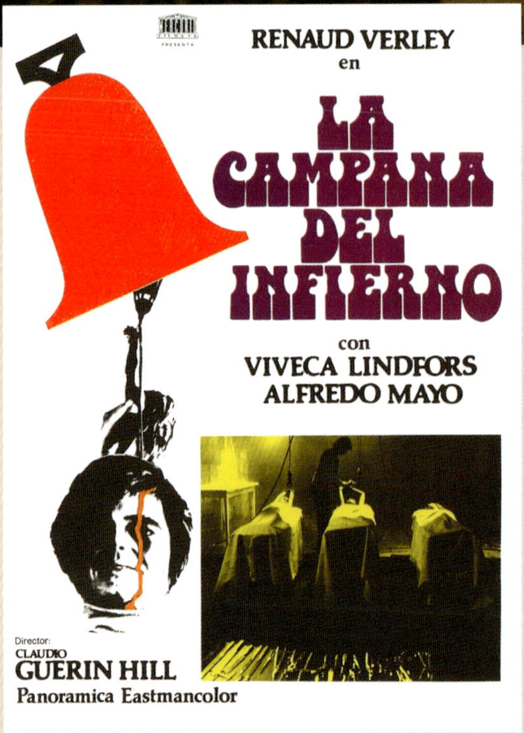

RENAUD VERLEY
en
LA CAMPANA DEL INFIERNO
con
VIVECA LINDFORS
ALFREDO MAYO
Director:
CLAUDIO
GUERIN HILL
Panoramica Eastmancolor

THE BELL OF HELL

Spain/France, 1973
Directors: Claudio Guerín Hill, Juan Antonio Bardem [uncredited]. Producer: Claudio Guerín Hill.
Screenplay: Santiago Moncada. Music: Adolfo Waitzman.
Cinematography: Manuel Rojas.
Cast: Renaud Verley, Viveca Lindfors, Alfredo Mayo, Maribel Martín, Nuria Gimeno, Christine Betzner [Christina von Blanc].

In one of the most tragic and ironic twists of horror movie fate, director Claudio Guerín Hill fell to his death from the bell tower featured prominently in the climax of this Spanish masterpiece on the very last day of shooting. Completed by his film school professor and mentor Juan Antonio Bardem (**The Corruption of Chris Miller**, 1973), the genre world clearly lost a major talent based on this thinly veiled pitch-black indictment of the Franco regime. Scripted by Santiago Moncada, and sharing much of the same imagery the writer brought to his screenplay for Mario Bava's **Blood Brides** (1970), Juan (Renaud Verley) is released from a mental asylum after five years and returns home to his wheelchair-bound Aunt Marta (Viveca Lindfors) and her three daughters, one of whom charged him with rape when she couldn't seduce him out of his share of the family fortune. Those slaughterhouse skills he learned are about to come in useful after abducting the three sisters and hanging them naked in his makeshift abattoir. Shocking in its day for shifting between morbid practical jokes and galvanising terror, like the work of Narciso Ibáñez Serrador, this represents an important chapter in the Spanish horror progression.

THE CORRUPTION OF CHRIS MILLER

Spain, 1973
Director: Juan Antonio Bardem.
Producer: Xavier Armet.
Screenplay: Santiago Moncada.
Music: Waldo de los Ríos.
Cinematography: Juan Gelpí.
Cast: Jean Seberg, Marisol, Barry Stokes, Perla Cristal, Rudy Gaebel, Gérard Tichy.

Night Must Fall (1937/64) again in director Juan Antonio Bardem's solid if over-familiar Euro-pudding. It was Bardem, Javier's uncle, who completed **The Bell of Hell** (1973) for his friend Claudio Guerín Hill after his tragic fatal on-set accident. Written again by Santiago Moncada, handyman drifter Barney (Barry Stokes, **Prey**, 1977) moves into a remote country mansion with weird couple Chris (former Spanish child star Marisol) and her artist stepmother Ruth Miller (Jean Seberg, still desperate for cash after her Black Panther/FBI scandal). Chris has been in a mental clinic due to stress over her father's strange disappearance and both women find Barney a sexual panacea for their shared grief. But could he also be the scythe-wielding serial killer who has recently been in the news for preying on wealthy older women? Great cinematography by Juan Gelpí (**Summertime Killer**, 1972), and a super score from Waldo de los Ríos (**Would You Kill a Child?**, 1976) allows Bardem to increase the ominous drumbeat of **Psycho** (1960) links with stylish tension and portentous undercurrents of simmering threat. If you saw the Spanish version, the female duo gets away with murder. For export, peas growing through a section of highway give away a dead body's location.

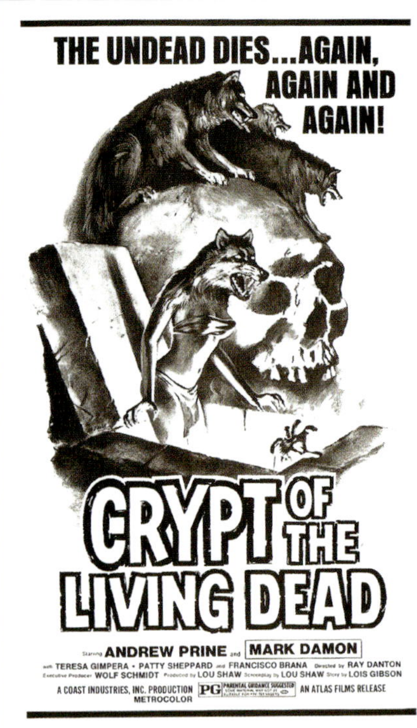

CRYPT OF THE LIVING DEAD

Spain/USA, © 1972, first public screening 1973
Director: Lou Shaw.
Producers: Julio Salvador, Ray Danton (new footage).
Screenplay: Julio Salvador, Lou Shaw (US version).
Music: Phillip Lambro. Cinematography: Juan Gelpí.
Cast: Andrew Prine, Mark Damon, Patty Shepard, Teresa Gimpera, Ihsan Genik [Ihsan Gedik], Mariano García Rey.

Move along, nothing much to see here under its original Spanish title **La tumba de la isla maldita** or its second American one, **Hannah, Queen of the Vampires**. Think of every undead cliché you can and its represented here in the bare bones plot of engineer Chris Bolton (1970s Exploitation mainstay Andrew Prine) travelling to Vampire Island when his archaeologist father (played by the movie's special make-up artist Mariano García Rey) is crushed under a tomb. Lifting the stone lid they awaken Hannah (Teresa Gimpera, **Naked Girl Murdered in the Park**, 1972), vampire wife of 12th Century crusader King Louis VII, who starts killing the islanders by floating out of her coffin as green mist and transforming into a wolf. Hannah's version of Renfield is The Wild Man (Turkish B-movie staple Ihsan Gedik) who juggles with disembodied heads, and she's soon put failed writer Peter (Eurotrash regular Mark Damon) under her evil influence. Directed by Julio Salvador (**They Killed a Corpse**, 1962), who died a year later, the American distributor Atlas Films cut out the gore to gain a child-friendly PG rating and hired actor/director Ray Danton (**Deathmaster**, 1972) to shoot extra scenes to keep the running time stable.

HEX

USA, 1973
Director: Leo Garen. Producer: Clark L. Paylow.
Screenplay: Leo Garen, Stephen Katz.
Music: Charles Bernstein, Patrick Williams [uncredited]. Cinematography: Charles Rosher Jr.
Cast: Keith Carradine, Tina Herazo [Cristina Raines], Hilarie Thompson, Scott Glenn, Robert Walker Jr., Mike Combs.

Before she went mainstream (**Nashville**, 1975, **The Sentinel**, 1977) after changing her name to Cristina Raines, Tina Herazo starred in one of the best cult movies of the decade. Sadly the sole feature directed by Leo Garen (who won an Avoriaz Fantasy Festival award), this sublime oddity collided horror, Western and Hells Angels genres to brilliant effect as it told the story of returning First World War veterans motorcycling to California to find their fortunes. In the Nebraska town of Bingo they seek shelter with two Native American sisters (Herazo and Hilarie Thompson). But after attempted rape on the younger sister, the elder calls on her ancestral powers and curses them with unusual death. Gored by an owl, impaled on a scythe, aged into an old hag and turned into a flock of doves are the beautifully realised fantasy moments all geared to preserving the inherent theme of retaining one's cultural identity and sexual purity. Acquired on the festival circuit by 20th Century Fox, 'Grasslands' – the shooting title – was shelved for two years and re-cut into a more straightforward occult chiller. Yet it still emerged a minor masterpiece with the final jet liner shock one for the ages.

America's first biker gang roars into town to raise some Hell... but Hell fights back!
KEITH CARRADINE GARY BUSEY SCOTT GLENN DAN HAGGERTY
HEX
A Magical Tale of Love and Terror.

Weekdays 7:00, 9:10 Sat.-Sun. 2:30, 4:45, 7:00, 9:10
CENTURY CINEMA II
Now Showing!
There is a place at the edge of the wild where two young sisters are waiting to enchant you. One can make things grow. One can make things die.
They'll scare the HEX out of you!
HEX
20th Century-Fox Presents "HEX" Starring KEITH CARRADINE • SCOTT GLENN with HILARIE THOMPSON as Acacia and TINA HERAZO as Oriole
Directed by LEO GAREN • Produced by CLARK PAYLOW
Executive Producer MAX L. RAAB • Associate Producer WILLIAM H. McCUTCHEN
Screenplay by LEO GAREN and STEVE KATZ • Story by DORAN WILLIAM CANNON and VERNON ZIMMERMAN • Music by CHARLES BERNSTEIN • COLOR BY DE LUXE®

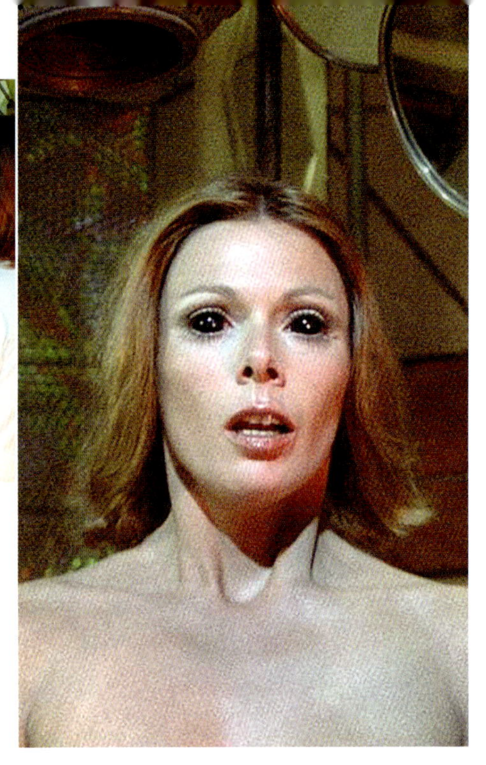

INVASION OF THE BEE GIRLS

USA, 1973
Director: Denis Sanders. Screenplay: Nicholas Meyer.
Music: Charles Bernstein. Cinematography: Gary Graver.
Cast: William Smith, Anitra Ford, Victoria Vetri, Cliff Osmond, Wright King, Ben Hammer.

Incredibly written by Nicholas Meyer (**The Seven-Per-Cent Solution**, 1976, **Time After Time**, 1979, **Star Trek II – The Wrath of Khan**, 1982) who tried to get his credit removed – then thought everyone has to start somewhere – this is a bizarre Bee Movie in every sense. Peckham, a Californian town with a scientific research facility, is the site for a number of deaths of men from heart attacks and sexual exhaustion. Government agent Neil Agar (burly Exploitation stalwart William Smith) is sent to investigate and traces the cause to Top Secret mutation experiments being conducted by entomologists. Dr. Susan Harris (Anitra Ford, **The Big Bird Cage**, 1972) turns out to be behind the deadly seductions, recruiting widows to be Royal jellied and radiated into her homicidal hive. Directed by Oscar-winning documentary filmmaker Denis Sanders (also the mystery melodrama **Shock Treatment**, 1964) with the accent on juvenile eroticism rather than any true insight into female empowerment or male sexual inadequacy, the leering attempted rape of Victoria Vetri (star of **When Dinosaurs Ruled the Earth**, 1970) is the nadir of this horny variation on creature feature science fiction. The multi-faceted 'bee's eye view' POV shots, stolen from **The Fly** (1958), add more OTT cheapness.

THE PYX

Canada, 1973
Director: Harvey Hart. Producer: Julian Roffman. Screenplay: Robert Schlitt.
Music: Harry Freedman. Cinematography: René Verzier.
Cast: Karen Black, Christopher Plummer, Donald Pilon, Jean-Louis Roux, Yvette Brind'amour, Jacques Godin.

It took a decade to get to the screen after being first announced with James Mason attached as star and producer. But when director Harvey Hart's underrated satanic thriller, based on John Buell's 1959 source novel, was finally released it got totally eclipsed by the sort-of-similar box-office tsunami **The Exorcist** (1973). A real shame, because this surprisingly potent supernatural chiller shows keen *giallo* influences of the Sergio Martino kind as heroin-addicted hooker Karen Black is found dead after falling from a swanky Montreal penthouse. Christopher Plummer is the hard-boiled detective on the case who uncovers a sinister occult explanation behind the weirdly accumulating killings. Deftly jumping between two timelines – the ongoing investigation and Black flashbacks – **The Pyx** (referring to a small round container used by Catholic priests to carry a consecrated host to the bedridden) is very Seventies, quite sleazy and culminates in a striking revelation. Terrific Black, who was turning her enviable indie career into a viable mainstream one, adds nuance to the Holy tart with a heart cliché, and wrote and performed the three songs featured (just as she did later for **Nashville**, 1975). A real discovery even under its eventual crass re-titling as **The Hooker Cult Murders**.

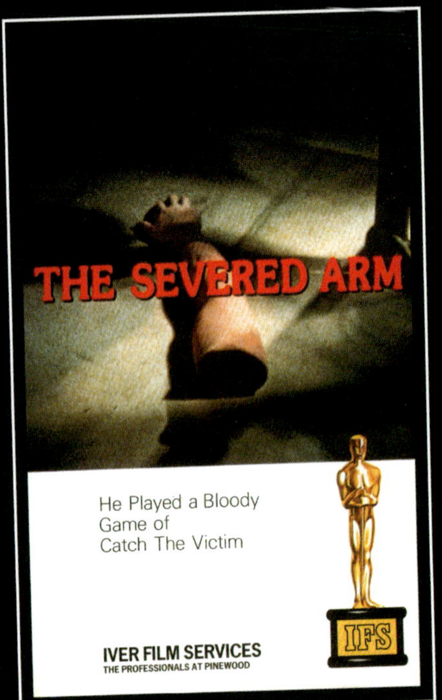

THE SEVERED ARM

USA, 1973
Director: Thomas S. Alderman. Producer: Gary Adelman.
Screenplay: Thomas S. Alderman, Darrel Presnell.
Music: Phillan Bishop. Cinematography: Bob Maxwell.
Cast: Deborah Walley, Paul Carr, David G. Cannon,
Marvin Kaplan, John Crawford, Vince Martorano, Ray Dannis.

Anyone who saw director Thomas S. Alderman's second and last movie (after **Coed Dorm**, 1971) during its apologetic Grindhouse release was completely thrown by the fact it starred Gidget/ Beach Party good girl Deborah Walley, ramped up super suspense, displayed decent gore and featured a cracking electronic score by Phillan Bishop (**Messiah of Evil**, 1973). So an embryonic slasher before that term had even been coined. The terrific story has six friends potholing down an old mineshaft when it collapses and traps them. Starving after two weeks, they know cannibalism is the only option and draw straws to decide whom to kill for food. But moments after they cut off Ray Dannis's arm to eat, they are rescued. Five years later David G. Cannon gets a severed arm in the post and his old pals think ex-mental asylum inmate Dannis is after axe-wielding revenge. First previews did not augur well for the cheaply-made and grainily-shot low-budgeter so Alderman reshot the twist ending to give it an extra gut punch. With the death scenes ominous and nicely choreographed – one in a radio station DJ studio is exceptional – the pointers to the slice-and-dice genre coming down the pike are plain.

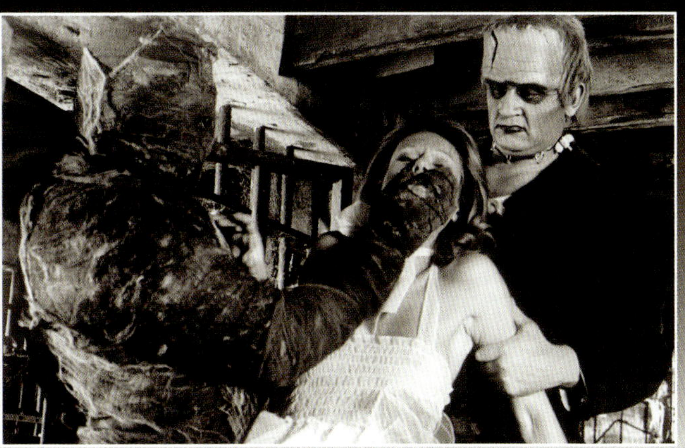

SON OF DRACULA

UK, 1973
Director: Freddie Francis. Producers: Ringo Starr, Jerry Gross [uncredited]. Screenplay: Jay Fairbank [Jennifer Jayne]. Music: Paul Buckmaster. Cinematography: Norman Warwick. Cast: Harry Nilsson, Ringo Starr, Freddie Jones, Suzanna Leigh, Dennis Price, David Bailie.

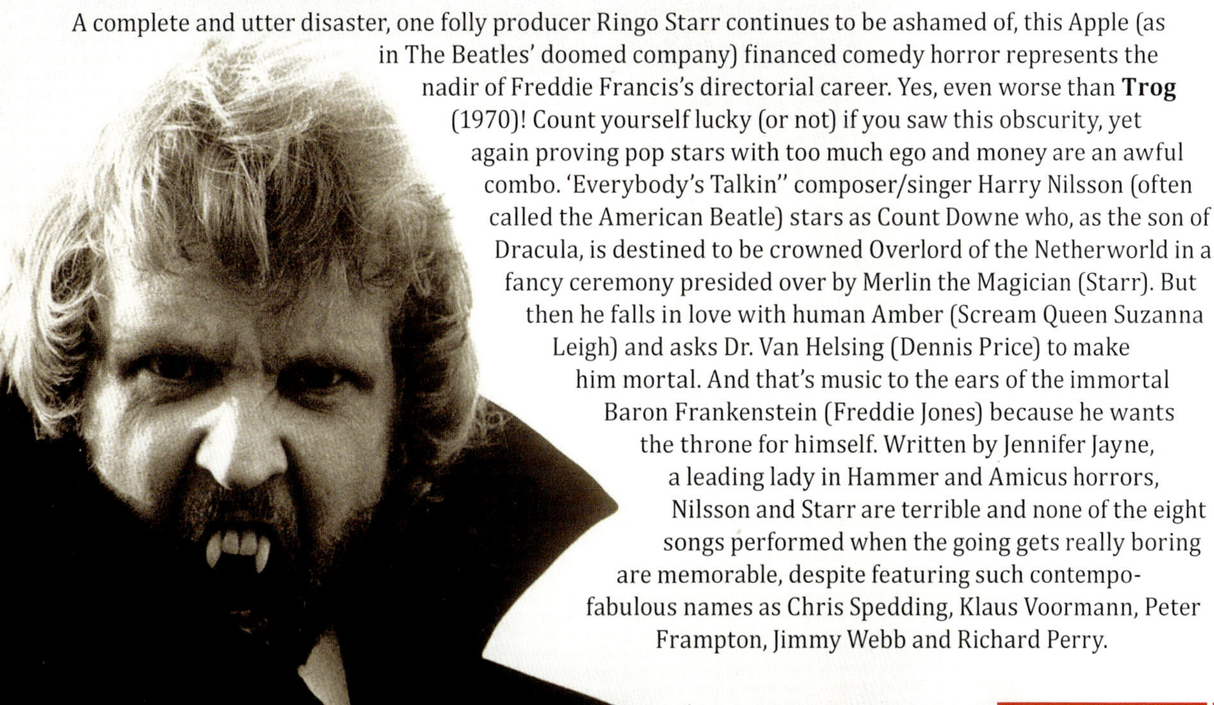

A complete and utter disaster, one folly producer Ringo Starr continues to be ashamed of, this Apple (as in The Beatles' doomed company) financed comedy horror represents the nadir of Freddie Francis's directorial career. Yes, even worse than **Trog** (1970)! Count yourself lucky (or not) if you saw this obscurity, yet again proving pop stars with too much ego and money are an awful combo. 'Everybody's Talkin'' composer/singer Harry Nilsson (often called the American Beatle) stars as Count Downe who, as the son of Dracula, is destined to be crowned Overlord of the Netherworld in a fancy ceremony presided over by Merlin the Magician (Starr). But then he falls in love with human Amber (Scream Queen Suzanna Leigh) and asks Dr. Van Helsing (Dennis Price) to make him mortal. And that's music to the ears of the immortal Baron Frankenstein (Freddie Jones) because he wants the throne for himself. Written by Jennifer Jayne, a leading lady in Hammer and Amicus horrors, Nilsson and Starr are terrible and none of the eight songs performed when the going gets really boring are memorable, despite featuring such contempo-fabulous names as Chris Spedding, Klaus Voormann, Peter Frampton, Jimmy Webb and Richard Perry.

THE SPOOK WHO SAT BY THE DOOR

USA, 1973
Director: Ivan Dixon. Producers: Ivan Dixon, Sam Greenlee.
Screenplay: Sam Greenlee, Melvin Clay.
Music: Herbie Hancock. Cinematography: Michel Hugo.
Cast: Lawrence Cook, Janet League, Paula Kelly, J.A. Preston, Paul Butler, Don Blakely.

In a 1970s landscape awash with commercial-minded Blaxploitation that took advantage of every Afro-American cliché in their sensational guns, gangs and pimptastic plots, director Ivan Dixon's radical thriller was something else. The fact you may never have heard of it could be down to United Artists pulling it from distribution soon after release due to 'outside influence' concerns, whereupon all prints were destroyed, the negative stored under another title and distressed novelist Sam Greenlee claiming FBI interference. What was so provocative about Dixon's follow-up to his seminal **Trouble Man** (1972), based on the homeboy required reading manual? Basically it concerned a CIA-trained black man, Dan Freeman (Lawrence Cook), with a revolutionary agenda. Freeman is recruited as the token agent of colour so the government agency could declare integration but once trained in white supremacist ways he goes underground and organizes a Chicago street gang into a unit of rebel soldiers with knowledge of the Man and how to use it against their racist suppressors. OK, while not a complete success artistically or technically, its raging mix of prophetic passion, prejudice and pain feels authentically real. No wonder the black anger highlighted was seen as incendiary in some quarters.

CHOSEN SURVIVORS

USA/Mexico, 1974
Director: Sutton Roley. Producers: Leon Benson, Charles W. Fries.
Screenplay: H.B. Cross [Harry Spalding], Joe Reb Moffly.
Music: Fred Karlin. Cinematography: Gabriel Torres.
Cast: Jackie Cooper, Alex Cord, Richard Jaeckel, Bradford Dillman, Pedro Armendáriz Jr., Diana Muldaur, Barbara Babcock.

A crappy sci-fi melodrama maybe, but it was this bland and batty yarn that paved the way for the Academy of Motion Pictures Arts and Sciences to universalize the methods of treating animals in a humane fashion in American movies shot in other countries. Stars Jackie Cooper and Barbara Babcock were so horrified at the casual slaughter of the vampire bats caught on a daily basis for the New Mexico based production that they complained to AMPAS and ensured their concerns were dealt with. All so much more exciting and relevant than the actual locked-bunker movie itself, about eleven people selected by the US government to participate in a subterranean survival experiment in case of a nuclear attack. With every strata of society represented – paranoid drunk, congresswoman, black athlete, crazed commander and bumper sticker activist novelist – how will they deal with the deadly bloodthirsty bats that have found an open electrical vent? Especially in the dark! The catastrophes pile up along with the clichés and director Sutton Roley barely lets the laborious action rise above the TV standard for which he had become well known with such popular series as 'Lost in Space' and 'The Man from U.N.C.L.E.'

CHRISTINA

Canada, 1974
Director: Paul Krasny. Producer: Trevor Wallace.
Screenplay: Trevor Wallace. Music: Cyril Ornadel.
Cinematography: Richard C. Glouner.
Cast: Barbara Parkins, Peter Haskell, James McEachin, Marlyn Mason, Barbara Gordon, Audry Kniveton.

Who is Christina? What is She? The relentless hype around **Valley of the Dolls** (1967), and its financial success against all the critical lambasting odds, was meant to jet its three leading ladies into the superstar stratosphere. Sadly it did no such thing for either Barbara Parkins or problem child star Patty Duke, while Sharon Tate… well, who knows? After a massive TV profile with 'Peyton Place' once past the Jacqueline Susann based cult trashterpiece, Parkins was quickly relegated to action horror B-movies of minimal interest aside from **The Mephisto Waltz** (1971) and **Asylum** (1972). And this reasonable mystery thriller by TV series aristocracy Paul Krasny ('V', 'Dallas', 'Hart to Hart'), in which Parkins asks an unemployed aeronautical engineer to marry her for $25,000 so she can get a U.S. Visa. But when he tries to make the relationship actually work, she disappears, and investigating why puts his life in danger. Spoiler alert: Deviant Parkins plays her drug-addict twin sister Katy, a Fever Dream features prominently and a cynical cop, phoney medium, porn-brokers and trio of transvestites, 'The Fabulous Freaks', also play a decisive part in the convoluted explanation, given away anyway by the crass US poster blurb.

DEVIL TIMES FIVE

USA, 1974
Directors: Sean MacGregor, David Sheldon [uncredited].
Producers: Michael Blowitz, Dylan Jones. Screenplay: John Durren.
Music: William Loose. Cinematography: Paul Hipp, Mike Shea.
Cast: Sorrell Booke, Gene Evans, Taylor Lacher, Joan McCall, Shelley Morrison, Carolyn Stellar, Leif Garrett, Dawn Lyn.

Killer kids have run the gamut from **The Bad Seed** (1956) to **The Children** (2008) via **Village of the Damned** (1960) and **Would You Kill a Child?** (1976). But while the production problems on this overlooked gem (aka **Peopletoys**) are legendary – original director Sean MacGregor (**November Children**, 1972) fired after a few weeks of difficult filming, noticeably replaced due to continuity errors by **Grizzly** (1976) writer David Sheldon – it's an unsettling and perversely moralistic shocker. Five wandering homeless children are offered shelter in Gene Evans's swanky winter retreat, where his self-important guests are unaware they've just escaped from an asylum for the criminally insane. The fun comes from seeing the affluent and snotty adults fall prey to the five-pack's charms before the sudden reality of their true homicidal natures erupts. The memorable death scenes include human torching, eaten alive by pet piranhas in the bath and chained to death, the latter shown in a chilling sequence of grainy still photos. Carolyn Stellar (playing Lovely), was the mother of Leif Garrett (David) and Dawn Lyn (Moe), two of the children. Four years later Garrett was in the Top Ten with the evergreen Disco hit 'I Was Made For Dancin''.

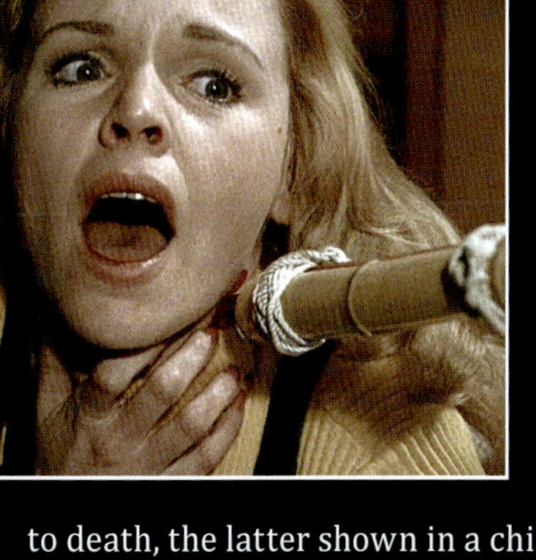

THE HAND THAT FEEDS THE DEAD

Italy, 1974
Director: Sergio Garrone.
Producers: Amedeo Mellone, Claudio Sinibaldi, Sakir Sözen.
Screenplay: Sergio Garrone. Music: Stefano Liberati, Elio Maestosi. Cinematography: Emore Galeassi.
Cast: Klaus Kinski, Katia Christine, Marzia Damon, Carmen Silva, Ayhan Isik, Erol Tas.

Filmed back-to-back with **Lover of the Monster** (1974), with more-or-less the same cast, sets and some shared footage, the reason they keep on being confused, **Django the Bastard** (1969) director Sergio Garrone's **The Hand That Feeds the Dead** (aka **Evil Face**) is a pedestrian mad doctor affair treading over-familiar ground. When his mentor dies in a laboratory fire, Professor Nijinski (a subdued Klaus Kinski) is determined to continue his skin grafting experiments, mainly because his disfigured wife Tanja (Katia Christine, **Pussycat, Pussycat, I Love You**, 1970) is keen to be the first transplant recipient. Before you can say **Eyes Without a Face/Les yeux sans visage** (1960) she's cajoled her husband's horny hunchback henchman (Erol Tas) into kidnapping a honeymooning couple in the woods as operating table guinea pigs. Carlo (**E.T. the Extra-Terrestrial**, 1982) Rambaldi's gory face-lift special make-up effects, Kinski's weird monologue to a doll and a little light lesbianism aside, Garrone's time-waster is often a sleep-inducing endurance test. Nowhere is the coming-soon **SS Experiment Love Camp** (1976) notorious grossness and bad taste fervour to be seen. For the record, **Lover of the Monster** was more a Jekyll and Hyde meets Frankenstein combo with Kinski as Nijinski fighting the murderous impulses of his evil alter ego.

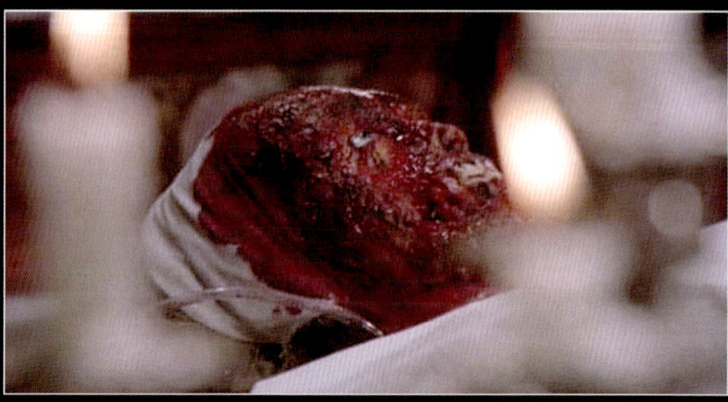

HOMEBODIES

USA, © 1973, first public screening 1974
Director: Larry Yust.
Producer: Marshall Backlar.
Screenplay: Howard Kaminsky, Bennett Sims, Larry Yust. Music: Bernardo Segall.
Cinematography: Isidore Mankofsky.
Cast: Peter Brocco, Frances Fuller, William Hansen, Ruth McDevitt, Paula Trueman, Ian Wolfe, Kenneth Tobey.

The elderly have always been a creepy trope in horror and can be found in everything from the cult pensioners of **The Brotherhood of Satan** (1971) and **Rosemary's Baby** (1968) to the more obvious **Rabid Grannies** (1988). In the same year senior citizen Sheila Keith wielded a power tool in **Frightmare**, a group of retirees got even with the construction tycoon wanting to destroy their tenement building to make way for a luxury apartment skyscraper.

Shot on location in Cincinnati, Ohio, director Larry Yust's follow-up to the crime drama **Trick Baby** (1972) was a rare example of a black comedy shocker that worked well because of its juxtapositioning of down home gentility with social comment and graphic violence. Populated by a familiar cast of character actors – industry bible Variety reported the elderly troupe "had appeared in 900 films collectively, but were receiving top-billing for the first time in their lives" – the murderous geriatrics included Peter Brocco (**What's the Matter with Helen?** 1971), William Hansen (**Fail-Safe**, 1964), Kenneth Tobey (**It Came from Beneath the Sea**, 1955) and Ruth McDevitt (**Mame,** 1974). Well shot and directed, with a wicked sense of humour prevalent throughout, this macabre joy was a welcome Grindhouse discovery.

MAGDALENA, POSSESSED BY THE DEVIL

West Germany, 1974
Director: Michael Walter [Walter Boos].
Screenplay: Jean Christian Aurive [August Rieger].
Music: Hans-Martin Majewski.
Cinematography: Ernst W. Kalinke.
Cast: Dagmar Hedrich, Werner Bruhns, Michael Hinz, Peter Martin Urtel, Rudolf Schündler, Karl Walter Diess.

The Exorcist (1973) rip-offs never stopped coming throughout the latter half of the 1970s, be they Blaxploitation, Italian or Turkish, and always ever-decreasing in scare mongering value. This German sleaze machine by **Schulmädchen Report** veteran director Walter Boos/Michael Walter follows the William Friedkin format but makes both the horror and obscenities far tamer and less impactful – "You just want to fuck me, ass-licker" being the only really outrageous line of dialogue in the dubbed export version. Virgin student Magdalena Winter (Dagmar Hedrich) finds her Satanist benefactor crucified in the courtyard and his evil spirit moves into her body. Soon she's showing all the demonic symptoms we've come to expect, only far cheaper. Once again doctors are clueless, but when the church's exorcism word is finally heeded, the devil slips out of her mouth as a serpent, to be killed with one stomp of a priestly foot. Yes, really! Workman-like, trite and featuring shoddy special effects – Magdalena's clothes levitating, whoopee – Boos relies on romantic bicycle interludes to pad out the running time. Shorn by 30 minutes before being unleashed internationally, the U.K. distributor had frames blown up to keep the running time consistent but Magdalena's heaving thighs off-limits.

MANIA

Italy, 1974
Director: Ralph Brown [Renato Polselli].
Producer: Renato Polselli.
Screenplay: Renato Polselli. Music: Umberto Cannone. Cinematography: Ugo Brunelli.
Cast: Brad Euston, Ivana Giordan, Isarco Ravaioli, Mirella Rossi, Eva Spadaro, Max Dorian.

Barely released in any overseas territories once past its initial Italian exposure many years after it was shot, writer/director Renato Polselli's obscurity can now be seen as the bridge between his cod Hammer Gothic horror obsessions (**The Vampire and the Ballerina**, 1960) and sleazy Mondo deviance (**Revelations of a Psychiatrist on the World of Sexual Perversion**, 1973). It's a total mess saddled with fractured narratives, disjointed editing and a dizzying style pitched somewhere between artful Jess Franco and unhinged Antonio Margheriti. Shot in the same villa and torture chamber locations as **Delirium** (1972), Freudian scientist Professor Brecht (Brad Euston) is madly experimenting to prove his theory that the human body can be cured more easily when it is in a cataleptic state. When he finds out his wife Lisa is having an affair with his twin brother Germano (Euston again), he decides to kill his sibling and take his place. But his actions turn Lisa into a crazed murderer and his assistant into an investigative force. Overloaded with non-stop screaming matches, ludicrous emotional outbursts, dicey disfigurement, sadistic laughter echoing through corridors and secret labs, floating heads bursting through smoke, and mirror effects, **Mania** couldn't be a more apt title.

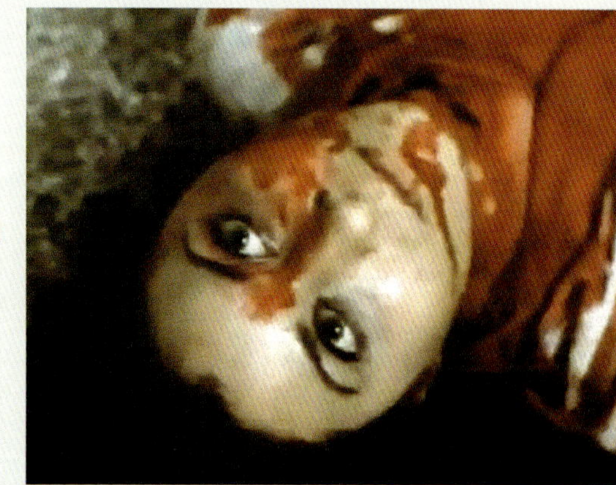

MOUSEY

UK/USA, 1974
Director: Daniel Petrie. Producer: Aida Young.
Screenplay: John Peacock. Music: Ron Grainer.
Cinematography: Jack Hildyard.
Cast: Kirk Douglas, Jean Seberg, John Vernon, Bessie Love, Beth Porter, Sam Wanamaker.

A precedent was set in the 1960s for making extended feature length versions of American TV pilots like 'The Man from U.N.C.L.E.' taster **To Trap a Spy** (1964). But it wasn't until the 1970s that many exploitable TV movies ended up on British cinema screens as the main attraction (**The Sex Symbol**, 1974) or the bottom half of a double bill. A prime case of the latter, **Mousey** accompanied the voodoo chiller **Craze** (1974) on the EMI circuit, retitled to the more obvious **Cat and Mouse**. Director Daniel Petrie followed his underwater yawnathon **The Neptune Factor** (1973) with this equally waterlogged, increasingly deflating thriller about meek-and-mild schoolteacher Kirk Douglas, nicknamed 'Mousey' by the snide student body. Thrown into psychosis when his wife Jean Seberg (the definition of a 'pay cheque' role) and son leave him, he quits his job and tracks her down to the big city hell bent on razor-sharp revenge. Despite a terrific central performance by Douglas, at this point game for anything in his career – **Once Is Not Enough**, 1975, anyone? – and a climax that would be stolen wholesale by both **Black Christmas** (1974) and **When a Stranger Calls** (1979), **Mousey** is lousy.

RUN, RUN, JOE!

Italy/France/Spain, 1974
Director: Giuseppe Colizzi. Producers: Carlo Ponti, Wolfdieter von Stein. Screenplay: Giuseppe Colizzi, Miguel de Echarri. Music: Guido De Angelis, Maurizio De Angelis. Cinematography: Marcello Masciocchi. Cast: Keith Carradine, Tom Skerritt, Cyril Cusack, Pepe Calvo [José Calvo], Raymond Bussières, Sybil Danning.

With **God Forgives... I Don't!** (1967), director Giuseppe Colizzi became responsible for the first pairing of Terence Hill (Mario Girotti) and Bud Spencer (Carlo Pedersoli)... by accident, because Peter Martell was originally cast in the Hill role but withdrew after breaking his foot. An Italian comedy double act was launched to become box-office sensations in further Colizzi adventures **Ace High** (1968) and **Boot Hill** (1969). But when the duo found more fame in the **Trinity** series, Colizzi thought he could strike charismatic camaraderie gold again with Keith Carradine (**Hex**, 1973) and Tom Skerritt (**Fuzz**, 1972) – a last minute replacement for Peter Fonda – as best friends Joe and Margherito. The result was **Run, Run, Joe!**, which tried to replicate the easy-going buddy formula but failed miserably. The story, such as it is, has Joe assigned to protect Mafioso Don Salvatore (José Calvo, **A Fistful of Dollars**, 1964) before he escapes to America. But Salvatore is murdered by plane crash and Joe must go on the run from even shadier criminals. By pretending to be English and hiding on glamorous marina boats! Pitched awkwardly between juvenile schtick and jokey violence, the tone is perfectly captured in the ubiquitous Oliver Onions theme song, 'Take It Easy, Joe'.

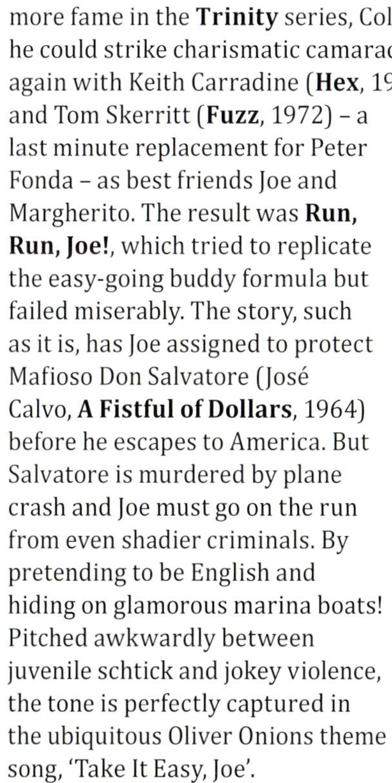

SEEDS OF EVIL

USA, © 1973, first public screening 1974
Director: Jim Kay [James H. Kay].
Producer: Tony Belletier.
Screenplay: Jim Kay [James H. Kay].
Music: Marc Fredericks.
Cinematography: Michael Zingale.
Cast: Katharine Houghton, Joe Dallesandro, Rita Gam, James Congdon, Anne Meacham, Teodorina Bello.

Andy Warhol superstar Joe Dallesandro never could escape his **Flesh** (1968) defining full-frontal nude pin-up, the counterculture equivalent of Raquel Welch's career-boosting **One Million Years B.C.** (1966) pose. The most beautifully photographed yet equally troubled member of The Factory arthouse crowd, Little Joe soon got disillusioned with Hollywood and managed to find gainful employment in Europe where he didn't just have to disrobe to show his full talent range. And this was the movie that precipitated his Continental move, a wretched killer tree horror even worse than **The Navy vs. the Night Monsters** (1966). When one of her friends dies mysteriously, socialite Katharine Houghton (Katharine Hepburn's niece) hires her monosyllabic gardener Dallesandro. Soon her house is filled with horticultural delights and glorious blooms, but when she looks further into his past, it seems death or insanity has a habit of inflicting itself on prior employers. The upshot, after should-have-known-better Hollywood veteran Rita Gam also falls in lust with his naked torso, finds Dallesandro transforming into an unearthly fusion of man and tree. Responsible for this black forest of excessive, banal dialogue, half-strength performances and unimaginative leadenness is director Jim Kay who, unsurprisingly, only made this one barking mad feature.

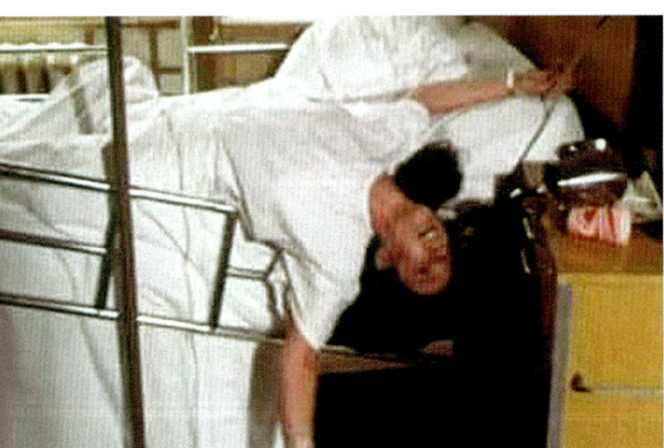

SEIZURE

Canada, © 1973, first public screening 1974
Director: Oliver Stone.
Producers: Garrard Glenn, Jeffrey Kapelman, Michael Thevis [uncredited].
Screenplay: Edward Mann, Oliver Stone.
Music: Lee Gagnon.
Cinematography: Roger Racine.
Cast: Jonathan Frid, Martine Beswick, Joseph Sirola, Christina Pickles, Henry Baker, Hervé Villechaize, Anne Meacham, Troy Donahue, Mary Woronov.

While **The Beast Must Die** (1974), a minor Amicus trifle, was top-billed with Brian De Palma's stunning **Sisters** (1972) in Great Britain, in America it was twinned with Oliver Stone's superb feature debut that dared take its audience on a magically dreamy, if harrowing, carpet ride through a cyclical nightmare laced with darkly philosophical questions. Horror writer Edmund Blackstone (Jonathan Frid) invites a group of friends (including Troy Donahue and Mary Woronov) to his lakeside house in Quebec for the weekend. Hearing on the news that three psychos have escaped from a nearby asylum, the guests are terrified when three apparitions start testing their physical endurance. Are evil Queen Kali (Martine Beswick), sadistic dwarf The Spider (Hervé Villechaize) and disfigured executioner Jackal the Giant (Henry Baker) the fugitive maniacs or are they just figments of Blackstone's imagination, conjured up for his new macabre children's book? Made with the skill, imagination and deft touch that Stone would bring to his later works – **Salvador** (1986), **Platoon** (1986), **Wall Street** (1987) – **Seizure** was smarter than the average horror at the time and with its freeze-framing techniques and striking special make-up effects emerged an oddball but intriguing calling card that would pay future dividends.

THE SEX SYMBOL

USA, 1974
Director: David Lowell Rich. Producer: Douglas S. Cramer.
Screenplay: Alvah Bessie. Music: Jeff Alexander. Cinematography: J.J. Jones.
Cast: Connie Stevens, Shelley Winters, Jack Carter, William Castle, Don Murray, James Olson.

Another American TV movie that sidled into UK cinemas due to its supposed commercial value, master of artlessness David Lowell Rich took once-blacklisted writer Alvah Bessie's trashy 1966 novel 'The Symbol', about self-destructive fame, and turned it into a thinly disguised version of the life of Marilyn Monroe. The result is an even more insulting and tarnished glitter attempt to squeeze the last vestiges of exploitability from the **Some Like It Hot** (1959) icon's fragile essence. The Movie Star is named Wanda Oliver in the book, but it's Kelly Williams in the film, a part turned down by A-List sexpot Stella Stevens and finally taken by B-List entertainer Connie Stevens (no relation). Very much in the Harold Robbins bestseller-to-blockbuster movie mode of **The Carpetbaggers** (1964), this redundant faux biopic hurtles through Kelly's problematic childhood, her model and bit player days, first real film role, phenomenal rise in Hollywood, disastrous affairs and marriages, a growing dependence on alcohol and pills, her studio battles and then the final suicidal tragedy. Been there, done that and so much better, this ended up on a hilariously thematic double bill with its complete polar opposite, **No Sex Please - We're British** (1973).

THE SPECTRE OF EDGAR ALLAN POE

USA, © 1972, first public screening 1974
Director: Mohy Quandour. Producer: Mohy Quandour. Screenplay: Mohy Quandour. Music: Allen D. Allen. Cinematography: Robert Birchall. Cast: Robert Walker Jr., Cesar Romero, Tom Drake, Carol Ohmart, Mary Grover, Mario Milano.

The directorial debut of the very mysterious Mohydeen Izzat 'Mohy' Quandour was a little late to the Poe party that Roger Corman had so expertly mined in the early 1960s. But putting the actual literary figure of Poe (played by Robert Walker Jr.) in the fear frame was a fun move, even if ultimately completely wasted as the notion that what happened in this made-up biography would influence his most famous works 'The Premature Burial' and 'The Pit and the Pendulum'.

Poe's traumatic romance with his great love Lenore (Mary Grover) ends when she's buried alive after being assumed dead, the trauma sending her insane and committed to a private asylum run by Dr. Grimaldi (Cesar Romero). But a series of bloody murders at the sinister facility leads Poe to investigate and discover a basement torture chamber and snake pit where Grimaldi is carrying out uncanny human experiments and his homicidal wife (Carol Ohmart) is killing patients and their visitors. Supposedly set in the 1830s with a teeny budget than cannot in any way do the period justice, a few eerie sequences summon up Poe's nightmarish atmosphere and dark imagination, but overall it's better to stick with **Two Evil Eyes** (1990).

TANGO OF PERVERSION

Greece, 1974
Director: Dacosta Carayan [Kostas Karagiannis]. Screenplay: Elio Montanari [Lazaros Montanaris] . Music: Yani Spanos [Giannis Spanos]. Cinematography: Billy George [Vasilis Vasileiadis].
Cast: Larry Daniels [Lakis Komninos], Erika Raffael, Dorothy Moore, Harry Cooper [Vagelis Voulgaridis], Jennifer Wynne, George Moss [Giorgos Moshidis].

More a homegrown comedy director until market changes forced him to diversify into horror thrillers – **The Rape Killer/ Death Kiss** (1974), **The Devil's Men** (1976) – Greek director Dacosta Carayan/ Kostas Karagiannis indulged in sordid Sexploitation with this venture that, despite revolving around necrophilia, voyeurism and lesbianism remains quaintly tasteful and humorously tongue-in-cheek. Rich kid Harry Cooper/Vagelis Voulgaridis can't find a cure for his impotence so lets his best mate and cocaine dealer Larry Daniels/Lakis Komninos use his swanky bachelor pad for sex with pick-ups from the swingers Club Tango (the original title was **Tango 2001**). But unbeknownst to Daniels, Cooper is watching and filming everything through a one-way mirror. Things turn weird when Cooper films Daniels murdering his abused girlfriend's lesbian lover and faced with disposing of the body finds he's aroused by the sexual opportunities her corpse provokes. Blackmail and more murder ensue until the police discover Cooper's secret home movie stash. Always good to see actors going for it bigtime even though they know the material is pretty wonky and Komninos goes manic sleazeball on overdrive, with the sexually frustrated Voulgaridis almost matching him in arch frenzy. All this and totally unexpected dance numbers in the Club Tango sequences.

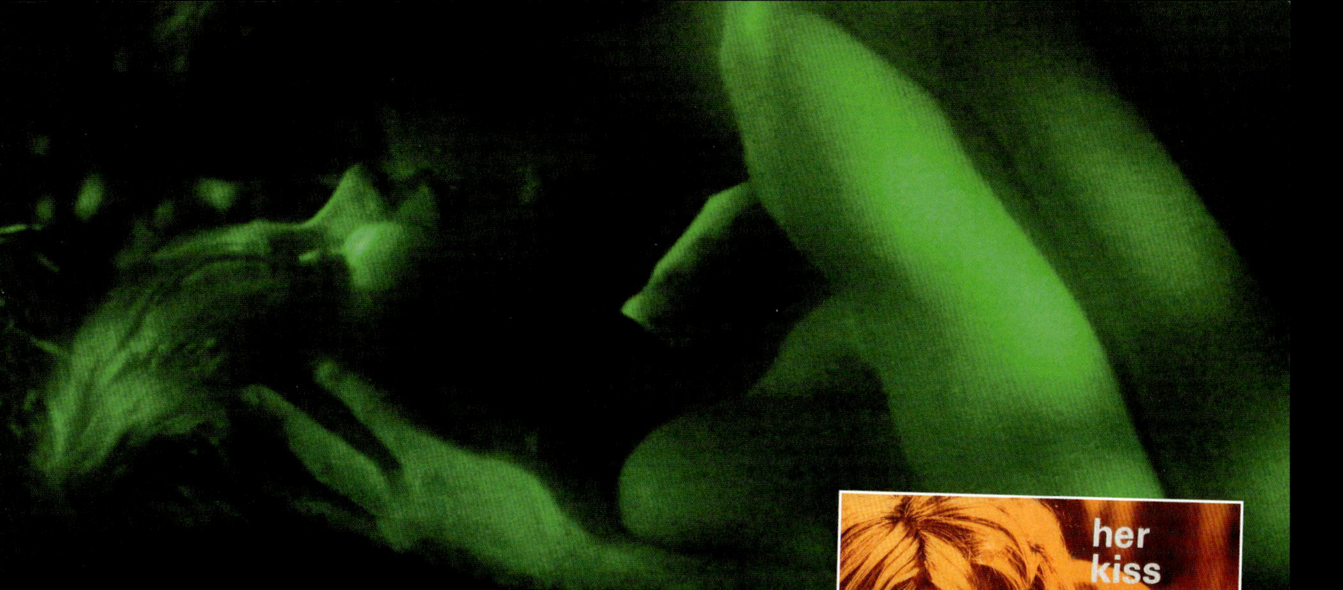

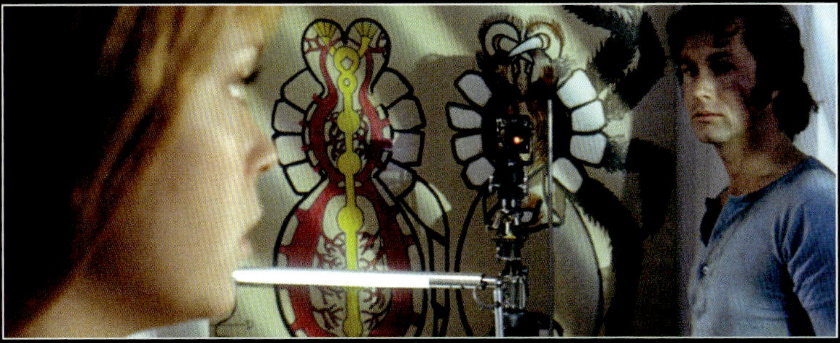

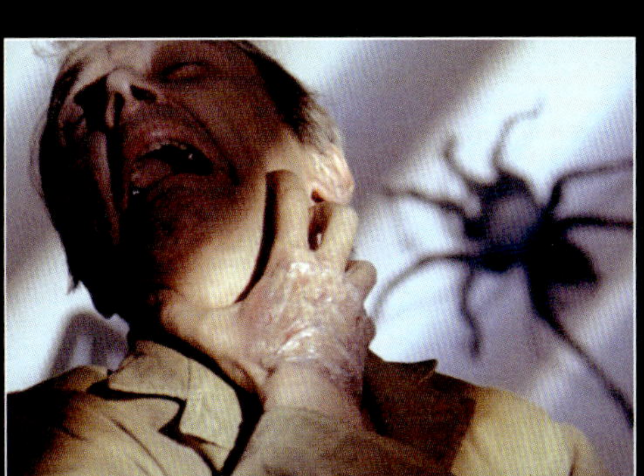

VENOM

UK, © 1971, first public screening 1974
Director: Peter Sykes. Producers: Michael Pearson, Kenneth F. Rowles. Screenplay: Derek Ford, Donald Ford, Christopher Wicking. Music: John Simco Harrison. Cinematography: Peter Jessop.
Cast: Simon Brent, Neda Arneric, Sheila Allen, Derek Newark, Terence Soall, Gerard Heinz.

An artist (British TV veteran Simon Brent) on holiday in Bavaria for new vistas to paint becomes involved with the mysterious and feral Anna (Serbian Neda Arneric) whose renegade Nazi scientist father (Terence Soall) is experimenting with spider venom to develop a new form of nerve gas in the first horror film directed by Peter Sykes. The transplanted Australian parlayed his stint on 'The Avengers' series into a variable genre career with the super **Demons of the Mind** (1972) – even though **Venom** was shot in 1971 it was not seen by the general public until 1974; Sykes claims that he was hired by Hammer after company execs saw an early preview screening. His subsequent films include the likeable **The House in Nightmare Park** (1973) and the awful last Hammer gasp **To the Devil a Daughter** (1976). Co-scripted by Sexploitation specialists Derek and Donald Ford (**A Study in Terror**, 1965) and lit by future Pete Walker cinematographer Peter Jessop, **The Legend of Spider Forest** as it was named in America is a ragged affair overdoing the Black Widow symbolism with agreeable glimpses of imitation Terence Fisher style as it staggers clumsily through vague erotica and fluffed horror. All made increasingly worse when New Line Cinema cut twelve minutes of plot and extreme imagery for its Stateside release. Who knew there were that many tarantulas in Bavaria, and how Anna actually kills her numerous lovers is anybody's guess?

THE VIOLATOR

USA, 1974
Director: Robert Kelljchian [Bob Kelljan]. Producer: Buzz Feitshans. Screenplay: Betty Conklin [David Kidd], H.R. Christian.
Music: Bill Marx. Cinematography: Brick Marquard.
Cast: Jo Ann Harris, Peter Brown, Jennifer Lee, Lisa Moore, Connie Strickland, Patricia Estrin.

After making money for AIP with three ace Exploiters in a row – **Count Yorga, Vampire** (1970), **The Return of Count Yorga** (1971), **Scream Blacula Scream** (1973) – director Bob Kelljan/Robert Kelljchian took an unexpected nosedive with this terrific distaff vigilante saga. Without doubt his finest hour, its surprisingly dismal box-office put him on the TV series conveyor belt ('Starsky & Hutch', 'Charlie's Angels') from which he never escaped. But the 'Jingle Bell' rapist's hockey mask disguise surely influenced Jason's iconic look in the **Friday the 13th** franchise, from Part III onwards? Jo Ann Harris is the rape victim who reports the crime to disinterested local cops who hint she must have been asking for it. Teaming up with other sexual assault casualties to learn karate and form a Rape Squad (the original title), they soon move from settling scores to entrapment as the 'Jingle Bell' attacker plots stalking vengeance using cages in the local zoo. Very much a product of its Women's Lib conflicted times – serious female issues discussed while naked in a hot tub, Harris's boyfriend calling her a 'diesel dyke' for her proactive stance, fighting in skimpy outfits – **Act of Vengeance** (another title) is way above average trash with a sobering message.

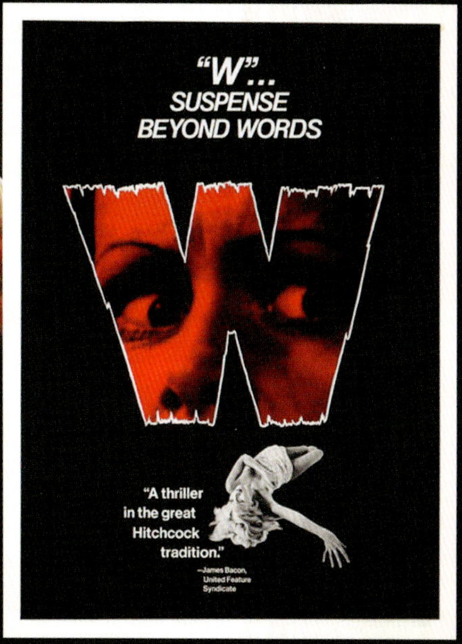

W

USA, © 1973, first public screening 1974
Director: Richard Quine. Producer: Mel Ferrer.
Screenplay: Gerald Di Pego, James Kelley. Music: Johnny Mandel.
Cinematography: Jerry Hirschfeld [Gerald Hirschfeld].
Cast: Twiggy, Michael Witney, Eugene Roche, Dirk Benedict,
John Vernon, Michael Conrad.

W is no **M** (1931/51). Fashion model icon Twiggy got great reviews in Ken Russell's **The Boy Friend** (1971), but this dismal psycho thriller follow-up did nothing for her burgeoning showbiz career and was dubbed "The worst with a capital W"! Produced by Bing Crosby Productions, the veteran crooner's company that hit big with **Willard** (1971), then lost it with **Terror in the Wax Museum** (1973), it was astonishingly scripted by James Kelley, **The Beast in the Cellar** (1971) and **Night Hair Child** (1972) director, Ronald Shusett, future **Alien** 1979) co-writer, and teleplay royalty Gerald Di Pego (**Born Innocent**, 1974). Obviously Kelley had his eye on the prize until Crosby insisted on director Richard Quine (**The World of Suzie Wong**, 1960) to handle the now 'Big Deal' Twiggy. She's the remarried housewife apparently being stalked by her first husband William (Dirk Benedict) because the letter W is scrawled at their near-fatal 'accidents'. But why is the private detective called in to investigate making matters worse? Quine's direction is virtually non-existent and slows the pace down even more than necessary in an all-round shockless bust. Co-star Michael Witney married Twiggy but tragically died of a sudden heart attack in 1983.

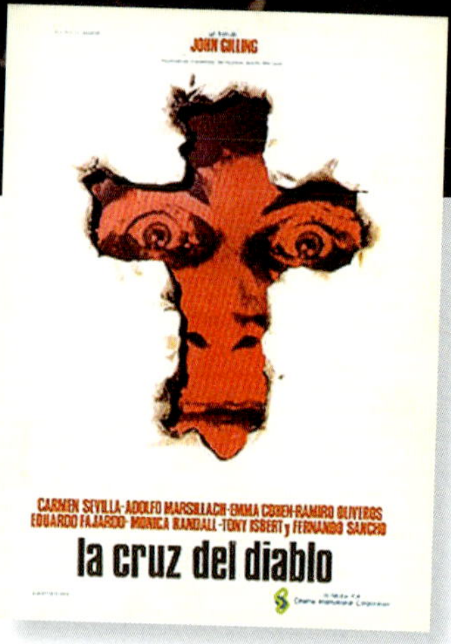

LA CRUZ DEL DIABLO

Spain, 1975
Director: John Gilling. Producer: Enrique Herreros.
Screenplay: Jacinto Molina [Paul Naschy], Juan José Porto, John Gilling [uncredited, Félix Martialay [uncredited]. Music: Ángel Arteaga.
Cinematography: Fernando Arribas.
Cast: Ramiro Oliveros, Carmen Sevilla, Adolfo Marsillach, Emma Cohen, Eduardo Fajardo, Mónica Randall.

Resolute horror director John Gilling made two of Hammer's most resonant works, **The Plague of the Zombies** (1966) and **The Reptile** (1966), the Cornish-set duo also considered amongst the best the studio ever produced. Gilling brought their rococo nightmare quality to his swansong, this criminally ignored **Confessions of an Opium Eater** (1962) affair that was shot in Spain and penned by Paul Naschy based on three stories, 'Miserere', 'El monte de las ánimas' and 'La cruz del diablo', by the 19th Century writer, Gustavo Adolfo Bécquer, the Iberian Edgar Allan Poe. Although written to star himself, Naschy was replaced by Ramiro Oliveros as the drug-addicted writer Alfred Dawson, travelling to Spain for rehab purposes, where he encounters the very dark visions that made him a junkie in the first place. Is he really a serial killer? Did his murdered lover arise from her tomb to scrawl the number 13 in blood? Do the Knights Templar pursue a damsel in distress, the reason **Cross of the Devil** keeps being erroneously lumped with the Blind Dead franchise? As ever the Devil is in the details in a gorgeously photographed (by Fernando Arribas, **The Blood Spattered Bride**, 1972), thoughtfully directed, Gothic-disturbed nervous breakdown.

DEAFULA

USA, 1975
Director: Peter Wechsberg [Peter Wolf]. Producer: Gary R. Holstrom.
Screenplay: Peter Wechsberg [Peter Wolf]. Music: Jerry Gregorius.
Cinematography: J. Wilder Mincey.
Cast: Peter Wechsberg [Peter Wolf], James Randall, Lee Darel, Dudley Hemstreet, Katherine Wilson, Cindy Whitney.

There are certain niche markets where off-the-wall concepts go to lose fortunes for misguided producers who think the world is ready for them, like the Esperanto language twosome **Incubus** (1966) and **Angoroj** (1964). And writer/director/star Peter Wolf's Portland, Oregon, shot sniff-of-a-shoestring budget horror, the first using American Sign Language. Its heart is clearly in the right place: of course audiences with hearing disability should have their own entertainment. But this utter fiasco featuring grainy Black and White stock, a terrible script that thinks it's funny, awful acting, papier-mâché special effects and nil production value was never going to cut it in the cutthroat distribution world, even considering its saleable vampire trappings. Wolf is the son of a preacherman who regularly channels Jekyll and Hyde by sporting fangs, a Satanic goatee beard and false nose to bite people to death. Can bumbling British policeman (Dudley Hemstreet) get to the bottom of the mystery – he is a Dracula expert after all? With a voiceover for those unable to read sign language, adding an even eerier disconnect, and sometimes referred to as **Young Deafula** for misguided Mel Brooks associations, the 'hearing' cast and crew are given in the credits in italics.

GIOCHI EROTICI DI UNA FAMIGLIA PER BENE

Italy, 1975
Director: Francesco Degli Espinosa.
Producer: Enzo Matassi. Screenplay: Renato Polselli.
Music: Felice Di Stefano, Gianfranco Di Stefano.
Cinematography: Angelo Baistrocchi.
Cast: Donald O'Brien, Erika Blanc, Malisa Longo, Maria D'Incoronato, Gianni Pulone, Carla Mancini.

Another efficient effort from the pen of ubiquitous genre luminary Renato Polselli (**The Vampire and the Ballerina**, 1960), who should have directed this low-rent *giallo* rather than leave it to no-mark Francesco Degli Espinosa (writer of **Emmanuelle on Taboo Island**, 1976). Originally titled **Thrilling Story** until someone in charge realised it wasn't and repositioned it more as a sex drama under the moniker **Erotic Games of a Respectable Family**, King of Italian B-movies Donald O'Brien plays Professor Riccardo Rossi who returns home early one evening to catch his adulterous wife Elisa (Malisa Longo, **Naughty Nun**, 1972) in bed with her lover. Determined to take revenge, he drugs Elisa during pretend make-up sex, stuffs her body in a sack and dumps it over a cliff into a lake. Not sure if he's been spotted by the suspicious passer-by in dark glasses and a hat, Riccardo starts an affair with prostitute Eva (the fabulous Erika Blanc). But the past comes back to haunt Riccardo when his teenage niece arrives wondering where her aunt is and seems to talk to Elisa on the phone... Rarely seen outside Italy for good reason, the multiple, if obvious, twist endings just about make it worth watching.

INFRA-MAN

Hong Kong, 1975
Director: Hua Shan. Producer: Runme Shaw.
Screenplay: Ni Kuang. Music: Chen Yung-Yu.
Cinematography: Ho Lan-Shan [Tadashi Nishimoto].
Cast: Danny Lee [Li Hsui-Hsien], Wang Hsieh, Terry Liu, Yuan Man-Tzu, Dana [Tsen Shu-Yi], Bruce Le [Huang Chien-Lung].

The first Chinese superhero movie and one of the most insane guilty pleasures ever. The Shaw Brothers manic comeback to their Japanese competition of Super Giant/ Starman/Spaceman and Ultraman, **Soul Brothers of Kung Fu** (1977) director Hua Shan's fantastic bombardment of monsters, make-up and mayhem is bright, brash and breezy comedy sci-fi. Inspired by 'The Six Million Dollar Man' series, this ridiculously scripted, badly dubbed action rush finds Professor Wang Hsieh turning his assistant Danny Lee into an indestructible superman customized with all sorts of electronic gadgets to battle against an attack by subterranean creatures led by the evil Princess Dragon Mom (Terry Liu, **The Bamboo House of Dolls**,1973) who lives in a volcano. After many trials, tribulations and karate chops, Infra-man wins the day with his nifty moves, boundless charm and a to-die-for red patent leather costume. The production design matches the overall zaniness – a communications centre that resembles six beach balls covered in silver foil – the mutant fiend design seems lifted from a bowl of mouldy pumpkins, and the dialogue is a cliché dream of, "The situation at this time is so bad that it's the worst in human history!" and, "Our destiny may depend on it" sort.

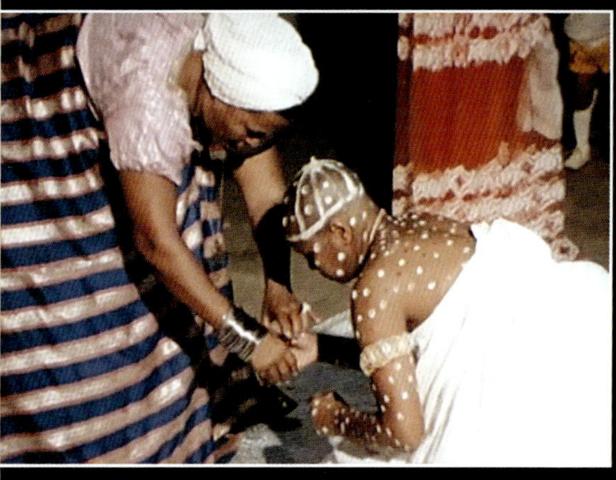

JOURNEY INTO THE BEYOND

West Germany, 1975
Director: Rolf Olsen. Producers: Rudolf Kalmowicz, Raphael Nussbaum.
Screenplay: Paul Ross. Music: Don Great.
Cinematography: Franz Xaver Lederle.
Cast: John Carradine (voice), Rolf Olsen, Paul Ross (voice), Edgar Mitchell, Othmar Fischer, Nina Kulagina.

Before **Shocking Asia** (1981) and **Shocking Asia II: The Last Taboos** (1985), Viennese director Rolf Olsen tried the Mondo genre out for size with this 'That's Entertainment' of psychic phenomena, which trailblazed his brand of horribly condescending, preachy and puerile narration (by John Carradine), with much exotic fakery or cultural traditions exaggeratedly twisted into shock sensation. Touted as being the winner of countless international awards and acclaim from renowned parapsychological groups – neither was true – and 'Three Years in the Making' – it wasn't – this somnambulistic excursion into the lowest form of reportage takes in the global delights of animal sacrifice for two mediums in Brazil, faith healing of polio victims in Italy, exorcism in the English home counties, dental surgery via hypnosis, psychic abdominal surgery, soul transference that isn't merely telepathy, 'doctors' pus-bursting tumours in the Philippines, necromancer levitation in Africa and witch doctor rain-making and eye-cataract removal. With tedious filler about religious occurrences such as statues, Madonnas and humans with unexplained stigmata or tears, only the sequence shot with special lenses showing ectoplasmic discharge comes close to being of marginal interest amongst the gruesome dross of what must surely be rejected outtakes from other, better, shockumentaries.

SEXY PARTY

West Germany, 1975
Director: Walter Boos. Producer: Wolf C. Hartwig.
Screenplay: Günther Heller. Music: Gert Wilden.
Cinematography: Klaus Werner.
Cast: Puppa Armbruster, Sandra Atia, Ulrich Beiger, Astrid Boner, Siggi Buchner, Kurt Bülau.

Or **Schulmädchen-Report 9.Teil**, from the master of that German Sexploitation staple, Walter Boos, who also directed the softcore pseudo-documentary reports **3** (1972), **5** (1973), **10** (1976), **12** (1978) and **13** (1980), the last in the globally profitable series. Subtitled **Matriculation Before Graduation** in its homeland, **Sophomore Sensations** in America, **When Girls Make Love** in the U.K. and **Sexy Party** in Italy, it delivers plenty of what the franchise is famous for in terms of polite nudity, sex, sin, salvation and dire warnings. An accident involving two cars lands twelve teenagers in hospital, the subsequent police enquiries ascertaining how they all ended up at a drunken orgy before the crash. The mixed bag statements run the gamut from rushed marriage disappointment, desperate virginity loss, date rape, lesbian blackmail, abortion and flasher trauma. The final hilarious collective analysis? Despite strict parenting it's completely ineffective once those adolescent hormones start coursing through hot-blooded veins. Only one true note is struck when two parents try to hiply engage with their daughter, whom they realise is no longer a child. Otherwise it's listless and tediously routine even by the low standards of the series. "Starring many uncredited adolescents and parents", says the opening crawl. Sure!

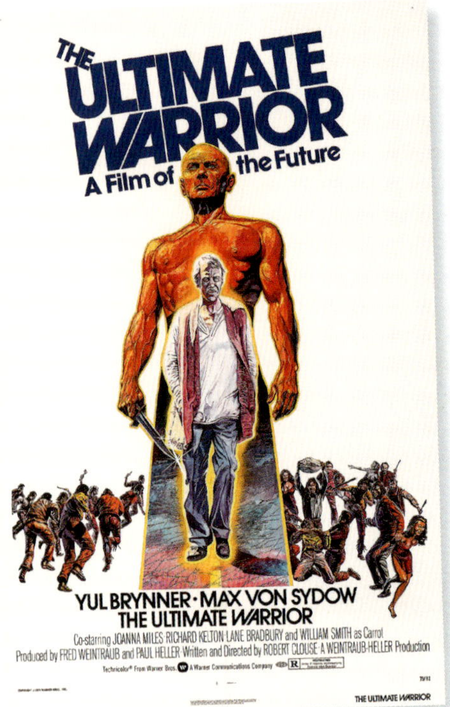

THE ULTIMATE WARRIOR

USA, 1975
Director: Robert Clouse.
Producers: Paul Heller, Fred Weintraub. Screenplay: Robert Clouse. Music: Gil Mellé.
Cinematography: Gerald Hirschfeld.
Cast: Yul Brynner, Max von Sydow, Joanna Miles, William Smith, Richard Kelton, Stephen McHattie.

Promoted as the first 'Kung Fu Science Fiction' futuristic thriller, mainly because Robert Clouse had found fame directing Bruce Lee's **Enter the Dragon** (1973), this stand-out comic strip adventure suffered the fate most pre-**Star Wars** (1977) sci-fi did. Dumped onto the Drive-In, quick play-off circuit just like the equally prescient **Westworld** (1973) before it, never given the chance to coast on rave reviews. In the virus-ridden New York City of 2012, society has disintegrated into barricaded communities. The Baron (a super Max von Sydow) hires fighter Carson (a never better Yul Brynner) to defend his peaceful neighbourhood from a marauding street gang led by Carrot (the ever great William Smith). With Carrot's mob gaining the upper hand, the Baron entrusts Carson to smuggle his pregnant daughter Melinda (Joanna Miles) and a single packet of plague-resistant seeds to island safety. Looking ahead to the **Mad Max** (1979) franchise and **Escape from New York** (1981) plus the Italian rip-offs **1990: The Bronx Warriors** (1982), etc, Clouse's influential flair for the unusual set up (the rat-infested pit challenge), atmospheric approach to the carelessness of death (Brynner's incredible demise) and thrilling violence (the lift shaft chase) made this the Grindhouse discovery of the year.

BLOODLUST

Switzerland, 1976
Director: Marijan Vajda.
Producers: Manfred Dohme, Dominik Huser. Screenplay: Mario d'Alcala. Music: David Llewellyn. Cinematography: Norbert Friedländer, David Khan.
Cast: Werner Pochath, Ellen Umlauf, Birgit Zamulo, Gerhard Ruhnke, Peter Hamm, Charly Hiltl.

It took the Swiss film industry and a Croatian film director to bring the true crimes of German serial killer Kuno Hofmann, the Vampire of Nuremberg, to the screen as failed art-house Exploitation. Marijan Vajda was expelled from Serbian cinema when his football comedy **Seki snima, pazi se** (1962) became a notorious flop. Moving to Austria, he made his only and final film a minimalist sicko starring Werner Pochath (the chauffeur in **The Cat O'Nine Tails,** 1971) as a deaf mute accountant with a doll collection and blood fetish, dubbed by the German police 'The Mosquito'. Haunted by childhood beatings and witnessing sexual abuse, he defiles women's corpses for erotic consolation, sucking their blood through a glass pipette and keeping their gouged-out eyeballs in a jar. Vajda problematically tries to make 'The Mosquito' a sympathetic victim indulging in the poignancy of perversion and poetry of violence. But so cack-handed is this approach to distasteful subject matter, it just emerges as laughable Eurosleaze. Not helping are the breathing 'dead' bodies and rubbish wax effigy substitutes for the mutilation sequences. While Pochath is blank to the point of catatonic, the remaining cast overacts hysterically, scuppering all interest in the cold case history.

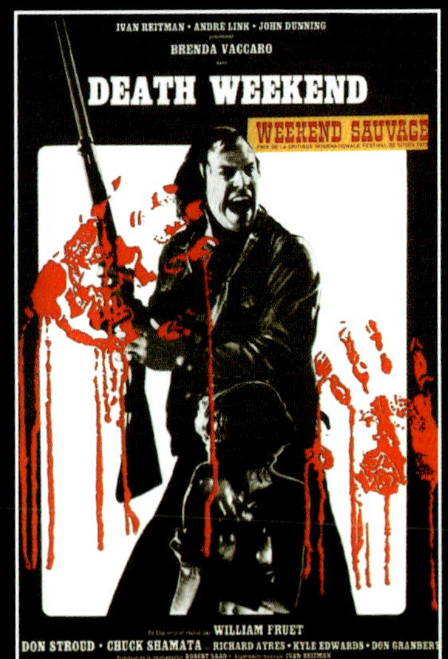

DEATH WEEKEND

Canada, 1976
Director: William Fruet.
Producer: Ivan Reitman.
Screenplay: William Fruet.
Cinematography: Robert Saad.
Cast: Brenda Vaccaro,
Don Stroud, Chuck Shamata,
Richard Ayrés, Kyle Edwards,
Don Granberry.

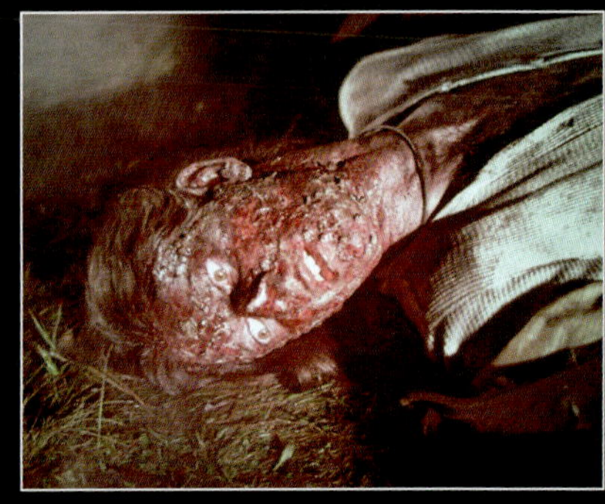

Giving a stunningly nuanced performance that in any other genre would have garnered her an Academy Award nomination, **Midnight Cowboy** (1969) star Brenda Vaccaro won the hearts of a whole generation of horror film buffs in director William Fruet's seat-edged shocker. Sporting the alternative title **The House by the Lake**, it's at this Ontario hideaway that playboy dentist Chuck Shamata takes his fashion model girlfriend Vaccaro for an ostensibly dirty weekend. But en route they run a foul-mouthed gang of thugs off the road, who then follow them to the remote location seeking brutal revenge. When her boyfriend is eventually murdered it's up to Vaccaro to survive a catalogue of sexual humiliations and turn her own tables on the gang, especially the leader of the pack Don Stroud, to whom she seems attracted. Soon an eye-grazing throat slashing with a glass splinter, fiery immolation and a nasty quicksand death lead to a heart-stopping fight over a getaway Land Rover. But while the concurrent thrillers **Lipstick** (1976) and **Open Season** (1974) exploited similar tropes in the grubbiest ways possible, Fruet expertly mines the true terror of the situation, keeping audiences engaged, horrified and eager to jump at every suspense-laden frame.

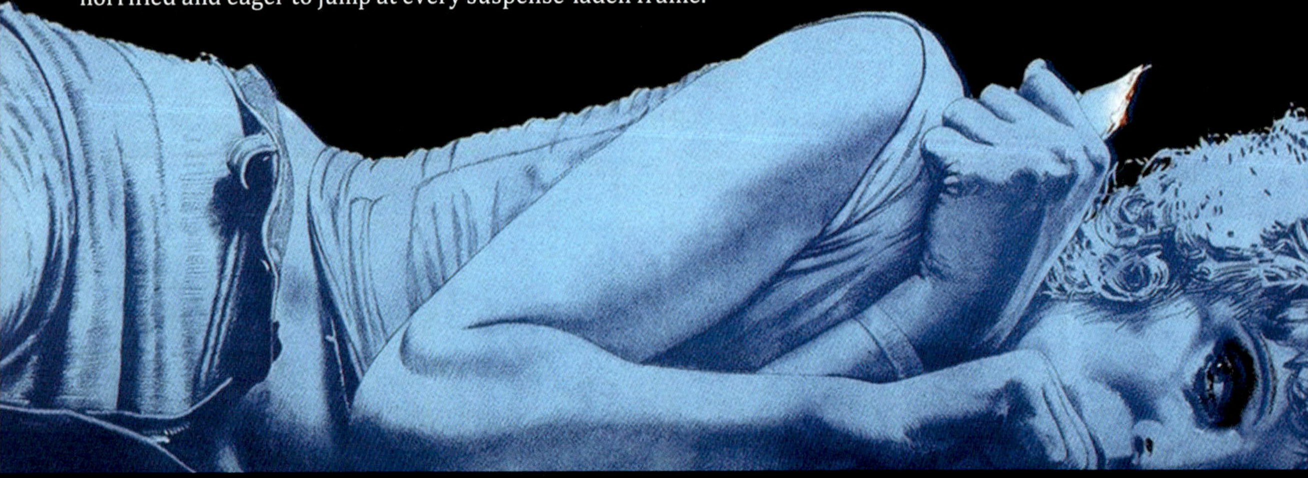

SCORCHY

USA, 1976
Director: Hikmet Avedis [Howard Avedis]. Producer: Hikmet Avedis [Howard Avedis]. Screenplay: Hikmet Avedis [Howard Avedis]. Cinematography: László Pal. Cast: Connie Stevens, Cesare Danova, John Davis Chandler, William Smith, Norman Burton, Joyce Jameson.

Pop princess and TV series cheesecake Connie Stevens had become an all-round entertainer by the mid-1970s, even adding commercial appearances that would hold her in good stead for her latter-day QVC product sales slots. In 1976 she gladly took the lead in AIP's big screen riposte to the hit 'Police Woman' cop show even though the material was clearly written with a bigger star in mind. She plays hot undercover Federal Agent Jackie Parker, out to bust a heroin smuggling outfit run by Philip Bianco (Cesare Danova, **Chamber of Horrors**, 1966). Posing as a charter plane pilot, Jackie offers her services to smuggle the drugs, contained in shipments of priceless antiques. Unfortunately, Bianco's greedy henchman Carl Henrich (good value go-to bad guy William Smith) nabs the smack stash and Jackie has to chase after him too, using bad wig disguises and hopelessly out-of-proportion stunt doubles to do so. With a tad more sex and tepid violence above the average Aaron Spelling produced network crime caper, **Scorchy** found little favour with its intended middle-market demographic and even less so when it got retitled to the even more dishonest **Race with Death**. Howard Avedis endured to direct the more interesting **Mortuary** (1983).

SNUFF

Argentina/USA, 1976
Directors: Michael Findlay, Horacio Fredriksson, Simon Nuchtern.
Producers: Jack Bravman, Allan Shackleton. Screenplay: Michael Findlay. Music: Rick Howard. Cinematography: Roberta Findlay.
Cast: Margarita Amuchástegui, Ana Carro, Liliana Fernández Blanco, Alfredo Iglesias, Enrique Larratelli, Mirta Massa.

It rocked the entire movie industry world in its day and became a watchword for the Grindhouse grift. But how did canny moviegoers fall for it to the extent that I was one of the first in line when **Snuff** opened in New York? Easy. 'Snuff' movies were the biggest story of the time and strongly featured across every contemporary media outlet. Porno was considered chic – Hollywood stars would soon have to go all the way by popular consensus – so when the first whispers of staged murder on film being made available to perverted punters began, it seemed the next horrendous step in the evolution of screen entertainment was here. Until it wasn't, and this con perpetrated by distributor Allan Shackleton was the defused bomb that exploded the myth. Taking directors Michael and Roberta Findlay's terrible Charles Manson-inspired flop **The Slaughter** (1971), full of grainy exposition and flashy dream sequences, and grafting on a fake disembowelling epilogue directed by Simon Nuchtern, Shackleton created Exploitation gold and became a Forty Thieves legend. Looking back, how could anyone have taken this clever cash-in seriously? Yet it has become an important part of Grindhouse folklore and an object lesson in supremely played hucksterism.

SPERMULA

con DAYLE HADDON UDO KIER · GEORGES GERET · ISABELLE MERCANTON
SUSANNAH DJIAN · ANGELA MAC DONALD · JOCELYNE BOISSEAU
CHARLES MATTON BERNARD LENTERIC
EASTMANCOLOR
Distribuzione: SUPERSTAR INTERNATIONAL

SPERMULA

France, 1976
Director: Charles Matton. Producer: Bernard Lenteric.
Screenplay: Charles Matton. Music: José Bartel.
Cinematography: Jean-Jacques Flori.
Cast: Dayle Haddon, Udo Kier, François Dunoyer, Jocelyne Boisseau, Ginette Leclerc, Isabelle Mercanton.

In the aftermath of the **Star Wars** (1977) phenomenon, Exploiters pounced on any sci-fi dog-and-pony show to palm off on the gullible public as similar. So French sculptor/director Charles Matton took his flop porn movie, removed 15 minutes of hardcore footage leaving just acres of merkins and mammaries, recut the time travel story to erase all reference to a 1935 genesis plot and upped the intergalactic quotient. Oh, and added an opening title crawl that fades off into infinity. The result is a confusing mess that seems to involve spiritual aliens from the dying Planet Spermula arriving on Earth to possess female bodies in a country chateau so they can seduce all mankind and cause total disinterest in sex. Apparently intercourse with the extra-terrestrials kills off the male sex drive, the twist here being it increases their own so that they abandon their invasion mission. Never-say-no-to-any-role actor Udo Kier appears as 'The Man who Came to Earth' scientific error with a tiny penis, and there's a tacked-on sideshow with dwarves and transsexuals to ensure it's slightly more far-out than the dire **Zeta One** (1969). With 'Thème de Spermula' performed by José Bartel, vocalist in **The Umbrellas of Cherbourg** (1964).

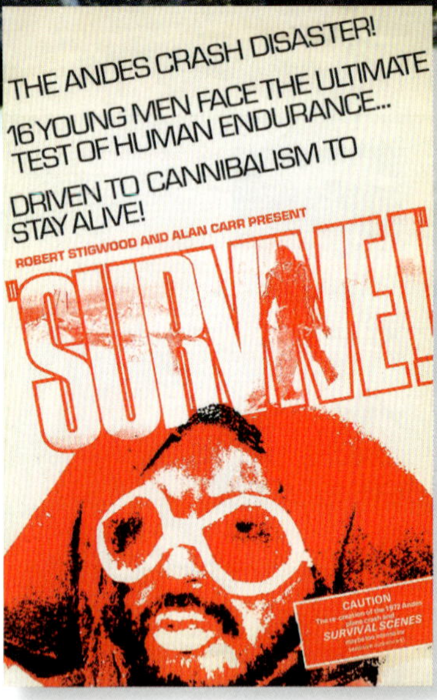

SURVIVE!

Mexico, 1976
Director: René Cardona. Producers: René Cardona, René Cardona Jr.
Screenplay: René Cardona Jr. Music: Gerald Fried, Raúl Lavista.
Cinematography: Genaro Hurtado, Luis Medina.
Cast: Hugo Stiglitz, Norma Lazareno, Luz María Aguilar,
Fernando Larrañaga, Lorenzo de Rodas, Pablo Ferrel.

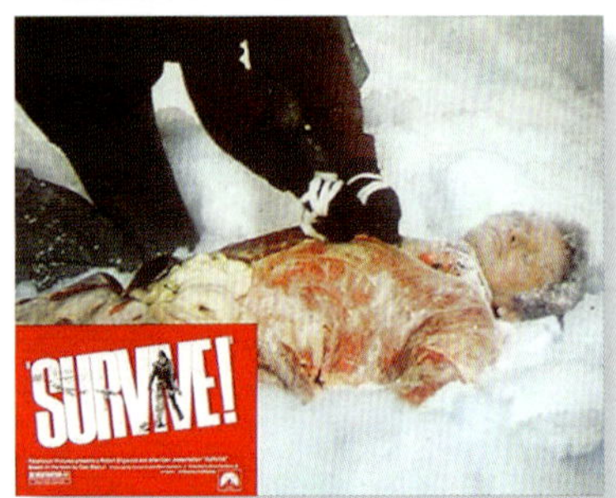

Before they combined to produce the mega-blockbuster **Grease** (1978), Allan Carr (**Can't Stop the Music**, 1980) and Robert Stigwood (**Saturday Night Fever**, 1977) foisted on the public one of the most reviled Exploiters of the decade. On 13 October 1972, a chartered plane carrying 42 passengers, mostly members of a Uruguayan college rugby team crashed into the Andes Mountains. How sixteen of them survived by eating the corpses of their dead companions made headline news around the world and became a bestselling book by Navy war veteran-turned-journalist Clay Blair Jr. But the film adaptation, directed by Mexploitation pioneer René Cardona (**Night of the Bloody Apes**, 1969) was lip-smacking schlock of the sleaziest kind that Carr and Stigwood made even more grotesque by adding optical effects to make the plane crash and avalanche more 'authentic' and extra cannibalistic gore – gut-spilling, body-skinning, limb severing, pus bursting – to ensure most critics walked out of the press showings. Raúl Lavista's original score was replaced with a more bombastic one by Gerald Fried (**The Killing of Sister George**, 1968) too. Hyped with the poster warning 'CAUTION: SURVIVAL SCENES may be too intense for sensitive audiences!' it was astonishingly nominated for an Ariel Award, Mexico's Oscars.

VORTEX

France/West Germany, 1976
Director: Sergio Gobbi. Producer: Jean Kerchner.
Screenplay: Catherine Arley, Lucio Attinelli,
Sergio Gobbi. Music: Stelvio Cipriani.
Cinematography: Jean Badal.
Cast: Rod Taylor, Bibi Andersson, Mathieu Carrière,
Paul Guers, Catherine Jourdan, Hans Meyer.

Or **Blondy** or **Germicide**, the latter title being more appropriate considering the submerged bio-warfare plot. Gonzo director Sergio Gobbi strikes again with this ill-fitting combo of suspense and suspenders erotic thriller and bacteria weaponizing shocker. Probably the worst movie Rod Taylor (**The Time Machine**, 1960, **Zabriskie Point**, 1970) starred in – even he called it "a dog" in contemporary interviews – Gobbi's ham-fisted adaptation of Pierrette Pernot/Catherine Arley's novel 'Duel au premiere sang' (she also wrote Sean Connery's **Woman of Straw**, 1964) just can't decide what it's trying to be. On one hand Taylor plays Christopher Tauling, United Nations bio-warfare disarmament official, warning global authorities about a new weapon threatening to wipe out mankind. On the other his wife Patricia (Catherine Jourdan) is lured into an S&M affair with a mysterious lover who nicknames her Blondy. All engineered by 'friend' Mitta (noted Ingmar Bergman star Bibi Andersson, who must have fancied the Paris locations), and when Blondy winds up murdered the political conspiracy theories come into frame. Apparently a conscious attempt by Gobbi to become wider known outside his French enclave, local critics panned it, ensuring the only life it could possibly have would be on the downmarket third-run Pacific Rim circuit.

THE CYNIC, THE RAT AND THE FIST

Italy, 1977
Director: Umberto Lenzi. Producer: Luciano Martino.
Screenplay: Ernesto Gastaldi, Dardano Sacchetti, Umberto Lenzi. Music: Franco Micalizzi.
Cinematography: Federico Zanni.
Cast: Maurizio Merli, John Saxon, Renzo Palmer, Gabriella Lepori, Robert Hundar, Tomas Milian.

Poliziotteschi superstar Maurizio Merli revived his Inspector Leonardo Tanzi role for director Umberto Lenzi after their shared success with **Rome Armed to the Teeth** (1976). In this rousing Euro-Crime entry, the ex-Milanese cop is now working as a mystery novel editor wanting a quieter life after putting Luigi 'The Chinaman' Maietto (Tomas Milian) behind bars. But when an attempt is made on his life, he flees to Rome and with American gangster Frank Di Maggio's (John Saxon) connections takes down The Chinaman's illegal operations in revenge. Obviously one of those businesses is pornography, allowing Lenzi to parade a gaggle of naked women across the screen. Tightly-paced with a droll edge and sporting almost 'Mission: Impossible' style action – rappelling between buildings, navigating infrared security – it's an elevated moustaches-at-dawn shoot'em-up perfectly accompanied by a great score courtesy of Franco Micalizzi (**The Devil Within Her**, 1974). Merli and Milian were at loggerheads on set but that professional mistrust of each other works well in context and gives the blood feuding characters an even nervier defensiveness. It doesn't quite deliver on the dialogue promise to "Make the St. Valentine's Day Massacre look like a baby's birthday party", but does come bracingly close.

HOLOCAUST 2000

Italy/UK, 1977
Director: Alberto De Martino.
Screenplay: Sergio Donati, Alberto De Martino, Michael Robson.
Music: Ennio Morricone. Cinematography: Erico Menczer.
Cast: Kirk Douglas, Simon Ward, Agostina Belli, Anthony Quayle, Alexander Knox, Virginia McKenna.

Take a *giallo* director (Alberto De Martino), a Spaghetti Western writer (Sergio Donati), an Italian Exploitation maven *par excellence* (Edmondo Amati), a top level cast led by Kirk Douglas, a threat of nuclear Armageddon and the Antichrist, and what have you got? This better-than-average, blatant Euro-pudding imitation of **The Omen** (1976), re-titled **The Chosen** in some markets to add even further copycat illusion. Amati and De Martino were already old hands at summoning up demonic scares in **The Antichrist** (1974) and here move the *de rigueur* decapitations and satanic imagery into a more spectacular dimension. Douglas is Robert Caine, an executive in charge of a Middle Eastern nuclear plant, who discovers his son Angel (Simon Ward) – see what they did there? – is the Devil incarnate and tries to stop him purifying mankind by setting off atomic explosions. If you saw the movie in Europe, Douglas is exiled with a new-born child as Angel stands poised to rule the world. In America Douglas blows up the plant and sacrifices himself to save humanity. With a stunning Ennio Morricone score and one terrifically eerie sequence of Caine's plant rising from the sea, towering above him and transforming into a seven-headed serpent.

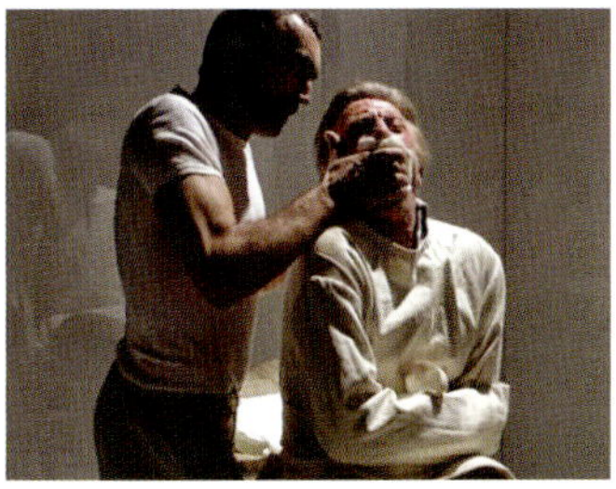

NINE GUESTS FOR A CRIME

Italy, 1977
Director: Ferdinando Baldi.
Producers: Mario di Nardo, Mario Forges Davanzati.
Screenplay: Fabio Pittorru.
Music: Carlo Savina. Cinematography: Sergio Rubini.
Cast: Flavia Fabiani [Sofia Dionisio], Massimo Foschi, Dana Ghia, Arthur Kennedy, Caroline Laurence, Loretta Persichetti, John Richardson.

Or Agatha Christie's 'Ten Little Indians' goes Italian with black-gloved knobs on. Coming on tepid like the never wanted bastard child of Michele Lupo's **The Weekend Murders** (1970) and Mario Bava's **Five Dolls for an August Moon** (1970), Ferdinando Baldi's late entry *giallo* is a fudged fiasco from the director who swore Ringo Starr off acting forever after his experiences on **Blindman** (1971). After an intriguing buried alive flashback prologue that then takes forever to be linked to the present action, wealthy Uberto (Arthur Kennedy, in one of the American actor's many 1970s Italian exploiters) takes his dysfunctional family – including **Cannibal** (1977) man Massimo Foschi, **Torso** (1973) star John Richardson, **Strip First, Then We Talk** (1975) pin-up Sofia Dionisio – on vacation to his remote private island. While everyone's dirty mind seems to be having it off with everyone else's partners, the guests start being offed by an unidentified assailant. Half-crazed Elisabetta (Dana Ghia, **Seven Deaths in the Cat's Eye**, 1973) blames the ghost of her dead lover but the truth of course is more mundane as the sole survivor discovers. Enough adulterous sex, blood and violence is on offer – the harpoon murder is particularly nasty – for undemanding completists though.

RUBY

USA, 1977
Director: Curtis Harrington. Producer: George Edwards.
Screenplay: George Edwards, Barry Schneider.
Music: Don Ellis. Cinematography: William Mendenhall.
Cast: Piper Laurie, Stuart Whitman, Roger Davis, Janit Baldwin, Crystin Sinclaire, Paul Kent.

Despite cult director Curtis Harrington's career spanning such wonderful movies as **Night Tide** (1961), **What's the Matter with Helen?** (1971), **Whoever Slew Auntie Roo?** (1972) and **The Killing Kind** (1973), it was this supernatural revenge saga that became his biggest commercial hit. Ironically, his last theatrical release was also the one most tampered with because he did not have control over the final cut. When a swamp-side Drive-In becomes the location for a series of gruesome murders, the unexplained crimes are traced to the autistic daughter (spookily effective Janit Baldwin, especially in the vocal reveal) of the cinema's owner – former gun moll Ruby Claire (Piper Laurie) – who is being possessed by the vengeful spirit of Ruby's assassinated gangster boyfriend. With the poster clearly coasting on the **Carrie** (1976) vibe, not to mention Laurie's attachment, Harrington crafts a series of arresting set pieces showcasing impaled bodies, hanging by celluloid, supernatural winds, telepathically controlled wheelchairs and severed heads in soda machines. Harrington's basic but clever concept here was to make a Drive-In movie within a Drive-In movie (notwithstanding the 1951 period being seven years too early for the main attraction **Attack of the 50 Foot Woman**, 1958), and by-and-large the conceit works.

BARRACUDA

USA/West Germany, © 1977, first public screening 1978
Directors: Harry Kerwin, Wayne Crawford (underwater sequences). Producers: Harry Kerwin, Wayne Crawford. Screenplay: Harry Kerwin, Wayne Crawford. Music: Klaus Schulze. Cinematography: Edmund Gibson. Cast: Wayne Crawford, Bert Freed, Jason Evers, Roberta Leighton, Cliff Emmich, William Kerwin,

One of the many creature feature cash-ins that swam into Drive-Ins after the game-changing success of **Jaws** (1975), file this one with **Tentacles** (1977), **Killer Fish** (1979), **Tintorera** (1977), **Devouring Waves** (1984) and **Mako: The Jaws of Death** (1976) rather than the above-average **Piranha** (1978). In fact that latter film's director Joe Dante was offered this carbon copy but wisely let it stay in producers Wayne Crawford and Harry Kerwin's clumsy hands. Stop if you've heard this one before… it's about a chemical plant in the small seaside town of Palm Cove illegally dumping waste into the ocean, turning the sharp-toothed barracuda population into man-eating machines. Frustrated marine biologist Mike Canfield (Crawford) is warning the authorities about the contamination, but because the plant is the main local employer… blah, blah, blah! Harry's brother William Kerwin (**Blood Feast**, 1963) is the sheriff turning a blind eye and Jason Evers (**The Brain That Wouldn't Die**, 1962) is the doctor whose emotional scenes cause more laughter than tears. Crawford directed the murky underwater sequences that barely frighten the fish extras, let alone the audience, as most of the running time is concerned with conspiracy theories rather than raising tension, aside from a terrible severed head.

LASERBLAST

USA, © 1977, first public screening 1978
Director: Michael Rae. Producers: Charles Band, J. Larry Carroll. Screenplay: Franne Schacht, Frank Ray Perilli.
Music: Richard Band, Joel Goldsmith.
Cinematography: Terry Bowen.
Cast: Kim Milford, Cheryl Smith, Gianni Russo, Ron Masak, Dennis Burkley, Barry Cutler.

Shot over three weekends for clearly no money by director Michael Rae for producer Charles Band to cream some cash thunder from the **Star Wars** (1977) juggernaut, this lame science fiction entry rocketed the genre back to the naff 1950s and is considered one of the worst extra-terrestrial flicks ever. Stage musical star Kim Milford had played Rocky in the first Broadway production of 'The Rocky Horror Show' and couldn't be more terrible as California small town scapegoat Billy Duncan, who stumbles on a powerful alien laser weapon in the desert and, in using it to even up the score with his persecutors, gradually transforms into a space invader himself. The intergalactic bazooka has an accompanying pendant (debris from an opening other-worldly battle stop-motion animated by David Allen of **Flesh Gordon**, 1974, infamy), the reason he turns into what looks like a green-faced member of the rock band Kiss. Girlfriend Cheryl Smith, aka Rainbeaux Smith star of **Caged Heat** (1974), hilariously perceives the 'darkness within' as turn-up-for-a-pay-cheque B-listers like Roddy McDowall do brief cameos before getting eliminated. The ho-hum in-joke scene where Billy resentfully obliterates a **Star Wars** poster was filmed after the main shooting had wrapped.

THE SKY IS FALLING

Spain/Liechtenstein, © 1975, first public screening 1978
Director: Silvio Narizzano. Producer: Andrés Vicente Gómez.
Screenplay: Gonzalo Suárez, Winfred Wells [Win Wells].
Music: Pepe Nieto [José Nieto]. Cinematography: Fernando Arribas.
Cast: Carroll Baker, Dennis Hopper, Win Wells,
Richard Todd, Faith Brook, Ivonne Sentis.

From Hammer's **Fanatic** (1965) and the Swinging Sixties Lynn Redgrave drama **Georgy Girl** (1966) to Joe Orton's **Loot** (1970) and the Glenda Jackson comedy **The Class of Miss MacMichael** (1978), director Silvio Narizzano's C.V. was eclectic to say the least. And he finished his illustrious career by reuniting **Giant** (1956) stars Dennis Hopper and Carroll Baker for this mind-boggling art-house curio. Shot in 1974, completed in '75 but not screened to the public until '78, it was retitled **Bloodbath** in the forlorn hope it would appeal to the undemanding Exploitation crowd. A band of desperate American ex-pats are living in a Spanish village and include drug-addict poet Hopper, alcoholic nympho actress Baker who still thinks she stands a chance of Hollywood fame, retired air force captain Richard Todd and his drunken wife, and jaded homosexual Win Wells (at the time, Narizzano's partner). Much is made of wild child Hopper's inability to separate fantasy from reality, so is the rash of unexplained deaths the responsibility of an invading Mansonesque cult of religious hippies? The often uproarious surrealistic episodes – a boy trampled to death, egg torture and cough-drop sex (no really!) – add new meaning to the word pretentious as the opening John Donne quotation highlights "But I do nothing upon myself... and yet I am mine own Executioner".

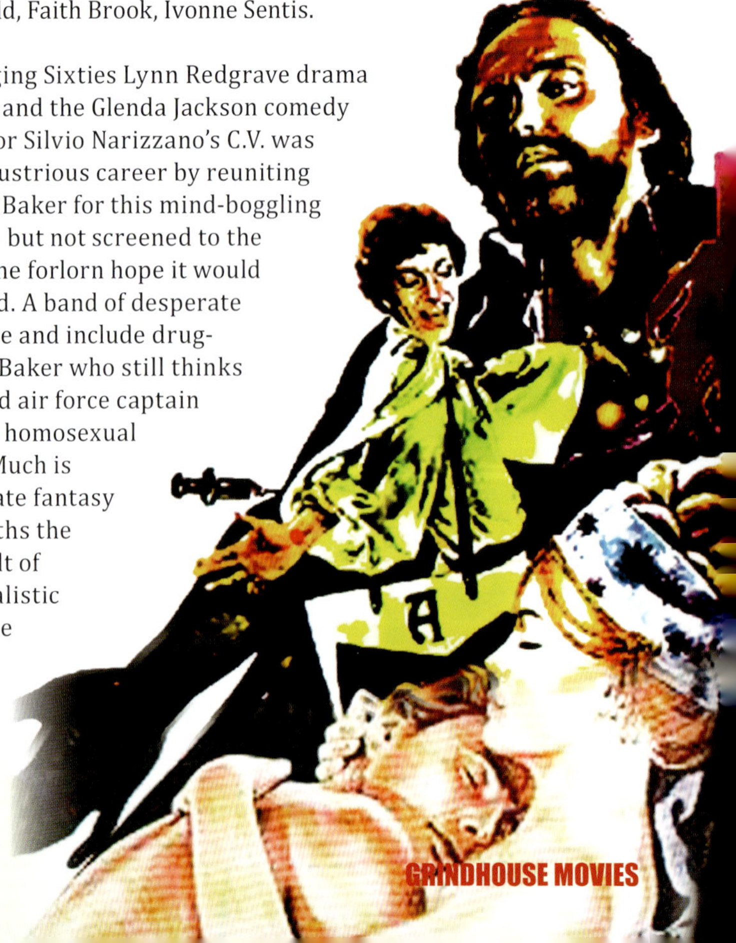

URANIUM CONSPIRACY

Italy/West Germany, 1978
Directors: Frank G. Carroll [Gianfranco Baldanello], Menahem Golan. Producers: Francesco Corti, Menahem Golan. Screenplay: Achille Grioni, David Paulsen, Jean Christian Aurive [August Rieger], Daniele Sangiorgi. Music: Coriolano Gori, Dov Seltzer. Cinematography: Adam Greenberg, Antonio Modica. Cast: Fabio Testi, Janet Agren, Assaf Dayan, Siegfried Rauch, Oded Kotler, Gianni Rizzo.

You have to give Menahem Golan his due. The director/producer would buy the Cannon name a year after pitching this lame Eurospy last gasp as being in the same bracket as Sir Lew Grade's ITC Films bloated epics like **The Cassandra Crossing** (1976) and **Capricorn One** (1977). He even hinted at the pre-production poster for **Raise the Titanic** (1980) to promote this co-directed, with Gianfranco Baldanello (**Blood River**, 1974), terrorist threat adventure starring Italian *poliziotteschi* hunk Fabio Testi, Assaf Dayan, actor/director son of Moshe Dayan (former Israeli defence minister), and love-interest *du jour* Janet Agren. Testi plays espionage specialist secret agent Renzo, who must secure a shipment of uranium targeted by an enemy power. Signal lots of low-rent boat/car/rooftop chases around gorgeous locations like Venice and Amsterdam, all shot through gauze and looking washed out. One 007-style stunt though, where a speedboat crashes through a house, gives **Puppet on a Chain** (1971) a proficient run for its meagre money. Originally titled **Agenten kennen keine Tränen**, loosely translated as 'Agents Don't Know Tears', and often playing the downmarket Pacific Rim territories as **Yellowcake Operation Uranium**, a better example of a proficiently made, mediocre late '70s potboiler would be hard to find.

DOMINIQUE

UK, © 1978, first public screening 1979
Director: Michael Anderson. Producers: Andrew Donally, Milton Subotsky. Screenplay: Edward Abraham, Valerie Abraham. Music: David Whitaker.
Cinematography: Ted Moore.
Cast: Cliff Robertson, Jean Simmons, Jenny Agutter, Simon Ward, Ron Moody, Judy Geeson.

The first Sword & Sorcery Film production from genre veteran Milton Subotsky was this creaky psychological thriller that the ex-Amicus doyen wanted promoted with the tag-line "**Dominique** will make you Shriek!" Sadly it didn't and the company with so many fantastic plans fizzled out after the equally lacklustre **The Monster Club** (1981). Cliff Robertson, fresh from Brian De Palma's exquisite **Obsession** (1976), is David Ballard, subtly trying to drive his wife Dominique (Jean Simmons) temporarily into a mental institution so he can delve into the family funds to help his near bankrupt business. Unexpectedly he drives her to suicide and in turn is driven to kill himself by ghostly visions of her tormented soul. **Diabolique** (1955) anyone? Now that really did make you shriek! Directed by the most boring helmer in the genre business, Michael Anderson (**Doc Savage: The Man of Bronze**, 1975, **Logan's Run**, 1976, you want more?), this is a slow and predictable gaslighter. Nor can the starry and obviously capable cast do very much with the old-fashioned theatrics on yawning display as they take their stagey places bathed in dramatic shades of red, green and blue to add something akin to a proxy Dario Argento/Mario Bava sheen.

HUMAN EXPERIMENTS

USA, 1979
Director: Gregory Goodell.
Producers: Summer Brown, Gregory Goodell. Screenplay: Richard Rothstein. Music: Mark Bucci. Cinematography: João Fernandes. Cast: Linda Haynes, Geoffrey Lewis, Ellen Travolta, Lurene Tuttle, Mercedes Shirley, Darlene Craviotto, Aldo Ray, Jackie Coogan.

Exploitation filler can often get by on central performance alone and that's definitely the case with this 'Women In Prison' sub-genre oddment, offhandedly directed by Gregory Goodell. Florida-born Linda Haynes was making a name for herself in a broad range of Drive-In titles, from **Latitude Zero** (1969) to **Coffy** (1973), and looked set to go big after terrific turns in **Rolling Thunder** (1977) and **Brubaker** (1980). But despite winning critical praise and fantasy festival awards for her sympathetic role here as country and western singer Rachel Foster, this was the movie that saw her reassess her career options and turn to the legal profession. Foster is touring the dive circuit with her solo act and ends up in small-town Puttnam, California, where sexually rejected bar owner Aldo Ray conspires with his equally venal sheriff brother Jackie Coogan to have her take the rap for a mass murder. Sentenced to life imprisonment, she finds herself at the mercy of doctor Geoffrey Lewis, who is experimenting with radical techniques involving aversion therapy with spiders to cure criminality. Arachnophobics might get freaked out but that's all the mild shock there is in this great-looking horror shot by porn industry favourite João Fernandes.

SUPERSONIC MAN

Spain, 1979
Director: Juan Piquer Simón. Producers: Faruk Alatan, Dick Randall. Screenplay: Sebastian Moi, Juan Piquer Simón. Music: Carlos Attias, Juan Luis Izaguirre, Gino Peguri. Cinematography: Juan Mariné.
Cast: Michael Coby [Antonio Cantafora], Cameron Mitchell, Richard Yesteran [José Luis Ayestarán], Patricia Morgan [Diana Polakov], John Caffarel [José María Caffarel], Frank Braña.

Is it a bird? Is it a plane? No, it's just another worthless dud from Spain. A desperate attempt to invade the Salkind family's blockbuster **Superman** (1978) territory, **Pieces** (1982) director Juan Piquer Simón's uneasy mixture of bland plot, flat comic relief and duff special effects is a classic case of hyped promise over zilch delivery. With the words "May the force of the galaxies be with me", private detective Paul Brown (Antonio Cantafora, who under his Michael Coby alias starred in the Disco classic **The Bitch** the same year) transforms into Kronos, the title superhero, sent to Earth to investigate experiments using stolen shipments of radioactive Iridium. At the centre of the raids is the maniacal Dr. Gulik (Cameron Mitchell), a cliché Mad Doctor made all the more forgettable by the gurning 'High Chaparral' TV Western star. Unsurprisingly Gulik wants to take over the world in the sort of juvenile matinee fantasy made completely redundant in the wake of the **Star Wars** (1977) high-end visuals era. NB: The last movie Spanish nude pin-up, photographer and singer Diana Polakov starred in (as Patricia Morgan) before retiring, her most notable role being in **The People Who Own the Dark** (1976).

CHRISTMAS EVIL

USA, 1980
Director: Lewis Jackson.
Producers: Pete Kameron, Burt Kleiner.
Screenplay: Lewis Jackson. Music: Don Christensen, Joel Harris, Julia Heyward.
Cinematography: Ricardo Aronovich.
Cast: Brandon Maggart, Jeffrey DeMunn, Dianne Hull, Andy Fenwick, Brian Neville, Joe Jamrog.

Pink Flamingos (1972) director John Waters' favourite Christmas movie – "I wish I had kids. I'd make them watch it every year, and if they didn't like it, they'd be punished" – is an engagingly oddball combo of psychotic wish-fulfilment, urban sleaze and distorted innocence. The product of a marijuana vision Sexploitation director Lewis Jackson had, imposing Brandon Maggart (**Dressed to Kill**, 1980) is the traumatised employee of a grasping toy company who keeps tabs on local children to see if they've been naughty or nice. Belittled remorselessly as usual on Christmas Eve for actually believing in the season of goodwill, he has a mental breakdown, and in a padded Santa Claus suit embarks on a Violent Night killing spree, giving away embezzled presents to the handicapped. With an uplifting climax straight out of **Miracle on 34th Street** (1947), inventive gore using lead soldiers and tree ornaments, the toy factory scenes were shot in **Sisters** (1972) producer Ed Pressman's family owned plant. While heavy on the unhinged anguish and twisted ideology, it wasn't this sweet slasher that caused American PTA groups to complain about the ill-effects on children of turning Santa homicidal, but the feeble and conventional **Silent Night, Deadly Night** (1984).

NOW! AN ALL-ACTION MAJOR MOTION PICTURE

INTERMEDIA PRODUCTIONS present

RISE AND FALL OF IDI AMIN

Introducing JOSEPH OLITA as IDI AMIN · GEOFFREY KEEN · THOMAS BAPTISTE LEONARD TROLLEY · DENIS HILLS as himself · LOUIS MAHONEY · MARLENE DOCHERTY
Produced and Directed by SHARAD PATE. Co Producer CHRISTOPHER SUTTON Screenplay by WADE HUIE Music Composed and Conducted by CHRISTOPHER GUNNING

AMIN: THE RISE AND FALL

UK/Kenya, © 1980, first public screening 1981
Director: Sharad Patel. Producers: Sharad Patel, Christopher Sutton.
Screenplay: Wade Huie. Music: Christopher Gunning.
Cinematography: Harvey Harrison.
Cast: Joseph Olita, Thomas Baptiste, Leonard Trolley, Geoffrey Keen, Louis Mahoney, André Maranne, Denis Hills.

Once Hammer Films dared to evoke more recent horrors with their wartime prison drama **The Camp on Blood Island** (1958), other companies followed suit, putting shocking headline events like the Charles Manson trials and the People's Temple mass suicide on celluloid display. This notorious Video Nasty chronicled the chilling exploits of Ugandan dictator Idi Amin (constantly raging Joseph Olita) and his 1971-79 reign of terror. The only film directed by Sharad Patel, who would claw back his soiled reputation by producing such Hollywood hits as **Bachelor Party** (1984) and **The Jungle Book** (1994), this low-budget examination of the cruel despot's savage regime focuses solely on the string of atrocities carried out to keep the crazed lunatic in power. Parading a graphic succession of hacked-up and blown-up bodies, beheadings, firing squads, cannibalism (Amin believed eating his enemies would transfer their strength to him), the tyrant's first big mistake was to gun down two Americans, his second to imprison British journalist Denis Hills, who incredibly plays himself in this head-rolling, eye-rolling sick-fest. To cap it all a promotional gimmick had cinemas given a life-size Amin cardboard cut-out, which patrons could hit with beanbags and was advertised as "Vent your spleen! Bean Amin!"

FRUITS OF PASSION

France/Japan, 1981
Director: Shûji Terayama. Producers: Anatole Dauman, Hiroko Govars, Eiko Kujo. Screenplay: Shûji Terayama. Music: J.A. Seazer. Cinematography: Tatsuo Suzuki. Cast: Isabelle Illiers, Klaus Kinski, Arielle Dombasle, Peter [Pîtâ], Keiko Niitaka, Sayoko Yamaguchi.

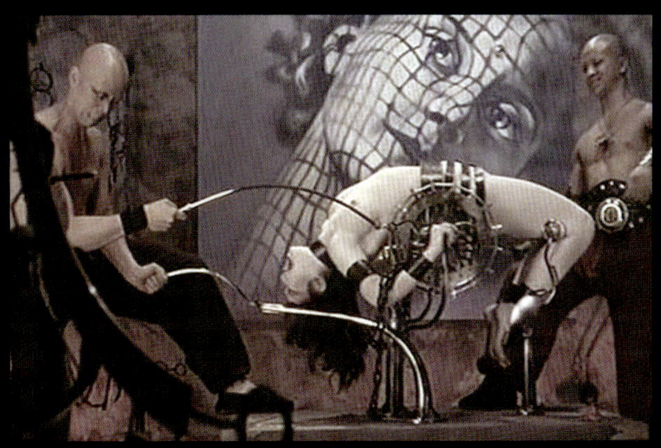

Sold as a sequel to Just Jaeckin's **Story of O** (1975), director Shûji Terayama's unofficial continuation really is just more of the gorgeously shot, stylized interior, lyrically presented and bondage fantasy same. Which was absolutely fine in those territories that didn't see Jaeckin's post-**Emmanuelle** (1974) S&M item because of censorship issues (like the UK). Loosely based on Dominique Aury's – under the alias Pauline Réage – follow up novel, 'Return to Roissy', the action shifts to 1920s Hong Kong, where the naïve and submissive O (Isabelle Illiers, **L'immorale**, 1980) is now being sexually degraded at the House of Flowers brothel by conflicted hedonist Sir Stephen (Klaus Kinski). Contentious scenes this time around included O whipped on a torture wheel – one of the many agonies along with starvation and gang rape should she refuse any client's demands – a kinky rough sex orgy and a hardcore oral sex insert. Produced by Anatole Dauman (**In the Realm of the Senses**, 1976) on an art-house budget – two-dimensional human cut-outs are used for peripheral scenes – Kinski swore blind in his autobiography the sex was real between him and Illiers but the little heat they generate together would belie that Shifty Shades of Grey remembrance.

THE WOMAN INSIDE

USA, © 1980, first public screening 1981
Director: Joseph Van Winkle. Producer: Sidney H. Levine.
Screenplay: Joseph Van Winkle, Steve Fisher [uncredited].
Music: Eddy Lawrence Manson.
Cinematography: Ron Johanson.
Cast: Gloria Manon, Dane Clark, Michael Champion,
Joan Blondell, Marlene Tracy, Michael Mancini.

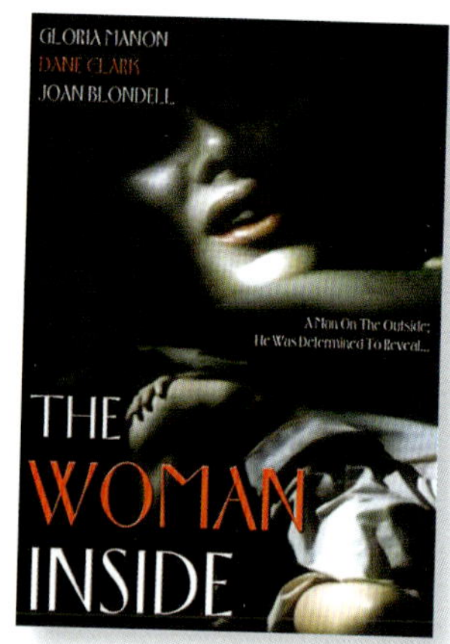

Incredibly picked up for shoddy distribution by 20th Century Fox two years after it was made, and marking the final nail in Hollywood glamourpuss Joan Blondell's career, this 1978-shot package of sex-change sensationalism, heavy-handed sincerity and overwrought seriousness, is yet another failed attempt to ride the emotional rollercoaster of transsexual experience. Closet queen Hollis Mackenzie (strident Gloria Manon) is the Vietnam veteran undergoing genital surgery to become Holly as flashbacks to the sub-genre's whole range of clichés are dragged out screaming. His hypocritical aunt (Blondell) is against the reassignment and his doctor insists he cross-dress as a woman before taking the final step. So out come the frocks augmenting the hormone treatment for the taxi-driving job needed to raise the cash for gash. Then Holly meets Irishman Nolan (Michael Champion) – boy, is he oirish! – and the angst about telling him the truth begins. Directed with a suspect candour by Joseph Van Winkle (the gay comedy **Mafia on the Bounty**, 1980) as a dewy-eyed paean to gender identification, this delightfully tacky mess is wrapped up in a soundtrack torn straight from **Valley of the Dolls** (1967) and a theme song titled 'Ain't Never Been a Love Like This One', sung by a suspect Silky.

BIG MEAT EATER

Canada, 1982
Director: Chris Windsor. Producer: Laurence Keane.
Screenplay: Phil Savath, Laurence Keane, Chris Windsor.
Music: J. Douglas Dodd. Cinematography: Doug McKay.
Cast: Big Miller, George Dawson, Andrew Gillies, Stephen Dimopoulos,
Georgina Hegedos, Ida Carnevali.

Illustrating just how good a deliberately made bad movie can be, director Chris Windsor's bizarre musical comedy horror isn't quite in the same class as the Queen Mother of the genre – **The Rocky Horror Picture Show** (1975) – but with its equally unique pace and warped reality, it's a cleverly orchestrated labour of B-movie love. Written in 1974, finessed in 1980 and made for $75,000, Windsor purposely followed the Roger Corman guidelines as laid down by **The Little Shop of Horrors** (1960), coincidentally turned into a smash Off-Broadway musical at the same time. An impossible movie to synopsise with clarity, suffice it to say space aliens hatch a plot to mine radioactive Balonium located underneath a butcher's shop in the Canadian town of Burquitlam, where the reanimated corpse of the mayor has decreed the new language of Adanaco must be learned for its redevelopment into the Vision of Tomorrowland. Songs by J. Douglas Dodd, musical director of the Canuxploitation thriller **Skip Tracer** (1977), including 'By the Banks of the Bonny Burquitlam', 'Bagdad Boogie', 'Atomic Radiation', 'Just Hanging Around', 'Mondo Chemico', 'Missile Love' and the title theme, all hit the spoof spot for a satisfyingly weird and wonderful show tune workout.

Pleased to meet you, meat to please you!
BIG MEAT EATER
"One of the best pictures of the year." - City Limits
"hilarious...
a superbly comical musical score underpins the insanity on the screen"
- Vancouver Sun

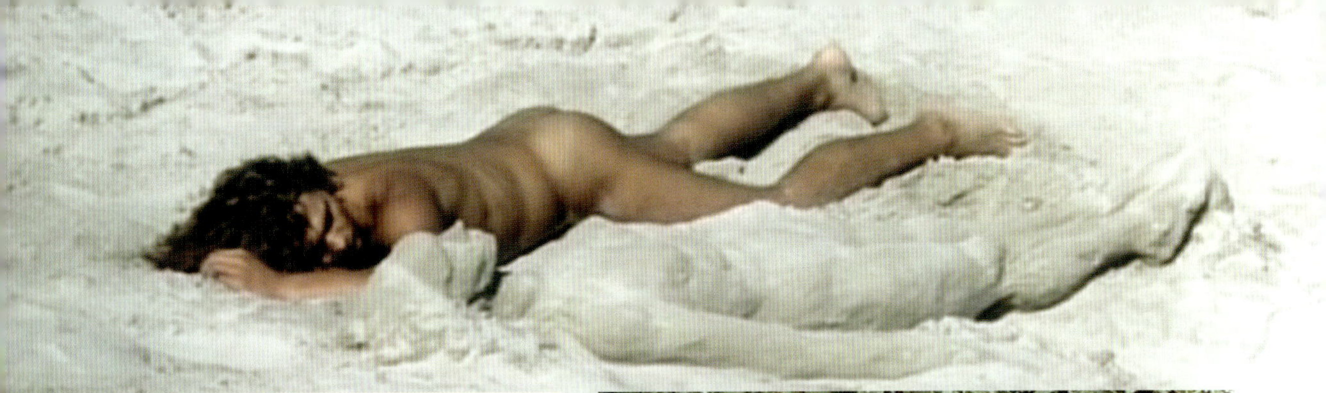

ADAM AND EVE: THE FIRST LOVE STORY

Italy/Spain, 1983
Directors: Vincent Green [Enzo Doria], John Wilder [Luigi Russo]. Producer: Enzo Doria. Screenplay: Mimo Rafele [Domenico Rafele], Lidia Ravera, Jaime Comas Gil, Eugenio Benito, Luigi Russo, Ezio Passadore [Enzo Doria].
Music: Guido De Angelis, Maurizio De Angelis.
Cinematography: Fernando Espiga.
Cast: Mark Gregory, Andrea Goldman, Ángel Alcázar, Costantino Rossi, Pierangelo Pozzato, Vito Fornari.

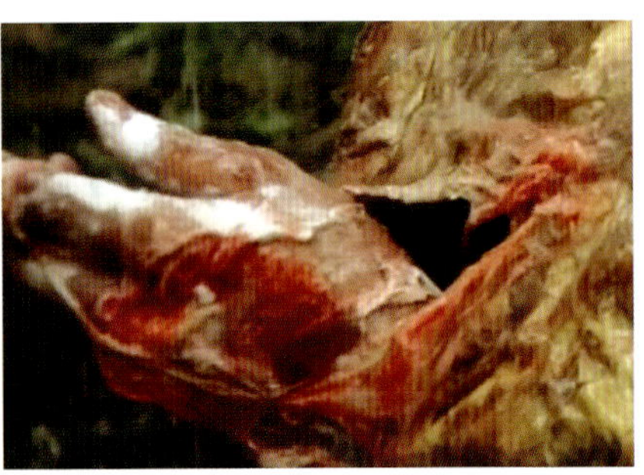

Want to know what the mysterious Roman gym discovery Mark Gregory did when not appearing in such nonsense as **1990: The Bronx Warriors** (1982) and **Thunder** (1983)? Look no further than **Blue Paradise** to give Enzo Doria and Luigi Russo's co-directed Bible thumper its export title, although another alternative, **Adam and Eve Meet the Cannibals**, is more fun. And God created Adam (Gregory) from a slimy egg sac and he made Eve (never seen again Andrea Goldman) out of sand. Together they get chucked out of Eden after eating forbidden fruit and having wild sex to brave volcanoes, hurricanes and mudslides, and battle a pterodactyl to make skin underwear. Soon Eve takes off with a rough and ready bear-killing Neanderthal but comes back to hunky Adam when he saves them both from hungry brain-bashing cannibals... And so this hilariously sexed and monstered-up Sunday School lesson continues by trashing the Old Testament with continual blasphemy, softcore tableaux and footage nicked from **One Million Years B.C.** (1966). Who knew the Bible could be this much fun? Half of the enjoyment comes in the actors playing it completely straight, without any hint they are fulfilling the Ten Commandments of Exploitation every which way and loose.

THE NEXT ONE

USA, 1984
Director: Nico Mastorakis. Producer: Constantine Vlachakis. Screenplay: Nico Mastorakis.
Music: Stanley Myers. Cinematography: Aris Stavrou.
Cast: Keir Dullea, Adrienne Barbeau, Peter Hobbs, Jeremy Licht, Phaedon Gheorghitsis [Faidon Georgitsis], Betty Arvaniti.

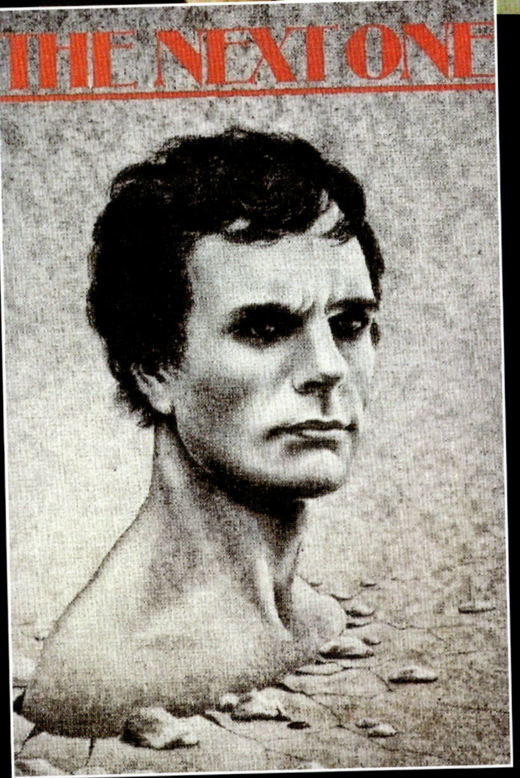

For a short period of time, radio/TV pioneer director Nico Mastorakis was Greeksploitation's singular purveyor, what with **Island of Death** (1976), **Blind Date** (1984) and **Edge of Terror** (1986) after gaining notoriety for writing **The Greek Tycoon** (1978), the thinly-veiled Aristotle Onassis biography. The political activist and one-time Vangelis record producer never rose above the B-movie doldrums despite earlier aspirations but this sci-fi romance was a good attempt at trying to reposition his moribund career. It didn't work because virtually no one saw it, and now it occupies a similar standing to that of Giulio Paradisi's equally bizarre **The Visitor** (1979). With all surprise wrung out because of its alternative title, **The Time Traveller**, American widow Andrea Johnson (Adrienne Barbeau) and her son Tim (Jeremy Licht) find a stranger washed up on a beach in Greece after an electrical storm. Glenn (magnetic Keir Dullea) is apparently suffering from amnesia but as he slowly recovers his memory he claims to be a prophet from the future. Andrea is more freaked out because she fears he may be an escaped child murderer. But as Glenn performs complex miracles, could he really have hurtled 2,000 years back in time to give mankind a warning?

MIRANDA

Italy, 1985
Director: Tinto Brass. Producer: Giovanni Bertolucci. Screenplay: Tinto Brass. Music: Riz Ortolani. Cinematography: Silvano Ippoliti, Erico Menczer [uncredited].
Cast: Serena Grandi, Andrea Occhipinti, Franco Interlenghi, Andy J. Forest, Franco Branciaroli, Malisa Longo.

To worldwide audiences the name Tinto Brass still means the controversial and scandalous **Salon Kitty** (1976) and **Caligula** (1979). But in his native Italy those notorious titles were just shrugged blips in a career devoted to bawdy romps mainly focused on the female silhouette. From **Nerosubianco** (1969) and **The Howl** (1970) to **The Key** (1983) and **Snack Bar Budapest** (1988), Brass's singular brand of saucy erotica always lit up the Italian box-office. **Miranda** is one of his endearing best, starring statuesque Serena Grandi (**Antropophagus**, 1980) in yet another screen adaptation of Carlo Goldoni's classic 1753 three-act farce 'La Locandiera/ Mistress of the Inn'. Miranda (Grandi) is the lusty landlady of a country tavern who beds the local talent in her effort to find a suitable soulmate to finally settle down with after her husband goes missing in World War II. Conquests include village stud Andrea Occhipinti, politician Andy J. Forest, and G.I. Franco Interlenghi, with her besotted bartender Franco Branciaroli tormented into sexual frustration by her wanton behaviour. Staying true to its racy source material and laden with double entendres and explicit puns, this is Brass at his lecherous best, while continuously parading Grandi's ample charms with ever arousing élan.

MONDO SEXUALIS

USA, © 1986, first public screening 1987
Director: David Adnopoz. Producer: Joan Huntington.
Screenplay: David Adnopoz. Music: Rod Ellis. Cinematography: Bruce Burnside.
Cast: Allan Rich (narrator), Ugly George, Al Goldstein, Gloria Leonard, Mistress Antoinette.

A blue metal door in a sleazy suburban alley; the judgemental narration by Allan Rich begins: "You will find the following surprising. You will be shocked. You may be offended". And it's through the doorway into the S&M fantasy nightclub Paddles where drag queens act out routines involving nipple clamping and jamming stiletto heels into various orifices. David Adnopoz's uneven journey through the sexual mores and lifestyles of the usual minority groups was a late addition to the shockumentary genre but a hugely entertaining one nevertheless. With personalised genital sculpting, an obviously staged occult orgy in Wisconsin, pussy shaving, impotency cures, voodoo love charms and sobering insights into the AIDS epidemic by transvestite nuns in San Francisco, it contained some extraordinary nuggets of information. Two segments set it apart from the usual fare: dominatrix Mistress Antoinette running her rubberwear mail order business by day and whipping clients at night, and tips on cross-dressing from an ex-marine who organises six-hour bondage sessions to help him achieve prolonged climax. It ends with a flashing 'Warning' sign and advice to leave the cinema if you have a weak stomach before the forensically filmed sex change operation begins. Sheer Mondo magic indeed!

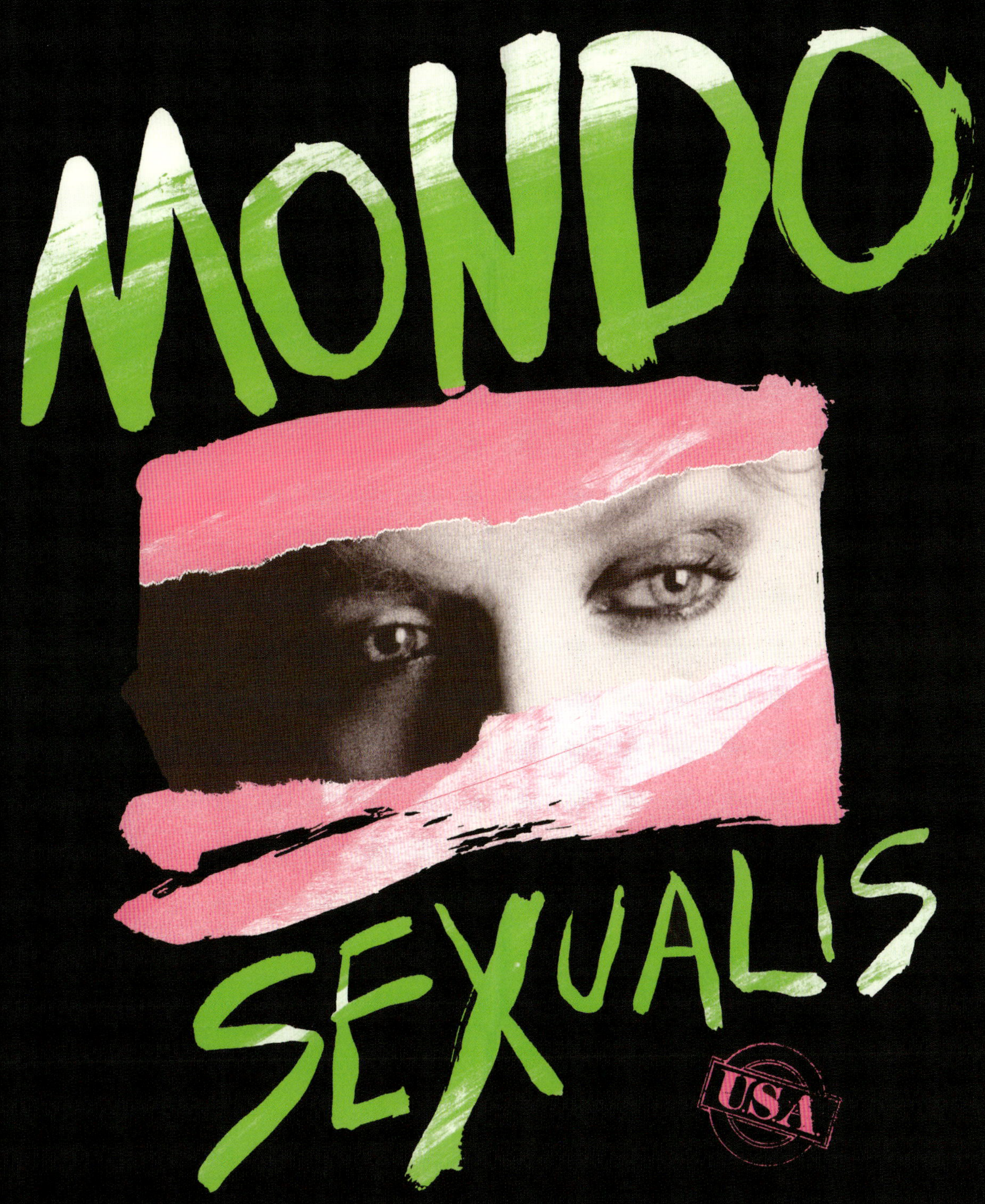

A K.E./BUCCANEER PRODUCTION MONDO SEXUALIS
PHOTOGRAPHED BY BRUCE BURNSIDE MUSIC BY ROD ELLIS EDITED BY CHIP BROOKS
NARRATED BY ALLAN RICH PRODUCED BY JOAN HUNTINGTON WRITTEN AND DIRECTED BY DAVID ADNOPOZ

INDEX OF FILM TITLES

Page references in **bold** refer exclusively to illustrations.

You have been reading Volume 5 in the FrightFest Guide series of books. Also available from FAB Press, Volumes 1, 2, 3 and 4 in this great collection...

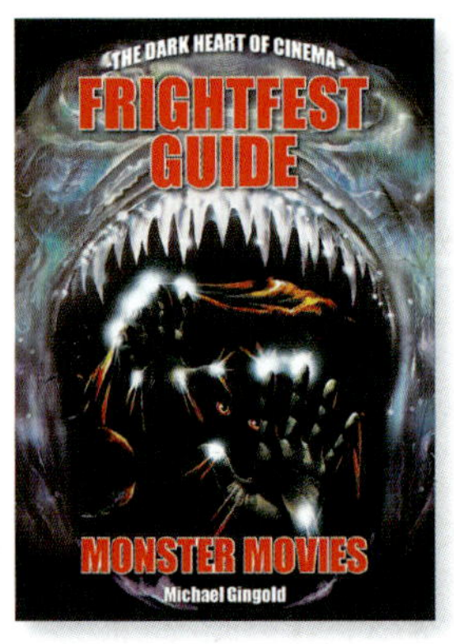

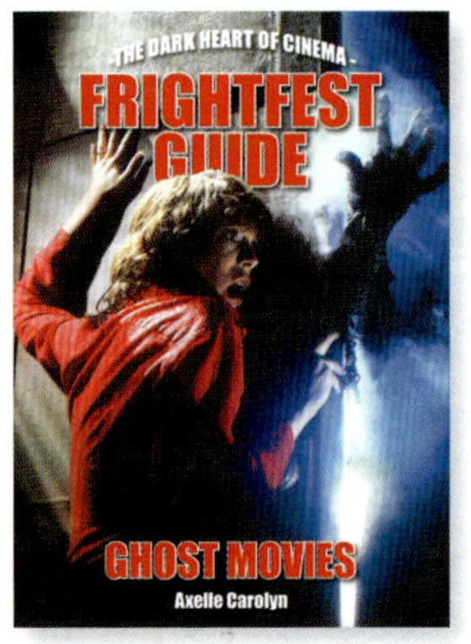

● Order the hardcover limited editions direct from the publisher, exclusively at www.fabpress.com